Praise for *The Education We Need for a Future We Can't Predict*

For decades Tom Hatch has been engaged in school reform as an observer, researcher, and participant—as well as the involved parent of three children. He has surveyed efforts across the United States and much of the world—notably Norway, Finland, and Singapore—sympathetically but not uncritically. In this magisterial work, he presents the lessons he has learned and offers sage advice to those who seek to improve our schools—anywhere, everywhere.

Howard Gardner, Hobbs Research Professor of Cognition and Education
Harvard Graduate School of Education
Author, *A Synthesizing Mind*
Cambridge, MA

You won't find a better book on system change in education than The Education We Need for a Future We Can't Predict. *It addresses all the key issues and does so from the ground up. We learn why schools don't change; how they can improve; what it takes to change a system; and, in the final analysis, the possibilities of system change. It has remarkable geographical range based on lived-in familiarity of the countries in question: the United States, Finland, Singapore, South Africa, Norway, and more. Above all,* The Education We Need *renders complexity into clarity as the writing is so clear and compelling. A powerful read on a topic of utmost importance.*

Michael Fullan, Professor Emeritus, Ontario Institute for
Studies in Education, University of Toronto
Toronto, Canada

It is highly unusual and wonderfully refreshing to read a book so carefully pitched to our turbulent times as Tom Hatch's The Education We Need for a Future We Can't Predict. *This magnum opus masterfully blends a moving personal memoir, trenchant social and political analysis, and an inspiring vision of a better world. This is must-reading for all serious educators and change leaders in the age of the coronavirus and beyond.*

Dennis Shirley, Duganne Faculty Fellow and Professor
Editor-in-Chief, Journal of Educational Change
Lynch School of Education and Human Development, Boston College
Chestnut Hill, MA

The Education We Need for a Future We Can't Predict *is an absolute must read for everyone interested in effective and equitable educational changes. Drawing on Tom Hatch's extensive expertise from research and direct involvement in educational improvement work, this book provides wise advice and practical actions ranging from micro-innovations for teaching, learning, and equity in classrooms, to school improvement and reform, and large-scale change to transform education systems. I cannot recommend this book highly enough—Tom tackles long-standing and emerging educational issues in new ways with an impressive understanding of the challenging complexities, but also feasible possibilities, for ensuring excellence and equity for all students.*

Carol Campbell, Associate Professor
Ontario Institute for Studies in Education, University of Toronto
Toronto, Canada

Thomas Hatch has been "in the arena" where policy, programs, people, and power converge to educate children. In his fantastic, informative new book, The Education We Need for a Future We Can't Predict, *Tom travelled the globe to study how individuals, classrooms, schools, school systems, and nations "try with despair and hope to change and transform educational opportunities." Whether you're a parent, practitioner, or policymaker, this book is written for you to take action to improve schools and communities and to create new educational possibilities.*

Pablo Muñoz
Superintendent of Schools
Passaic Public Schools
New Jersey

This educational odyssey is a fascinating story about why we need, now more than ever, to both improve our schools and transform education systems at the same time. In the era of global health crisis, political instability, and economic uncertainty, Tom Hatch and colleagues bring us a much-needed message of optimism and hope: We can change schools for the better and improve educational systems if we really want to do so. This book is a must-read for those who want to think differently about education and what it takes to have schools that our children need for a future we can't predict.

Pasi Sahlberg, Professor of Education Policy
UNSW Sydney
Author, *FinnishEd Leadership: Four Big, Inexpensive Ideas to Transform Education*
Sydney, New South Wales
Australia

Tom Hatch has worked at the center of some of the landmark school reform initiatives of our times. He has inside knowledge of the promise and the disappointments of school reform. In this perceptive book, Hatch shares his well-informed vision of what can work in efforts to improve our schools. The book is a timely and valuable contribution to our literature on school improvement.

William Damon, Professor of Education
Stanford Graduate School of Education
Director, Stanford Center on Adolescence
Stanford, CA

Very few books on school reform contain so many ideas and insights into how to develop and improve education and educational systems for the future challenges. This book underlines in a very interesting and absorbing way the fact that we do not know about the future and we can't predict it. We can, however, create a future together by offering a right to good teaching and learning in our systems. In this task, our education must focus on humanity, equity, democracy, sustainable way of life and at the same time take into account the uniqueness of a person and the richness of multicultures.

Mikko Salonen, Educational Leadership Consultant, Coach
Konsulttipaja Oy
Espoo, Finland

There are many reasons to feel discouraged about attempts to substantively transform public education these days. The grammar of schooling has proved remarkably hard to change, most reform efforts have failed to prepare our children for the messy world we're passing on to them, and we're now entering a world where disruptions to life and work will likely become part of our everyday realities. If you're one of those unwilling to give up to hopelessness, or if you're already on the verge of losing hope, you have to read this book by Tom Hatch. The Education We Need for a Future We Can't Predict *is at the same time thoughtful and pragmatic, American and global, micro and macro. Tom provides a thoughtful analysis of why it is so hard to change schools and what it takes to make meaningful change stick in classrooms and across entire educational systems. Tom's book is a good reminder that our way out of this mess and toward a brighter future is to be found in our human agency, understood as our capacity to exercise choice in the face of uncertainty. And it shows, through example, how and why it is so important—even urgent—for the United States to look beyond its borders to learn from the amazing educational transformation work going on abroad, all the way from Europe to Africa, from South-East Asia to Latin America.*

Santiago Rincon Gallardo, Education Consultant
Author, *Liberating Learning: Educational Change as Social Movement*
Toronto, Canada

Education is plagued by an absence of knowledge on the intricacies related to "making change happen," but the various conceptualizations of change strategies included in this book provide a much-needed resource for practitioners, reformers, and policy makers to consider in planning and implementing change in complex times in a variety of educational settings across the globe. Tom's personalized approach offers excellent case studies and a variety of ways to think about making change happen. Readers are certain to identify with a rich array of relevant research and practice whether planning change for an education-oriented non profit, schools, districts, or state and national change projects.

Larry Leverett, Retired Executive Director
Panasonic Foundation
Former Superintendent, Greenwich, CT, and Plainfield, NJ
Former Assistant Commissioner of Urban Education, New Jersey Department
of Education
New Jersey

Tom Hatch has written a deeply personal and reflective book that weaves decades of personal and global research evidence with his own personal experience as a student, parent, and scholar in different countries. As a result, The Education We Need *provides a unique, timely, and compelling argument for how lives within schools and educational systems are inextricably linked to local and national context.*

This book will be essential reading for my students!

Karen Edge, Reader in Educational Leadership
UCL Centre for Educational Leadership
UCL Institute of Education
London, UK

A well written and well-argued book, bringing in the value of small scale changes in improving whole educational systems across the developed and developing world. It is healthily critical, reflective and humble while seeking to be constructive and ultimately optimistic, too. The book shows that educational transformation without social transformation is extremely unlikely on any significant scale, but that substantial improvement of what already exists is feasible, desirable and, of itself, can make significant contributions to equity.

Andy Hargreaves
Research Professor, Boston College
Director of CHENINE (Change, Engagement &
Innovation in Education), University of Ottawa
President & Co-Founder, ARC Education

The Education
We Need for a Future
We Can't Predict

The Education We Need for a Future We Can't Predict

Thomas Hatch

With Jordan Corson and

Sarah Gerth van den Berg

FOR INFORMATION:

Corwin

A SAGE Company

2455 Teller Road

Thousand Oaks, California 91320

(800) 233-9936

www.corwin.com

SAGE Publications Ltd.

1 Oliver's Yard

55 City Road

London EC1Y 1SP

United Kingdom

SAGE Publications India Pvt. Ltd.

B 1/I 1 Mohan Cooperative Industrial Area

Mathura Road, New Delhi 110 044

India

SAGE Publications Asia-Pacific Pte. Ltd.

18 Cross Street #10-10/11/12

China Square Central

Singapore 048423

Acquisitions Editor: Ariel Curry

Associate Content

    Development Editor: Jessica Vidal

Editorial Assistant: Caroline Timmings

Production Editor: Gagan Mahindra

Copy Editor: Will DeRooy

Typesetter: C&M Digitals (P) Ltd.

Proofreader: Barbara Coster

Indexer: Integra

Cover Designer: Rose Storey

Graphic Designer: Rose Storey

Marketing Manager: Sharon Pendergast

Printed in the United States of America

Library of Congress Cataloging-in-Publication Data

Names: Hatch, Thomas, author. | Corson, Jordan, author. | Gerth van den Berg, Sarah, author.

Title: The education we need for a future we can't predict / Thomas Hatch, Jordan Corson, Sarah Gerth van den Berg.

Description: Los Angeles : Corwin, [2021] | Includes bibliographical references and index.

Identifiers: LCCN 2020039609 | ISBN 9781071802083 (paperback) | ISBN 9781071838495 (epub) | ISBN 9781071838501 (epub) | ISBN 9781071838518 (pdf)

Subjects: LCSH: School improvement programs. | Educational change. | Educational equalization.

Classification: LCC LB2822.8 .H38 2021 | DDC 371.2/07—dc23

LC record available at https://lccn.loc.gov/2020039609

This book is printed on acid-free paper.

SUSTAINABLE FORESTRY INITIATIVE

Certified Chain of Custody

Promoting Sustainable Forestry

www.sfiprogram.org

SFI-01268

21 22 23 24 25 10 9 8 7 6 5 4 3 2 1

Contents

List of Figures

List of Programs

More information on these programs and the
references and resources in this book
can be found on the companion website:
resources.corwin.com/educationweneed

Preface

Writing about change seems particularly strange as I sit here in my bedroom in a small town outside New York City in June 2020 in the midst of the coronavirus pandemic. It seems that, in March and April of this year, everything changed at the same time that everything slowed down. Closures at my youngest daughter's high school, at my two older daughters' colleges, and at my university kicked us all out of our classrooms and into online learning almost overnight.

The vicious spread of the virus, the subsequent lockdowns, and the inequitable impact on lives, livelihood, and everyday life exposed the systemic barriers to resources and opportunity that the world has never addressed. It's a gross luxury to be able to reflect and write at a time like this, while so many people are trying to reclaim their livelihoods or fighting for their very lives. But in many ways, this situation is not new; a hidden virus has just exposed these systemic inequities again. This experience reinforces for me the basic premise of this book: we have to find and create opportunities to make improvements in our daily life in schools at the same time that we rededicate ourselves to transforming the basic structures that perpetuate inequitable educational opportunities.

And then George Floyd was murdered. That murder, and the subsequent protests, made clear again some of the ways that racism contributes to the systemic inequities in educational opportunities addressed in this book. In Chapter 2, I originally focused on the ways in which inequitable opportunities in education add up for Black and Latinx students in particular, to highlight the connection between race and inequitable outcomes. But when I re-read the draft manuscript, I realized those drafts didn't go far enough. As I worked through the manuscript one more time, I tried to make those connections more explicit. But these discussions still don't adequately address the many policies and institutional and organizational practices in the

> We have to find and create opportunities to make improvements in our daily life in schools at the same time that we rededicate ourselves to transforming the basic structures that perpetuate inequitable educational opportunities.

United States today that systematically disadvantage Black people, indigenous peoples, and people of color. A number of powerful books document these racist policies and practices in many sectors, as well as offer critical ways to change them:

- Michelle Alexander's *The New Jim Crow: Mass Incarceration in the Age of Colorblindness* (2012)

- Darryl Pinckney's *Blackballed: The Black Vote and US Democracy* (2014)

- Elizabeth Hinton's *From the War on Poverty to the War on Crime: The Making of Mass Incarceration in America* (2016)

- Ibram X. Kendi's *Stamped From the Beginning: The Definitive History of Racist Ideas in America* (2017)

- Ruha Benjamin's *Race After Technology: Abolitionist Tools for the New Jim Code* (2019)

- Keeanga-Yamahtta Taylor's *Race for Profit: How Banks and the Real Estate Industry Undermined Black Homeownership* (2019)

These works leave no doubt that changing educational systems must be part of a larger movement to confront racism in every sector of society.

George Floyd's murder by a white policeman in May in Minneapolis was only the latest such killing of Black men, women, and children, following Breonna Taylor, Ahmaud Arbery, and so many others. But this time, like so many other people, I've been swept up in discussions about specific things that everyone can do to dismantle the policies and practices that create and maintain inequitable opportunities and perpetuate systemic racism. Yet even after working with my colleagues in the New Jersey Network of Superintendents on issues of race and equity for more than a decade, I'm still trying to deepen my understanding of the role of systemic racism in producing educational disadvantage for students of color; I'm still learning what it takes to be actively "anti-racist," and I'm still learning to talk about race explicitly. At the same time that I despair at the slow pace of progress, I remain convinced that everyone involved in education can take steps right now to create more equitable educational opportunities and to develop the broader social movements and long-term commitment that combating racism and producing more equitable outcomes demands (Rincón-Gallardo, 2019).

Writing about the importance of building relationships and working together while being isolated at home during the pandemic has also gotten me to think about where my community members are and how they support me even when we haven't been in touch directly. It has reminded me that developing relationships isn't just a matter of "luck"—of running into the "right" people or being in the "right" place at the "right" time. The relationships I've developed and the access and resources they bring are not an accident. Relationships have to be built out of the opportunities in our environment, and, in the United States, we've built schools and systems to segregate and sort people based on their race and other characteristics, not to bring people together. This system reflects a host of decisions and developments that are different from those made in Norway, Finland, Singapore, and other countries that have chosen to make education one part of a larger system that provides comprehensive support for the health and well-being of every citizen. Those countries haven't eradicated racism or eliminated inequality. But they offer hope that, as entrenched as they are, the school and educational systems in the United States and other parts of the world can be constructed differently. As the many examples in this book from both developing and developed contexts demonstrate, inequitable outcomes—for Black people, indigenous peoples, and people of color, for immigrants, and for low-income families in so many parts of the world—are neither "natural" nor universal.

In the later sections of this book, I explore the consequences for education of some of these decisions and consider what it will take for countries like the US to foster the common understanding and collective responsibility that can create a brighter future. But I begin by looking directly at some of the reasons why it is so difficult to improve the schools we have, and by describing some incremental, but crucial, steps we can take to make schools more efficient, more effective, and more equitable right now. The challenges are all around, but opportunities abound!

An Education in Schools

In third grade, I didn't get much out of school, but I learned more than I ever had before. That year, my family moved from Cleveland, Ohio, to Mexico City. My father was transferred from his job at a manufacturing company to help oversee a plant his company had acquired. For a few weeks before summer vacation, I went to a large, largely American international school, where I felt overwhelmed by the number of students in the classrooms and on the playground. In the fall, I switched to a small, bilingual, independent school: Colegio Peterson. Named after its founder, Colegio Peterson was a nice, quiet house, with small rooms organized around a large open staircase in an upscale neighborhood. I can still remember the warm welcome of all my teachers and peers, as well as the sudden recognition of the ways that school does and doesn't fit the interests and abilities of individual children. I didn't need the lessons in English grammar the teachers offered my peers; and, unable to speak or understand Spanish, I couldn't take much advantage of the math and history lessons designed for my bilingual classmates. Instead I often found myself outside, in the marble hallway, engaged in some other activity. The only specific activity I can remember is working happily on a puzzle that showed the states of Mexico.

But the whole year was glorious. I loved being in that hallway working largely on my own. We joined the little league. We regularly visited the Museo Nacional de Antropología and watched as the construction of new subway lines constantly unearthed the stones of the ancient Aztec city of Tenochtitlan that the Spanish razed to build their own capital. We took time off from school to visit the temples and pyramids of Monte Alban and Mitla in Oaxaca, and Uxmal and Chichen Itza on the Yucatan Peninsula. We flew over the jungles of Guatemala, in an old cargo plane with seats bolted to the floor. We watched as the tips of the pyramids of Tikal emerged out of the jungle canopy (just as they do in the approach to the hidden rebel base in the first *Star Wars* movie).

Looking back, I can't say that I really gained a deeper understanding of many aspects of Mexican society, and, unfortunately, I never learned to speak Spanish. But I remember the large school and the small school; learning happily on my own and the complete inability to understand Spanish; the puzzles with different states; the discovery of a different set of presidents; and the feeling of more than a thousand years of history beneath my feet.

But more than anything else, those experiences gave me a glimpse beyond the United States. They provided an early indication of how limited my perspective is and how the world around us always escapes our comprehension. These experiences also inspired me to continue to learn, to travel, to explore, and to try to see the limits of my own perspective.

That year is really the year my education began. That year convinced me that everyone should be able to have that kind of "sabbatical" experience—even, and perhaps especially—in third grade. It inspired me to pursue a career in academia, where I could continue to explore the world, and where I might be able to provide my children with the same kind of formative experience I had in Mexico.

That's why when my wife, Karen, was invited to be a visiting professor at the University of Leiden in the Netherlands in 2007, we figured out a way to spend the month of June there with our young family; and that's where Hannah and Clara were warmly welcomed into a local public school when they were just eight and six years old.

That experience in Mexico also inspired me to look for a way to take my family outside the States when I had a sabbatical in 2009 and 2010, and that's how we ended up in Norway. For Hannah and Clara, the timing was perfect; they were old enough to go to Norwegian schools and really remember their time there. But Stella, as she has repeatedly pointed out, was only five; she was still in preschool and too young to recall many of the Nordic experiences so central to the development of her sisters. As a consequence, when we went to Finland for a month a few years later, Stella insisted she get a chance to go to a "real school," and we found a way for her and her sisters to spend a few weeks in a Finnish school as well.

These opportunities to go to school in other countries that I and my children had were just brief experiences, but they've had a catalytic effect on my work and my life. They've given me the chance to look at "the forest *and* the trees," to think about the specific details of changing schools as well as the larger context in which schooling takes place. Going back and forth between the two can be jarring, but, as Peter Senge describes in *The Fifth Discipline* (1990), that's a crucial part of systems thinking and central to the aims of this book.

An Education in School Reform

My experiences of living and working in other countries have also made clear the extraordinary privileges that I've enjoyed, including the opportunity to attend private schools and the ability to move to and live in places where Karen and I think the schools will meet our hopes for our children's education. But my own educational experiences have been central in shaping my views on schooling and school improvement, and it felt appropriate to start the introduction with my family's educational experiences in Norway.

At the same time, beyond these experiences and my own studies of reform efforts, my work has been shaped by the people I've been able to meet: an incredibly supportive group of advisers, teachers, colleagues, and formal and informal mentors whose words and ideas have had a profound impact on me and on education more widely. My work as a graduate student in the 1980s with the psychologist Howard Gardner sparked my interest in the contexts that shape development (which I explore in Part 3). At that time, a focus on the cognitive development of individuals was shifting to look at "situated learning" and how the physical, sociocultural, and institutional forces in different contexts constrain and support development of all kinds (Hatch, 1997; Hatch & Gardner, 1993). I began working with Gardner shortly after he published the book *Frames of Mind* in 1983.

Frames of Mind introduced the term "multiple intelligences" to highlight that people have many different abilities which can and should be developed in schools. Although some academics have disputed Gardner's claims that there is a neurological basis for calling at least eight different abilities "intelligences," the fundamental idea—that children have all kinds of abilities that are worth recognizing and developing—took off almost before my eyes. As Gardner describes it, he started getting calls from people all over the United States and around the world who said they had always believed that the kind of general linguistic and logical-mathematical abilities assessed in IQ tests and focused on in schools weren't the only things that mattered, but that they had never had the language and the words to articulate that point of view (Gardner, 2006). That enormous public interest set off a wave of work and partnerships as Gardner and colleagues at Project Zero (where I worked) sought to explore and study what it might take to create learning environments that provide more holistic support for children's development.

As I discuss in Part 2, those partnerships, particularly my work with the ATLAS Communities Project, provided a crash course in the challenges of improving schools and school systems. Launched in 1992, ATLAS sought to create a "pathway" of primary, middle, and high schools based on the work of four of the best-known organizations involved in educational reform: Harvard Project Zero, led by Howard Gardner and David Perkins; the School Development Program at Yale University, headed by James Comer; the Education Development Center in Newton, Massachusetts, led by Janet Whitla; and the Coalition of Essential Schools, led by Ted Sizer. Those experiences demonstrated over and over again that the structures, practices, and culture of conventional schools can be changed, but many of those changes take place slowly and incrementally.

My experiences with ATLAS gave me an opportunity to work with Sizer and Comer, who instilled in me the importance of relationships— or, as Sizer put it (quoting Comer), the three most important things in school reform: "relationships, relationships, relationships." Sizer was an educational historian; dean of the Harvard Graduate School of Education; head of Phillips Andover Academy, one of the best-known elite boarding schools in the United States; and then founder of the Coalition of Essential Schools. The Coalition consisted of a grassroots network of schools that committed to "9 Common Principles" introduced in Sizer's 1985 book *Horace's Compromise*. Notably, Sizer launched the term "personalization" into common use. Today, "personalization" refers to almost any effort to differentiate or customize learning. But for Sizer, "personalization" meant much more than matching students with different activities and learning experiences based on the level of their abilities or the nature of their interests. Sizer emphasized the *personal*—or, really, the *interpersonal*— in personalization by stressing that personalization grows out of the relationships between teachers and students. For Sizer, personalization depended on teachers knowing their students well; therefore, he made reducing the course loads of faculty a central element of the Coalition's reform strategy (and, as I point out in Part 6, a critical issue for schools to address in the wake of the coronavirus pandemic and related school closures).

Dr. Comer (everyone calls him Dr. Comer), a psychiatrist at the Yale Child Study Center, established the School Development Program to build on the belief that strong relationships among all those involved in education—students, families, teachers, administrators, school staff, community members—provide the foundation for children's healthy and holistic development. Dr. Comer's approach grows out of his own experiences growing up in Gary, Indiana. In *School Power* (1980) and *Maggie's American Dream* (1989), Dr. Comer recounts how his successes, eventually leading to his graduate studies and work as a professor at Yale University, reflected the contributions of a host of relatives, neighbors, and community members in the neighborhood where he grew up. The support from that whole network of relationships epitomizes the idea that "it takes a village to raise a child," but it applies as well to careers like mine. My relationships with mentors like Gardner, Sizer, and Dr. Comer gave me access to a series of networks that were instrumental to my development and the development of this book. Among them, at the same time as my work on ATLAS in the early 1990s, Gardner introduced me to Ernesto Cortes Jr. and the Alliance Schools in Texas, where I learned powerful ways to connect community organizing and school improvement. My work with ATLAS also connected me to Richard Elmore, another faculty member at Harvard, whose ideas and work on the "instructional core" and school reform have shaped my views on the infrastructure for teaching and learning and system change. In turn, in 2008, Elmore introduced me to Larry Leverett, the president of the Panasonic Foundation. Leverett invited me to join the "design team" that created the New Jersey Network of Superintendents and gave me an opportunity to work with a host of teachers and administrators to learn what it takes to identify and address specific equity goals.

My work with Leverett and colleagues in the NJNS has had a particularly profound impact on my thinking and development. Modeled after a similar network that Elmore and colleagues started in Connecticut, the NJNS was designed initially to help improve outcomes for all students by engaging superintendents in a series of "instructional rounds" in one another's schools. In those visits, small groups of us made brief visits to a series of classrooms—spending ten minutes or so in four or five different classes. Those visits enabled me to work with dedicated teachers and administrators working to address issues of equity, race, poverty, and justice, but they also repeatedly revealed segregated classrooms and schools: places where Black and Latinx students were given relatively low-level texts and tasks while their white and Asian peers pursued more challenging, though not always more engaging, activities.

The meetings and observations took place almost every month over the last twelve years (up until the coronavirus hit and we moved our meetings online). And even with a multiracial group committed to addressing issues of equity, keeping the focus on equity and race—without slipping back into generic discussions of what's best "for all"—has been a challenge. As Mark Gooden put it, we need "color-conscious," not "color-blind," leadership (Davis et al., 2015; Gooden, 2012).

At the same time, even as we in the NJNS work to address explicitly the inequitable opportunities students of color face, the diversity of those districts accentuates that no set of categories adequately encompasses all the students who encounter discrimination and educational disadvantage because of their racial, cultural, or socioeconomic background; the language(s) they speak; their abilities; their gender identity; or their sexual orientation. Reflecting the growing diversity and patterns of movement and immigration in the United States, one of the NJNS suburban districts has become more and more integrated as middle- and upper-income Black families have moved into the area. The student population in another district, in a high-income suburb, has grown substantially and now has a majority of students from East Asia whose families have come to work in local pharmaceutical and technology companies. Another, more urban district, has an almost entirely Latinx population, many from low-income families who emigrated from Central America. And one of the NJNS districts grew so much more diverse as immigrants from India, China, and Mexico arrived that its schools shifted from a large white population to one with almost equal percentages of white, Black, Asian, and Latinx students.

In these districts in New Jersey and the other developing and developed contexts I discuss in this book, there are also indigenous groups whose interests, needs, and concerns deserve explicit attention. Throughout, there are also numerous students who see themselves as having a heritage reflecting a mix of races and cultures unrecognized by the conventional categories used in statistics and policies. I try to note here some of the many aspects of diversity, because the work in this book is based on the idea that substantive, broad change in education begins with attending to the specific students and local conditions in schools and other educational programs. I can't adequately explore what it takes to address the needs of each student, each group of students, or all the specific local conditions that matter in every situation. But I can stress that there are no generic issues of race and equity. The circumstances and conditions in each of the contexts I explore in this book create very different challenges and opportunities for improving education, and educators need to look explicitly at the ways in which race and other factors create inequitable opportunities in their communities. In this context, improving education for all is an important goal, but that goal can't be reached without creating more equitable educational opportunities and outcomes for each of those students who have been disadvantaged by the systems at work today.

Why This Book?

Together, all these experiences and connections, the inspiration and the deep frustration that go with them, created the impetus for this book. I wrote this book to try to explain the despair and hope that come along with efforts to change and transform educational opportunities—whether those efforts are carried out in a few classrooms,

within a school, throughout a community, or across districts, municipalities, and education systems. In the process, I attempted to get
beyond the false choice of either improving the schools we have or
blowing up the current system. In their book *The Fourth Way* (2009),
Andy Hargreaves and Dennis Shirley put the conundrum well
when they ask:

> Should schools be improving what they already do, and
> undertake everything in their power to make it better, and
> more effective? Or should they be embracing innovation . . .
> not merely making their existing practice more effective, but
> transforming that practice and perhaps even the nature of
> their institutions altogether?
>
> (p. 210)

My answer to that question is simply *yes*; the challenges in education are
so great that we have to do both.

In the midst of the current protests and renewed calls to address systemic racism, I know that any support for working within the existing
system could end up maintaining the status quo and preserving the
systemic advantages that many people, myself included, have had. But
given what I've seen and learned, dividing educational-improvement
efforts into either/or camps—advocates for *either* improvement *or*
revolution; *either* reformers *or* "non-reformers"; *either* tinkerers *or*
transformers—just produces more and more conflicting initiatives
that end up undermining the capacity for significant educational
change rather than building it. The systemic problems are so deep
that we have to figure out ways to confront these divides as we work
toward a more just and equitable society.

In spanning both efforts—to improve schools and to transform
education—I've written this book for educators who are committed
to making concrete improvements in their own work and interested
in how their work connects to the challenges and opportunities for
improving schooling and creating educational opportunities that so
many people are experiencing around the world. In that sense, this
book is for anyone who wants to be part of a global movement to
create new educational possibilities.

To that end, Parts 1 and 2 of the book are designed to help educators
place their efforts to improve learning opportunities and create new
ones in a global and historical context and understand that many of

the challenges and setbacks they face are not unique. In Parts 3 and 4, I highlight critical steps that anyone can take to launch systemic improvement efforts in their schools, districts, and communities. In this book, I don't go into depth on all the steps needed to carry out those efforts (as I do in my 2009 book *Managing to Change: How Schools Can Survive [and Sometimes Thrive] in Turbulent Times*), but these two sections are designed to introduce approaches and programs that are already demonstrating some success and that can serve as models and further resources. In Parts 5 and 6, I provide a systems perspective to help educators understand and navigate the conditions in their communities that can either imperil or propel their efforts to create more powerful learning experiences. Throughout the book (and listed after the table of contents) are descriptions of programs in the United States and other countries that can serve as models of success.

Given these different purposes and perspectives, you may have an interest in all the sections, or you may prefer to focus on how to start improvement efforts in the schools we have or how to find ways to stretch the limits of conventional schooling in Parts 3 and 4. If you're a policymaker or someone who takes more of a systems perspective, you may want to begin with the history and challenges of educational-reform efforts in Part 2 or the strengths and weaknesses of different systems in Part 5.

On the one hand, I remain enormously optimistic that educational opportunities and outcomes can be improved, particularly for members of groups that have been historically disadvantaged. On the other hand, we can never underestimate the remarkable intransigence of the schools and educational systems we have or the deep-seated beliefs about learning, teaching, schooling, and race that perpetuate inequitable educational opportunities and outcomes. Moving forward requires embracing the contradictions in both improving schools and transforming education and building on the diversity of perspectives and the differences that make new learning experiences possible.

Acknowledgments

This book builds on the support of many colleagues, friends, and family members. My work in education grows out of the generosity and continuing support of Howard Gardner, Lee Shulman, and Ann Lieberman. They, in turn, introduced me to a host of colleagues and mentors who have played pivotal roles in my own development and in the evolution of the ideas in this book, among them David Perkins, Bill Damon, James Comer, Ted Sizer, Janet Whitla, Edmund Gordon, Ernesto Cortes Jr., Dennis Shirley, Larry Cuban, Andy Hargreaves, Larry Leverett, and Bob Peterkin. Throughout, I've benefited from the opportunity to work with colleagues at Harvard Project Zero; the Carnegie Foundation for the Advancement of Teaching; the National Center for Restructuring, Education, Schools and Teaching (NCREST); and the New Jersey Network of Superintendents.

Funding from the Spencer Foundation and the Fulbright Scholar program made possible much of the research and many of the experiences described here, and my colleagues in the Fulbright offices in Norway and Finland welcomed my family warmly and made sure we had everything we needed during our stays. Kirsti Klette helped us make the initial connection to Norway and has remained a valued friend and trusted colleague ever since. In Finland, Auli Toom, Jukka Husu, and Lena Krokfors made possible my family's visit to Finland and, along with Pasi Sahlberg, Jari Lavonen, and Anneli Rautiainen, provided invaluable contributions to my understanding of education in Finland. Both the University of Oslo and the University of Helsinki served as wonderful hosts. In Singapore, I continue to benefit from the support of a wide group of colleagues who have hosted me at the National Institute of Education and made my visits there so enjoyable, productive, and inspiring, including Christine Lee, Pak Tee Ng, David Hung, Tang Heng, current director Christine Goh, and the late Sing Kong Lee. Margus Pedaste and Äli Leijen hosted and supported me in Estonia; Alma Harris and Michelle Jones did the same for me in Malaysia, and Brahm Fleisch made everything possible in South Africa.

I'm also indebted to all those who responded so thoughtfully to my inquiries and questions about their work, and many deserve special thanks for continuing those discussions and reviewing parts of this book: Saku Tuominen, Shelley O'Carroll, Pablo Muñoz, Rachel Goldberg, Charles Sampson, Lynette Guastaferro, Mathew Moura, Thulani Madondo, Nadia Naviwala, Joy Olivier, Mark Dunetz, Jefferson Pestronk, Brian Cohen, Danny Kahn, Santiago Rincón-Gallardo, Heini Karppinen, Pekka Peura, Caitlin Barron, Nikita Khosla, Maretta Silverman, and Eric Schwarz. Throughout, unless otherwise indicated, the quotations from these individuals and other members of their programs are taken from interviews conducted by me or my colleagues as part of the research that went into this book.

I also truly appreciate the efforts of my friends and colleagues who provided invaluable feedback on a draft of this manuscript: Sam Abrams, Larry Leverett, Kirsti Klette, Pekka Peura, Pak Tee Ng, and Karen Hammerness. While the work described herein couldn't have been done without their help and support, the views expressed are those of the authors.

I also thank my colleagues at Teachers College, particularly Felicia Smart-Williams and Alisha Arthur, and my co-director, Jackie Ancess, and Grazyna Hulacka at NCREST, as well as Anita Sicignano, Beatriz DaMotta, and Denise Recinos, who helped in the preparation of the references. The book's reviewers provided very helpful comments on an earlier draft, and I'm thankful for the guidance of my initial editor at Corwin, Arnis Burvikovs; his successor, Ariel Curry (who picked up the ball in the middle of the pandemic after Arnis's retirement); and Jessica Vidal, Gagan Mahindra, and Will DeRooy and all their colleagues who shepherded this book through the production process.

This book draws from a number of my previous publications, and I want to acknowledge the support of the many editors and colleagues who contributed to those publications:

Hatch, T. (2013). Beneath the surface of accountability: Answerability, responsibility and capacity building in recent educational reforms in Norway. *Journal of Educational Change, 14*(1), 1–15.

Hatch, T. (2014). Responsibility and accountability in (a Norwegian) context. In M. Kornhaber & E. Winner (Eds.), *Mind, work, and life: A festschrift on the occasion of Howard Gardner's 70th birthday* (Vol. 1, pp. 487–511). Cambridge, MA: The Offices of Howard Gardner.

Hatch, T., Roegman, R., & Allen, D. (2019). Creating equitable outcomes in a segregated state. *Phi Delta Kappan, 100* (5), 19–24.

Hatch, T. (2020). Building the capacity for collective responsibility in Norway. In M. Jones & A. Harris (Eds.), *Leading and transforming education systems: Evidence, insights, critiques and reflections* (*Education in the Asia-Pacific Region: Issues, Concerns and Prospects* series). Singapore: Springer Singapore.

Earlier versions of some parts of this book also appeared in blog posts on *internationalednews.com* and *thomashatch.org*.

All the work in this book reflects the continuing contributions of Jordan Corson and Sarah Gerth van den Berg. I benefited from their work and ideas throughout the writing of this book, and they were particularly instrumental in developing and carrying out the research and many of the interviews in New York City. I couldn't have asked for more thoughtful and supportive collaborators. I also want to thank Deirdre Faughey, who worked with me in developing my School Change course and helped launch much of the research that has gone into this book.

My extended family—particularly my aunt, my uncle, and my mother, who all became educators long before I did—has always supported me and education in general. My father brought me on that first trip to Mexico and provided a model for so much of what I do. Both of my parents, my brothers, and my sister have always been sources of immense support.

Finally, none of this would've been possible—or so much fun— without Karen Hammerness and her constant support and critical advice. And I cannot imagine doing any of this without the love, inspiration, and wisdom of Hannah, Clara, and Stella that continues to bring me joy and hope. For that reason, and for all the learning opportunities in the future, I dedicate this book to them.

Publisher's Acknowledgments

Corwin gratefully acknowledges the contributions of the following reviewers:

David G. Daniels, Principal
Susquehanna Valley High School
Conklin, NY

Tara Fortner, Assistant Professor of Education
Northern Vermont University–Lyndon
Lyndonville, VT

Clint Heitz, Instructional Coach
Bettendorf Community School District
Bettendorf, IA

Emily McCarren, High School Principal
Punahou School
Honolulu, HI

Cathern Wildey, Adjunct Professor of Education
Nova Southeastern University
Miami, FL

About the Authors

Photo by Alison Sheehy Photography

Thomas Hatch (Twitter: @tch960) is a professor at Teachers College, Columbia University, and director of the National Center for Restructuring Education, Schools, and Teaching (NCREST). His research includes studies of school-reform efforts at the school, district, and national levels. His current work focuses on efforts to create more powerful learning experiences, both inside and outside schools, in developed and developing contexts. He is also the founder of the *International Education News* blog (internationalednews.com) and has developed a series of images of practice (https://www.tc.columbia.edu/ncrest/images-of-practice/) that use multimedia to document and share teachers' expertise. He previously served as a senior scholar at the Carnegie Foundation for the Advancement of Teaching. His other books include *Managing to Change: How Schools Can Survive (and Sometimes Thrive) in Turbulent Times* (Teachers College Press, 2009); *Into the Classroom: Developing the Scholarship of Teaching and Learning* (Teachers College Press, 2005); and *School Reform Behind the Scenes* (Teachers College Press, 1999).

Jordan Corson is an assistant professor at Stockton University. He recently completed his doctorate at Teachers College, Columbia University, where he defended his dissertation, *Undocumented Educations: Everyday Educational Practices of Recently Immigrated Youth Beyond Inclusion/Exclusion.* Jordan has published research in the fields of education and philosophy and teacher education. His research takes up ethnographic and historical methods to interrogate issues of transnational migration and curriculum studies through anti-colonial and abolitionist praxis.

Sarah Gerth van den Berg is a doctoral candidate at Teachers College, Columbia University. Her research explores the design and theory of curriculum involving nontraditional spaces, materials, and processes. She has published in the fields of curriculum studies, participatory arts-based practices, and out-of-school learning.

Introduction

In 2008, after almost twenty years of working on school reform in the United States, I needed to get away. My experiences with educators and schools always inspired me, but inevitably the improvements were never enough. Over and over again, I saw that individual schools could be transformed or created with the right combination of people, resources, support, and relentless drive, but I also learned a lot about why improving schools is so difficult. In the end, most of my learning was summed up in one presentation, titled "How Much Is Too Little?" In it, my colleagues and I described the uncomfortable reality that in many cases the needs in schools were so great that without a massive redevelopment effort involving the entire community, little was likely to change.

With an opportunity for my first sabbatical, I wanted to get out of the country and spend time studying schools where something— anything—might be going better. I set out to study schools and school systems considered "higher-performing," and I hoped to visit places like Singapore and Finland, those at the top of the charts on international tests like the Program for International Student Assessment (PISA) and stars of many stories of educational success.

But I had a contact in Norway, and my wife Karen's grandparents on her father's side were Norwegian, and Norway was close to Finland. . . . One letter of inquiry led to an invitation and to Fulbright Fellowships for both of us, and there we were: my wife, my three daughters, and I in the middle of what seemed like a gray and drizzly afternoon in October. It was the middle of August, 2009, my oldest daughter Hannah's eleventh birthday, and the day before the start of school in Oslo. My wife was ready to expand her research on teacher education to Norway and other Nordic countries, and I was ready to learn about school improvement and what was "working" in education around the world.

While Norway shares many traits with Finland—both are relatively homogenous social-welfare states with cold, dark winters—only Finland regularly finds itself in discussions of educational "high performance." On the PISA tests so often used as a measure of education systems, Norway's fifteen-year-olds perform substantially worse than those in the top-performing countries and about the same as those in the United States in the three tested subjects of reading, mathematics, and science. Rather than trying to determine why the US educational system hasn't been as good as Finland's, I found myself exploring why Norway's educational system hasn't performed as well as Finland's either.

School Improvement in (Norwegian) Perspective

My wife and I first started learning about the Norwegian educational system when we tried to enroll Stella, our five-year-old, in kindergarten in Oslo. After waiting almost eleven years to get all our children into school for a full day, we discovered that compulsory schooling in Norway doesn't begin until first grade. By the time we heard in March that our fellowships for the 2009–2010 academic year had been approved, almost every private or public kindergarten we called was already overenrolled. At least, every *indoor* kindergarten was overenrolled. There were a few places in "forest kindergartens": kindergartens where children spend almost all day, all year round, in all kinds of weather, outside. The children did spend about an hour a day inside, usually in a hut-like structure with a kitchen and a bathroom, but since Stella liked to eat her breakfast in the winter under a table next to the heating vent, we thought the outdoor kindergarten probably wasn't a match for her. Instead, we found her a place in an international preschool. Although she never got much exposure to the Norwegian educational system, she gained friends from all over the world, and she learned to read in the same British accent as her teachers.

The surprises continued once Clara and Hannah started fourth and sixth grade in their Norwegian school. Typically, they left our house in Smestad at about 8:45 in the morning, scootered a block or so to the T-bane (Oslo's metropolitan subway), and traveled two subway stops to school. By about 2:15 in the afternoon, Karen and I had to race back from our offices at the University of Oslo to greet them. More accustomed to sending the girls off on a bus at 7:30 a.m. and then picking them up again at 3:30, we found our workday in Norway almost two hours shorter and wondered how we would get anything done. (We also began to wonder how anyone else got anything done when we realized that Oslo's subways were always packed during a "rush hour" that appeared to start between 2:30 and 3:00 in the afternoon as many other parents traveled home.)

We had so much trouble adjusting to a primary-school day that was only about five and a half hours long that it took us several weeks to realize that Clara wasn't getting out of school at the same time as her older sister. When Karen called Clara's teacher in September to set up a parent conference, we were invited to come in at 1:30. "What will the children be doing then?" Karen asked. "That's when they're done with school," her teacher responded. When we asked Clara about it, we learned that she had been spending an hour hanging out with several of her friends while waiting for her sister. For that hour, they played on the playground or lingered around an after-school program hoping to get leftovers from the hot meal served to enrolled students. On one occasion, Clara excitedly told us that one of the staff let them roast hot dogs over a fire in a trash can in the parking lot.

Our perception of the differences in instructional time in Norway and the United States was also shaped by regular dinner-table conversations in which Hannah and Clara told us about arts and crafts like woodworking and handwork (like knitting) and about the "ute" time (outside time) they had every day. They did have substantial time for Norwegian, math, English, and German, but their Norwegian schedule looked nothing like their schedule back home, where they had daily double doses of language arts and math, art and music once or twice a week, and only twenty minutes for lunch and twenty minutes for recess every day. For homework in Norway, the main things they had to do were the math worksheets we gave them to "keep up" with their peers back in the States.

The differences in the emphases in Hannah and Clara's Norwegian and American school experiences should have been obvious from the start, but the middle of the Norwegian winter was when things really hit home for us. By the end of January, we realized that Clara had spent an entire day, once a week, for four weeks in a row, cross-country skiing with her class. She took her skis with her on the T-bane; walked to school; put on her skis with her classmates, her teacher, and a few parents (some of whom had logs strapped to their backs for the lunchtime campfire for roasting more hot dogs); and skied off into the woods. After lunch, she skied back to school with her classmates, got on the T-bane, and went home.

Hannah and Clara had a great time in Norway. Not only that, but they learned Norwegian. They learned to cross-country ski. Hannah went on a weeklong camping trip with her class and climbed Galdhøpiggen, the tallest peak in Scandinavia. (We found out later that the climb included a trek across a glacier with the sixth-graders tied together with ropes in case they slipped into one of the deep crevasses.) Clara made a project out of inviting every girl in her class over to play, and, toward the end of the year, turned to my wife and announced, "Mommy, I used to be shy, but I'm not shy anymore." And she was right. She and Hannah returned to the United States and picked up their academic work right where they left off. Clara became much more outgoing and much more likely to speak up in class. Hannah went on to read *Harry Potter* in Norwegian.

My research on the Norwegian educational system confirmed the commonality of many of my children's experiences. Middle-school students in Norway, like those in other Nordic countries, spend about 700 hours with their teachers each year, while those in the United States spend almost 1,100 hours with their teachers. Students in Norway spend much less time on homework than those in the United States—about 75 percent of eighth-graders in the United States receive homework in math, but less than 40 percent of their peers in Norway do—yet debates over whether children are being assigned too much homework continue in Norway as well (Matharu, 2015; OECD, 2019). In terms of assessments, educational policy stipulates that students in Norway should receive no grades—no written marks of any kind—up until eighth grade. While some national standardized tests were introduced in Norway (with great controversy) in selected grades and subjects in 2004, for the most part students can still get to eighth grade with almost no written documentation about whether they're performing below, above, or at the level of their peers. On top of that, almost all elementary students (nearly 95 percent) are enrolled in the regular classroom; there's no tracking by ability; and elementary students can't "fail" or be held back.

Slowly, as Karen and I reflected on these personal experiences and our own research, it dawned on us: with less instructional time, less emphasis on academics, less homework, no written marks, and limited testing, Norwegian students still perform about as well as students in the United States. By the end of our year in Norway, we told our friends and colleagues that the Norwegians are doing as well as the United States without even trying.

Improving Schools and
Transforming Education

Although I set out to see what I could learn from "high-performing" systems, I ended up learning about the strengths and weaknesses of many different systems. In some ways, it wasn't as uplifting as I'd hoped, because I found problems everywhere I looked, but I also gained an appreciation for the possibilities that emerge from the unique conditions and contexts that shape learning opportunities around the world.

In this book, I describe what I learned from my experiences studying both the strengths and the weaknesses of educational systems from Singapore to South Africa. I draw as well from a series of studies of the evolution of organizations that have helped expand learning opportunities both inside and outside schools in places like New York City and Helsinki and in rural Rwanda and neighborhoods across Pakistan. Many of those studies, particularly those in New York City, were carried out with my coauthors, Jordan Corson and Sarah Gerth van den Berg.

As detailed in Part 1, those studies around the world and in New York City show that some things in education *have* changed. Globally, more children are enrolled in school than ever before; across the United States and in New York City, high-school graduation rates have reached their highest levels. What's more, those improvements have been accompanied by a host of new and more powerful learning experiences inside and outside conventional schools. Some districts and networks have developed a small set of alternative, magnet, or "innovative" schools. A handful of organizations—such as Success for All, EL Education, and KIPP in the United States and The Citizens Foundation and the Second Chance Program in Asia and Africa—have created their own programs or school models and replicated them in a number of places. In New York City alone, between 2001 and 2015, more than 700 new small school and charter schools were created, some of them featuring unusual and unconventional themes, organizational structures, and learning arrangements.

But the limits of these developments are apparent as well. Whether I looked at a "Future school" in Singapore, explored new small high schools or charter schools in New York City, or visited IkamvaYouth, an after-school program in South Africa, I heard similar stories with a common refrain: it's extremely difficult to develop, sustain, and spread approaches to instruction and schooling that look substantially different from the teacher-centered, age-graded, academically oriented, standardized-tested classrooms that have developed over the past century all over the world. In order to have an impact on large numbers of students, these educational-improvement efforts still have to deal with the conventional structures, practices, and beliefs that define educational experiences for so many children. Having to deal with these conventional structures means that improvements take place slowly, incrementally, over long periods of time; and those improvements are still unlikely to reach many of the children who have never benefited from the schools we have today. As a consequence, those who seek to improve educational outcomes have to confront the fundamental reality that the more radical their approaches are, the more difficult it will be for those approaches to take hold and to spread across many schools and communities.

That means that, instead of hoping that new developments will suddenly cascade across schools and benefit all students, we need to transform the prevailing conception that equates education with schooling. The current logic suggests that

If students go to school, get an adequate education, and graduate high school . . .

then they should be able to succeed in college and/or get a job.

But this simple linear equation ignores the many learning opportunities inside and outside schools that support all aspects of students' development and help prepare them for life and work beyond schools.

Expanding conceptions of education build on the recognition that children in the United States spend only about 20 percent of their time in a given year in school (National Science Foundation, 2014). When we try to improve life outcomes by focusing solely on what happens in schools, we severely limit our ability to support children's development, and we ignore the ways in which differences in access to all kinds of educational opportunities and resources inside and outside schools contribute to inequities (National Commission on Social, Emotional, and Academic Development, 2018). Supporting the development of every child depends on recognizing that "success in life"—whether we define it as graduating from college and getting a job, developing into a responsible person, or making a contribution to a healthy community—depends on far more than formal schooling; it depends on establishing educational systems that embrace and support the development of the whole child, for the whole day.

In short:

- We can use the knowledge and the understanding gained from years of efforts to improve schools to make the next generation of educational-reform efforts much more efficient, effective, and equitable than in the past.
- But changing schools on a large scale also depends on changing our conception of schooling and recognizing that education has to embrace all the opportunities to support learning both inside and outside schools.

To that end, in this book, I explore what it takes to make the schools we have more efficient, more effective, and more equitable at the same time that we create more powerful opportunities to support all aspects of students' development both inside and outside schools.

To achieve this goal, I strive to address a frequent problem with many policies and reform initiatives that aim to make improvements in learning on a large scale across many schools and districts:

Many large-scale school-reform efforts are both too big and too small.

They are too big in the sense that they focus on general issues where it's extremely difficult to make visible progress "on the ground," in schools and classrooms in the short term. At the same time, these large-scale efforts are often too small because they fail to take into account all the aspects of the educational system that have to be improved, and they fail to address the ways in which our improvement efforts are shaped by their cultural, social, economic, and geographic contexts.

In order to tackle this dual challenge, the approach to educational change outlined in this book describes the practices that can make specific, concrete, and visible improvements in the schools we have; demonstrates what can be accomplished when programs think beyond the boundaries of conventional schooling; and describes what it takes for educational systems to develop comprehensive and coherent approaches to support students' development.

Design and Organization

To explain why we need to both improve schools and transform education, the six parts of this book draw on different aspects of my work and different perspectives on educational change. In Parts 1 and 2, I focus on broader questions related to school change—what has changed, what hasn't, and what might—in the United States and around the world. These chapters highlight that the kind of education we need can't be summed up in a single list or laid out in a grand vision. The education we need has to be responsive, flexible, and forward-looking, and it will always be somewhat beyond our comprehension. In Part 2, I take up the question of why it's so hard to change schools and what it will take to create the foundation for the education we need in the future. In the process, I draw on the work of scholars like David Tyack and Larry Cuban (1995), who provided me with the tools and concepts to try to make sense of my early experiences working on a variety of school-reform efforts. Parts 3 and 4 detail some of the specific improvements that can be made in schools right now by focusing on what I've learned throughout my career from working with a variety of organizations and improvement initiatives in both developed and developing contexts. Part 5 returns again to my experiences and work in Norway, Finland, and Singapore. In that section, I look at educational change from a systems perspective and describe the materials, expertise, and relationships it takes to create more comprehensive and coordinated approaches to improving schools. In Part 6, I explore the implications of this approach to look at improvement on the ground and at the policy level and consider some avenues for transforming schools and school systems over the long term. Throughout the book, I highlight a series of principles of school improvement that explain why so many of the conventional structures and practices of schooling endure and explore how we can use that knowledge to develop more effective, equitable, and meaningful educational opportunities in the future.

KEY PRINCIPLES OF SCHOOL IMPROVEMENT

1. *Improvement initiatives are most likely to take off when their goals, capacity demands, and values fit the common needs, existing capabilities, and prevailing conditions in the schools and communities they're supposed to help.*

2. *The more complicated and demanding the changes are, the more difficult the initiatives will be to put in place.*

3. *When problems are widely shared among the stakeholders involved, initiatives that address those problems are more likely to be seen as worth pursuing.*

4. *The demands and pressures of conventional schooling make it easier to transform learning experiences in niches rather than across entire school systems.*

5. *The more radical the changes are, the less likely they are to spread and take hold across large numbers of schools.*

6. *Large-scale improvements in the practices and structures of schooling depend on building capacity throughout the educational system.*

7. *Educational systems and the efforts to improve them reflect the social, cultural, geographic, political, and economic conditions in which those improvement efforts take place.*

8. *The structures and practices of conventional schools are most likely to change in concert with changes in other aspects of society.*

Here are a few things to keep in mind when reading:

Inequitable opportunities and outcomes are intertwined with race, but the realities of racism and the work on equity and justice is different in different contexts. Even high-performing systems—whether measured in terms of education, the economy, human rights, or well-being more generally—fall short of the goals of "perfect social equality" and mutual respect that Sonya Horsford (2011) describes as central to the development of integrated and inclusive schools and societies. Indigenous populations have been displaced and disenfranchised in each of the contexts I discuss in this book, and those whose racial and ethnic background are different from the elite and those in power have been systematically disadvantaged around the world. Language has been used as a marker, often forcing assimilation through the adoption of the language of power, even though there's ample evidence that instruction in a child's first language is crucial.

But in Finland and Norway, issues of race and equity are taken up in contexts where the population is overwhelmingly white and where immigration has been largely voluntary. In Singapore, the educational system evolves in a context where over 70 percent of the population is Chinese, but where political choices were made explicitly to support a multiethnic society and to both adopt English as a national language and preserve and support instruction in Mandarin Chinese, Malay, and Tamil. In South Africa, almost 80 percent of the population is Black African, but a white minority created and maintained the apartheid system and enacted racist policies for years, enforcing segregation and criminalizing many aspects of interaction among racial groups. But it's also a context where apartheid ended in 1994 and a Truth and Reconciliation Commission publicly documented crimes against humanity and, in some cases, provided reparations for the victims.

In the United States, the demographics have recently shifted as the white population has now dropped below 50 percent, but it's also a place where issues of race and equity have to be discussed in a context of colonization, where indigenous people have been displaced and never recognized in the way that they have been in countries like New Zealand and Australia. It's a context in which waves of immigrants from many parts of the world have and continue to arrive, despite the inhumane treatment many have encountered at the border. It's a country where Japanese Americans were forced into prison camps during World War II. And it's also a country that Black people were forcibly brought to and enslaved. Although slavery was abolished by law 150 years ago, numerous policies and accepted practices have perpetuated systematic and systemic racism. The responses to the inequitable opportunities and other inequities described in this book therefore have to go hand in hand with explicit efforts to understand and address the specific conditions in each society and all the ways that people of different races, different backgrounds, different genders and gender identities, different means, and different capabilities have been disadvantaged.

This book focuses on improving school improvement, not on "fixing" schools. Creating more effective and equitable outcomes begins by strengthening the "instructional core"—the relationship between students, teachers, and content in the classrooms and other contexts in which learning takes place (City et al., 2009; Cohen & Ball, 1999; Elmore, 2002). But much of this book focuses on what can be done outside the classroom to create a stronger infrastructure for teaching and learning so that students and teachers can engage in much more effective and equitable learning experiences inside classrooms and across their communities. This choice is deliberate. It reflects the belief that students and teachers around the world are ready to learn together, but we've failed to provide the support that will allow them to take best advantage of the time spent in schools. Too often, when outcomes don't match our aspirations, we blame students and teachers, rather than looking to see what everyone involved in education could be doing better. In that sense, instead of focusing on schools or the nature of the learning experiences inside them, in this book I focus on the work of educational improvement more broadly and what all of us can do to make improvement efforts more effective. I emphasize the work that needs to be done so that students and teachers can do theirs.

Everyone can be an education leader. This work challenges the division between learning inside and outside schools—and the separation between "leaders" and "followers." In this work, rather than talking about administrators and teachers or about "education leaders," I use the more general term "educator," because the changes that have to be made ultimately have to support the work of all the educators who work directly with students and because everyone can play a role in leadership. The examples in recent years of movements to address gun violence in schools as well as the growth of the climate change movement demonstrate that students and parents can be education leaders—as can teachers and school staff, school and district administrators, superintendents, policymakers, and politicians. *All have to play a role* if we are to distribute and share the responsibilities for creating more powerful and equitable educational opportunities. But none of that work will matter if it doesn't support and sustain the crucial work that teachers do with students.

> All have to play a role if we are to distribute and share the responsibilities for creating more powerful and equitable educational opportunities.

No single "solution" will work across all contexts. In this book, I show that no single approach to school improvement—no one model, system, or set of resources and practices—will work for every child in every community. Schools can be successful in systems like Singapore's, with a strong central authority; in Finland, where there's a strong role for a central social-welfare state, but also considerable autonomy at the local level; and in highly decentralized systems like the Netherlands', where almost anyone can start a public school. Even in the United States, successful schools can be found in districts that provide little central direction and those that take a strong system-wide approach; successful schools can also be found in centralized charter networks and among independent, private or public mom-and-pop alternative schools started by parents or community groups. Rather than pitting one approach against another, I take the perspective that the approaches to education discussed in this book have both strengths and weaknesses. I look at where, when, and for whom schools and school systems are working and then strive to understand what we can do to create the local conditions in many different contexts that support the development of all children, in every community.

There is no "one best system." Along those same lines, what counts as higher-performing in education—as in everything else—varies widely. The higher-performing educational systems like Finland's and Singapore's have various strengths and weaknesses. Both countries have ranked near the top on PISA's tests of reading, mathematics, and science for some time. Finland shows more equitable results than many countries, with one of the lowest percentages of low performers in reading and with consistency in high scores across schools and regions. Finland also ranks high on broader measures of development, including work-life balance, overall living conditions, and happiness (Legatum Institute, 2019). At the same time, Finland's PISA scores in reading, mathematics, and science have been declining since 2006, although the nation continues to rank among the top performers (Legatum Institute, 2019; OECD, 2020; Schleicher et al., 2019). Singapore has continued to top the PISA charts in reading, mathematics, and science—even showing improvement since 2009—and leading all other educational systems in the test of collaborative problem-solving, as well (OECD, 2017; Smith, 2019). Nonetheless, Singapore's students report significantly higher levels of stress than the OECD average (86 percent said they were worried about grades at school, compared to the OECD average of 66 percent) (Legatum Institute, 2019). Further, Singapore continues to have high levels of income inequality—almost as much as in the United States and much higher than in Finland—with more constraints on personal freedom than in the United States or Finland.

Even systems that are "lower-performing" on PISA can excel on a wide range of other measures of success. Norway, like its neighbor Finland, routinely tops the charts in adult development, health, economic performance, and other areas. Therefore, in this book, I consider what it takes to develop and improve each educational system within its social, cultural, political, economic, and geographic context. The goal is to use that information to enhance and deepen our understanding of our own educational systems and the benefits and drawbacks of pursuing different approaches to improving them—not to advocate for a particular policy or for universal best practices.

Why Should Schools Change?

Every fall, I teach a class called School Change. I inherited the class when I arrived at Teachers College in 2003. If I'd had a choice, I would've called it School Improvement or Educational Reform, but going through the paperwork to officially change the title never seemed worth it. Instead, I now produce a syllabus with "School" crossed out, so that the title reads Educational Change.

In that course, I routinely begin the semester with an activity in which I ask the students to close their eyes and to think back to what they were doing in their classroom when they were a student in first grade. They sit quietly for a few moments and then turn and talk to a classmate. After five or ten minutes of conversation, I ask the students to close their eyes again, this time to imagine what's happening in first-grade classrooms today and then to share their perspective with their partner.

The activity moves on to a discussion of whether anything has changed since they were in first grade. Usually, some students point to what they think of as clear differences—there are now laptops, iPads, and even cell phones, for example—and many students from the United States argue that testing and homework have increased. But the fact that sometimes as many as half the students grew up and went to school outside the United States deepens the discussion. Relatively quickly, changes that at first seemed "obvious" become more ambiguous: Is there really more hands-on learning? Are teachers and students really more stressed and anxious than they were twenty years ago? Have there really been effective efforts to create more equitable learning opportunities? To ground the conversation, we talk about why the students might have different perspectives on what's going on today. What evidence are they drawing on? Research? Media portrayals? Their own experiences? All are worth considering, but in the end, I ask them to answer an either/or question: "Have schools gotten better or worse?"

Invariably, students try as hard as they can not to answer. "It depends," many argue. That conversation starts a new one as students begin to generate all the conditions and factors that make it hard to decide. Crucially, that conversation brings to light that schools may have changed for some people, in some places, in some ways . . . all of which makes it difficult to decide whether things have gotten better or worse and for whom.

And that's the point.

Like the act of "changing" the course without going through the paperwork of changing the title, this activity highlights that whether we believe the world has changed depends on how we think about the world. We can see the world as changing, or we can see the world as staying remarkably the same, but what matters is what we *do* about what we think.

> We can see the world as changing, or we can see the world as staying remarkably the same, but what matters is what we *do* about what we think.

In the next three chapters, I introduce the key motives for improving schools and transforming the educational system by exploring this question of how schools have and have not changed. I look at some of the improvements in schooling that have been made around the world, but I show some of the ways that those efforts continue to fall short. I outline a series of barriers in the United States that perpetuate inequitable learning opportunities for Black students, indigenous students, students of color, and students from many other historically underserved groups; and I argue that even with drastic improvements on typical academic outcomes, conventional schools still won't address the many aspects of development or the broader purposes that support meaningful lives. Together, these three challenges provide the motive and rationale for this book: increase access to and quality of education, establish equitable educational opportunities and outcomes, and broaden the purposes of schooling.

Increasing Access and Quality 1

A wide variety of educational statistics fuel the debates over whether schools have improved. To illuminate those debates, in this chapter, I first look at some of the changes in access and quality of education in the developing world and then consider what has and has not yet been accomplished in the United States and other established educational systems.

What Has Improved in Schooling in the Developing World?

On the one hand, education in the developing world has shown remarkable improvements in both access and quality:

- Enrollment rates in primary school reached their highest levels ever, with over 90 percent of school-aged children enrolled in 2015.

- The years of school completed by the average adult in developing countries more than tripled, from two years to more than seven years, between 1950 and 2010.

- The percentage of literate youths (ages fifteen to twenty-four) around the world has increased to over 90 percent since the 1980s.

- Almost 60 percent of all countries for which data are available have largely eliminated illiteracy among youths (UNICEF, 2019).

Reflecting the continuing challenges, however, numerous statistics expose the limits of progress toward the educational targets of the Sustainable Development Goals endorsed by the United Nations in 2015 (UN General Assembly, 2015). Those targets focus on ensuring inclusive and equitable quality education and promoting lifelong learning opportunities for all, yet the numbers show how much farther we have to go:

- More than 260 million children and youths aged six to seventeen were still out of school in 2017.

- Roughly 617 million primary-school-aged and lower-secondary-school-aged children—more than 50 percent—didn't achieve minimum proficiency levels in reading and mathematics in 2015 (UN Economic and Social Council, 2020).

- Even after having spent four years in primary school, almost 130 million children won't have developed basic skills—by one estimate, only 14 percent of students in low-income countries master basic mathematical skills (such as making simple calculations) by the end of primary school, compared to over 98 percent of students in high income countries like Japan and Norway (UNESCO, 2015; World Bank, 2018).

- Many developing countries still lack basic infrastructure and facilities to provide effective learning environments (sub-Saharan Africa faces the biggest challenges: at the primary and lower secondary levels, less than half of schools have access to electricity, the internet, computers, and basic drinking water).

What these statistics mean to children all over the world became clearer to me when I got to see schools and classrooms in South Africa. I spent one morning at a gleaming public school, with stone walls and marble hallways, surrounded by manicured athletic fields and a pool. Under apartheid, the school had been a part of the school system reserved for white students, but, post-apartheid, it had a multiracial student population, drawing students from mixed middle- and higher-income neighborhoods in the area. When I arrived, the entire school body was assembled, seated outside on a beautiful day, listening to a well-known journalist who described his efforts to cover wars and human-rights violations around the world.

The very next day, I found myself in a neighborhood with a growing middle class. I passed yard after yard of ranch houses, some well-kept and others that appeared to be abandoned. There I found a smaller school with trailers for some classrooms, surrounded by dusty fields. When I was ushered into a darkened office to talk to the principal, he apologized for the lack of lights and air conditioning, explaining that the electricity was out. We talked for almost two hours while he described the work the school was doing to improve. In many ways, the story he told—the careful steps he was taking to build support in the community and to hire and develop a capable and committed staff—sounded like the stories of successful school improvement I had heard from the community organizers and educators in my work in El Paso, Dallas, and the Rio Grande Valley in the United States. But our conversation was just beginning, and for the next hour and a half, the principal laid out a litany of issues related to the basic needs for learning that were common across a number of schools in South Africa, particularly the township schools that had been a part of the educational system under apartheid. As he put it, in some places where he had worked, "there was no teaching and learning—none." Students dutifully showed up day after day, and year after year, but received no sensible instruction in any sensible sequence, epitomizing what *The Economist* has called the world's worst educational system (*Economist*, 2017). Under these conditions, despite some improvements, 27 percent of students who have attended school for six years can't read; 34 percent of ninth-graders still can't do basic computations and haven't acquired a basic understanding of whole numbers, decimals, operations, or basic graphs; and one in four students fail their end-of-school exams (Spaull, 2017).

What Has Improved in Established Educational Systems?

The experiences and evidence from the developing world demonstrate how much has been accomplished and the depth of the problems that remain; but, even in developed countries like the United States, this same "the more things change, the more they stay the same" scenario repeats itself. On the positive side, there are some encouraging numbers from the United States:

- High-school graduation rates rose from barely over 70 percent in 2001 to almost 85 percent in 2017 (though debates continue over how accurate these figures are) (America's Promise Alliance, 2019; Dynarski, 2018).

- From 1990 to 2016, the dropout rate for Hispanic youths fell from 32 percent to about 9 percent. For Black youths, it dropped from 13 percent to about 6 percent (Snyder et al., 2019).

- For the first time, low-income students are enrolling in college at the same rate as middle-income students, and college enrollment has grown substantially for youths from all racial and ethnic groups, including a 240 percent increase for Hispanic students and a 72 percent increase for Black students (America's Promise Alliance, 2019; Child Trends, 2018; Krogstad, 2016).

- On the National Assessment of Educational Progress (NAEP) ("the Nation's Report Card"), students at the fourth- and eighth-grade levels performed at higher levels in 2017 than they did in 1992 (Nation's Report Card, 2017).

These are meaningful improvements for the society as a whole and especially for the students (and those students' families) who have been able to get a high-school diploma that may have been out of reach in their parents' generation. Nonetheless, roughly 4 to 5 percent of American high-school students—almost 500,000 students—drop out each year, a number that has gotten only marginally better than the almost 6 percent who dropped out in 1976. Estimates suggest that, altogether, about 4.5 million youths are neither in school nor working. That's roughly 11 percent of sixteen-to-twenty-four-year-olds overall. For Black young adults, that percentage rises to 18 percent, and for Native American youths the percentage is almost 24 percent (Lewis, 2019).

As American demographics have changed in recent years, the percentage of white public-school students has dropped below 50 percent, with the largest increase in the percentage of Hispanic students (National Center for Education Statistics, 2019). At the same time, high-school graduation rates for emergent bilinguals (those learning to speak English) and students with disabilities have risen, but only to about 67 percent, substantially below the graduation rate for all students.

Student performance, as measured by test scores on the National Assessment of Educational Progress, also remains far behind graduation rates. Although graduation rates overall surpassed 80 percent in 2017, only about 40 percent of fourth-graders and 34 percent of eighth-graders could demonstrate proficiency in math. Roughly 37 percent of fourth-graders and 36 percent of eighth-graders demonstrated proficiency in reading (Nation's Report Card, 2017; National Center for Education Statistics, 2018). For students classified as English language learners or identified as having a disability, the results are much, much lower. Only about 15 percent of emergent bilinguals and of students identified as having a disability reach proficiency in reading, with a similar percentage reaching proficiency in math, at fourth grade. Those percentages get even smaller at eighth grade (Advocacy Institute, 2020; Heasley, 2019; U.S. Department of Education, 2018).

Even in Massachusetts, where improvements in education have been dubbed "the Massachusetts Miracle" and the state routinely ranks highest in terms of NAEP scores, not all students have benefited. In fact, as of 2017, almost half of Massachusetts' students still failed to demonstrate proficiency in reading at fourth grade, and 46 percent didn't demonstrate proficiency in math. Massachusetts also has one of the largest gaps in outcomes between students from families with lower incomes and those from families with higher incomes, and that gap has been widening (Balonon-Rosen, 2016; Nation's Report Card, 2019; Wong, 2016).

The hope and frustration reflected in these statistics crystallized for me in one study my colleague Doug Ready and I carried out in New York City. To inform the policy discussions leading up to the city's mayoral election in 2012, we were asked to examine how the odds and outcomes for students in New York City had changed since the year 2000. For our analysis, we focused on the performance of the 77,501 students who started ninth grade in 2005 and who had been in New York City public schools since kindergarten. Those analyses showed that 67 percent of the students in that cohort graduated by 2009, a substantial increase from the 51 percent graduation rate in 1999. But when we looked at another measure—improvements in annual test scores in English language arts (ELA)—the numbers told a very different story. Of that same cohort of students who started high school in 2005, less than 3 percent of those who had failed to meet the ELA standard when they were in third grade had gone on to meet or exceed the standard in eighth grade. These findings showed that there was a significant group of students in New York City for whom five years of education, from fourth to eighth grade, produced virtually no improvement.

Statistics like these demonstrate that, despite reasons for hope, there's no reason to believe that the improvements made so far will lead in the near future to a system that supports the development and serves the needs of all students. In the United States, the No Child Left Behind Act of 2001 (NCLB) famously contained provisions designed to ensure that all students—100 percent—would be on track to achieve proficiency by 2014. That policy included requirements for testing students in math and reading every year from third to eighth grade and penalties for schools and districts that weren't making "average yearly progress" toward the goal of universal proficiency by 2014. The results? Although researchers continue to debate whether some improvements in test scores can be attributed to NCLB, by 2011, almost half of all schools in the nation were considered "failing"; in six states, that label was applied to *75 percent or more* of all public schools (Ladd, 2017; Usher, 2011).

With these kinds of problems, many of the strictest requirements of NCLB were loosened, and with the subsequent Every Student Succeeds Act of 2015 (ESSA), states now have the right to develop their own measures of average yearly progress (which can now include a much wider range of indicators, including indicators related to absences, socio-emotional learning, and school climate). But the predictions about when such average yearly progress might translate into a basic level of educational success for all students have been abandoned.

Improvement Is Not Enough

> Working in education demands an ability to see the glass of water as both "half full" and "half empty" at the same time.

Working in education demands an ability to see the glass of water as both "half full" and "half empty" at the same time. The progress made in education in developing countries deserves to be celebrated, but the rate of progress in increasing access to primary education has declined significantly since 2007. The difficulties of reaching basic levels of educational success for all are evident even in those places where some of the most rapid improvements in educational performance have occurred, and even children from the richest 20 percent of households haven't reached universal mastery of basic reading and math by the age of thirteen (Akmal & Pritchett, 2019).

The development of the highest-performing educational systems also illustrates both the possibilities and the problems in improving schooling. On the one hand, the relatively rapid development of comprehensive schooling in countries like Singapore and Finland demonstrates that significant, large-scale improvements in education can be made. Beginning with the election of Singapore's first independent prime minister in 1959, Singapore created a comprehensive public education system out of a disparate set of English, Chinese, Tamil, and Malay schools that previously served only a small portion of the population. In tight coordination with the development of Singapore's economic policy, new schools were created, free textbooks were distributed, new teachers were hired, and universal lower-secondary education was achieved by 1970 (OECD, 2011). In the 1970s, Finland launched a nationwide effort to turn a highly inequitable and inefficient group of schools into a comprehensive school system that offered a consistent, high-quality education to all students (Sahlberg, 2011). By the end of the century, both educational systems ranked among the highest performers on international tests.

On the other hand, many of the Singaporean and Finnish educators and policymakers I talked to on my visits recognized the problems with their educational systems as well. In Singapore, I saw the obsession with tests and academic achievement in bookstores and even on newsstand kiosks, where parents could select from row after row of workbooks and exam study guides. I saw it again in the shopping centers and malls whose directories listed numerous businesses that provide endless tutoring and homework assistance options. And I saw it again, out at night with a Singaporean educator who shared her concerns about the extent of academic pressure but nonetheless felt compelled to phone her daughter at 10:00 p.m. to make sure she was still studying. In Finland, along with the recent declines in PISA scores, I heard concerns about low levels of student engagement and the increasing gap between low and high performers in what has been one of the most equitable educational settings in the world.

To address these issues, both systems are pursuing new initiatives designed to overhaul the teacher-centered, academic instruction characteristic of conventional schooling and shift to what they hope will be more engaging, interdisciplinary, and student-centered approaches. Consistent with other efforts to support the development of "21st-century skills" in the United States and other countries, these initiatives seek to develop social, emotional, and cognitive abilities that will enable students to work together, solve problems, persist in the face of adversity, and adapt to an unpredictable future. Nonetheless, making such a substantial shift in these educational systems has been no easier than it has been in places like the United States.

The Bottom Line

Almost any statistic can spark a debate, but, from my perspective, the evidence recounted here should contribute to a broad consensus: improvements in access and quality of schooling have benefited children across the globe, but the efforts to improve education have not gone far enough. Educational-improvement efforts have failed to reach millions of children—even some children in the most developed educational systems in the world—and even the highest-performing systems have problems that need to be addressed.

What should we do? For some, the improvements are evidence that we're on the right track: that if we can keep increasing access and quality, double down on the improvement efforts that have worked, then we can improve schooling for all. But the evidence suggests that we have to develop a much better understanding of which children have been left behind and why, and then we have to take specific steps that can create more equitable and powerful learning opportunities for every one of them.

Improvements in access and quality of schooling have benefited children across the globe, but the efforts to improve education have not gone far enough.

Establishing Equitable Learning Opportunities   2

All children have a right to a strong educational foundation, but focusing on creating educational systems that serve students in general ignores the differences in opportunities that shape each child's development. Beyond improving access to and quality of education overall, developing an explicit focus on equity and justice and eliminating the barriers to educational opportunities that so many children face serves as a crucial second goal for systemic educational improvement.

Equity, Opportunity, and Education

Equity in education means ensuring that all students have the opportunities and support they need to reach the same meaningful outcomes. That means eliminating the predictability of students' educational accomplishments based on their racial and ethnic backgrounds, their gender, their family's level of income, where they live, and other characteristics.

A comment from Dr. Comer sums up for me why creating equitable educational opportunities needs to be an explicit focus of efforts to improve and transform schools and why confronting systemic racism has to be a part of that work. The comment came during an interview I was doing with him about the evolution of the organization he founded, the School Development Program. That organization had a multiracial staff, with a particularly large number of Black members at all levels of the organization, including in leadership roles. Toward the end of the interview, I asked him about the significance of having an organization with so many Black members as senior leaders. He paused for a moment and then said, "White people just don't understand, deep in their hearts, what it means to be disconnected."

Over the years, that conversation and that comment have stayed with me. There have been times when I have felt disconnected. When Karen and I moved to California, far from our network of family and friends on the East Coast, we had to find doctors and navigate the healthcare system when Karen was pregnant. In Norway, where we couldn't understand the language, we often found ourselves confused, missing out or misunderstanding key information. Unaware of the "potato vacation" in September (so named, we were told, because it used to coincide with the potato harvest), we suddenly found ourselves with our children home from school for a week. Later in the year, one day we dutifully took our children to school only to find the building completely empty; our confusion lifted later when a neighbor told us it was Kristi Himmelfartsdag (Ascension Day), a national holiday. But when I think of that conversation with Dr. Comer, I am reminded that those were just minor inconveniences. Those experiences gave me only a momentary glimpse of what it might be like to be disconnected from the information, resources, and support that are denied to so many around the world. That conversation with Dr. Comer pointed as well to the systemic racism—the policies, practices, and norms—in the United States that enforces that disconnection and limits access by promoting segregation, advancing white privilege, and perpetuating racial inequity.

In this chapter, I try to make visible the barriers and gaps that limit access to the networks of economic, social, educational, and political support that are the foundation for the healthy development and effective education of every child. To illustrate the challenges, I focus on ways that inequitable economic and educational opportunities add up, creating what Gloria Ladson-Billings (2006) calls the "education debt." Given the systemic racism that has affected Black students in the United States in particular, I highlight the statistics that frequently show that Black students continue to face some of the most significant opportunity gaps. To indicate the breadth and extent of the problems, however, I also draw on a few of the statistics that demonstrate that inequities and discrimination create significant opportunity gaps for people of many races, backgrounds, genders, means, and capabilities.

It's important to keep in mind that, despite the barriers and problems of racism and inequality, millions of people rise above these grim statistics every day and demonstrate how to overcome these conditions. Developing a common understanding of the challenges and the possibilities creates a foundation for the collective work that can accelerate those accomplishments and expand educational opportunities as the fight for racial and economic justice continues.

The Vicious Cycle: Economic Inequality + Inequality of Educational Opportunity

Despite having one of the largest economies in the world, the United States has a much higher rate of economic inequality than many other developed countries. Over the past forty years, the gap between those at the top and those at the bottom of the US income distribution has widened considerably. Even in 1980, those in the top 1 percent of adult wage earners earned twenty-seven times as much as adults in the entire *bottom half* of the income distribution. But by 2014, the top 1 percent, with an average pre-tax income of $1.3 million, were earning over eighty times as much as those in the bottom half of the income distribution, whose average income was $16,000 (Piketty et al., 2018). Black families have seen little progress: in 1968, the median Black family income was 57 percent—just over half—of the income of white families, and in 2016, Black family income remained almost the same, at 56 percent the income of white families (Manduca, 2018).

As the income gap increased, upward intergenerational mobility slowed. In the United States, those born in the 1940s had a better than 90 percent chance of earning more than their parents did at age thirty, but for those born in the 1980s, the odds dropped to almost fifty-fifty. This overall decline in mobility comes with important differences by race and other factors: middle-class white Americans tend to make slightly higher incomes than their parents, but middle-class Black Americans tend to earn slightly *lower* incomes (Philanthropy News Digest, 2018; Semuels, 2016; Smith, 2018).

These developments produce a vicious cycle: increasing inequality of outcomes exacerbates disparities in opportunities, which in turn contributes to more inequitable outcomes (Yellen, 2014). Simply put, wealthier families can take advantage of opportunities that poorer families can't, making it harder and harder to level the playing field. Under these circumstances, the failure to address existing inequalities

> The failure to address existing inequalities in educational opportunities means that education reinforces, rather than reduces, inequitable outcomes.

in educational opportunities means that education reinforces, rather than reduces, inequitable outcomes.

Separate and Unequal

Overwhelming evidence shows that many educational resources and opportunities in US schools remain inequitably distributed. Some of those inequities reflect the wide variations in funding that stem from public schools' reliance on local taxes. But the continuing segregation of communities by race and income makes those inequalities especially pernicious: 28 percent of Black children and almost 20 percent of Latinx children live in areas of concentrated poverty, compared to only 6 percent of Asian children and 4 percent of white children (Annie E. Casey Foundation, 2019).

That segregation contributes to the fact that Black and Latinx students are much more likely than white and Asian students to go to schools with a higher percentage of Black and Latinx students. In addition, in half of the "intensely segregated" schools—schools where students of color make up more than 90 percent of the student population—90 percent of the students also come from low-income households. In contrast, only 2 percent of those in schools where Black students make up less than 10 percent of the population come from low-income households (Kneebone & Holmes, 2016; Orfield et al., 2017).

This racial and economic segregation contributes to the substantial differences in access to money, resources, and opportunities. EdBuild, a nonprofit organization established explicitly to examine disparities in school funding, found that, on average, school districts with predominantly nonwhite students receive $2,226 less *per student* than predominantly white school districts. EdBuild also noted that districts that are poor and predominantly white receive about $150 less per student than the national average, but they still receive nearly $1,500 *more* than poor nonwhite school districts. When taking wealth into account, 20 percent of students go to schools in districts that are both poor and nonwhite, but only 5 percent live in districts that are poor and predominantly white (EdBuild, 2019).

How Inequality Adds Up

The debates over the impact of increased school funding continue, but few experts dispute the findings that *teachers* have the most significant impact on student learning of any school-based factors in the United States. Yet studies that show disparities in access to teachers remain as common as studies that show how important teachers are. Study after study shows that Black, Latinx, and low-income students are more likely to have less experienced, less qualified, and less effective teachers. These results generally hold whether the studies look at how teachers are distributed across districts, across schools, or within schools (Isenberg et al., 2013). One study of all districts in Washington State made the point bluntly, reporting that virtually every measure of teacher quality "is inequitably distributed across every indicator of student disadvantage— free/reduced-price lunch status, underrepresented minority, and low prior academic performance" (Goldhaber et al., 2015, p. 1).

Recent research also highlights that students benefit from having a teacher of a similar racial background (Bristol, 2019). Yet, with white teachers making up over 80 percent of the workforce, estimates indicate that 40 percent of schools have no teachers of color. As a result, thousands of students of color never have the opportunity to learn from a teacher of a similar racial or ethnic background. On the other hand, thousands of white students lose the chance to learn from a teacher of a different racial or ethnic background. That situation limits all students' opportunities to benefit from the diversity that can have a positive impact on their development.

Access to appropriate and challenging curricula ranks as another of the most important school-based factors for student learning. Nonetheless, tens of thousands of historically underserved students remain shut out of advanced coursework (NAEP, 2015; National Academies of Sciences, Engineering, and Medicine, 2019).

- Low-poverty schools are one and a half times as likely as high-poverty schools to offer advanced courses; 40 percent of graduates from low-poverty high schools completed biology, chemistry, and physics, compared to only 23 percent of graduates from high-poverty schools.

- One-quarter of high schools with the highest percentages of Black and Latinx students don't even offer Algebra II; a third of these same schools don't offer chemistry.

- One study found that more than 70 percent of white students go to schools that offer a "full range" of math and science courses— including algebra, biology, calculus, chemistry, geometry, and physics; just over two-thirds of Latinx students have access to those courses, but barely half of all Black students and less than half of Native American and Native Alaskan high-school students have access to those courses.

How Inequality Adds Up

Inequity in per-pupil funding

+

Inequity in access to teachers

+

Inequity in access to advanced coursework

+

Inequity in private contributions for public schools

+

Inequity in access to education outside school

+

Inequity in political and economic power

- Teachers of lower-performing students are less likely to ask them to engage in advanced tasks, such as identifying main themes or critiquing an author's craft, or to pursue higher-order activities emphasizing algebra.

And the list goes on. In addition to inequitable educational opportunities related to the distribution of teachers and access to advanced courses, a report from the National Academies of Sciences, Engineering, and Medicine (2019) identified five more areas where educational opportunities inside schools are often distributed inequitably—including the breadth of the curriculum, high-quality academic supports, school climate, and non-exclusionary disciplinary practices.

On top of all these inequitable opportunities, wealthier families have options and flexibility that poorer families don't (Aldrich, 2019; Goldstein & Patel, 2019):

- Wealthier families have a greater capacity to move to neighborhoods located in better school districts.

- Students in wealthier communities appear to be gaining accommodations for disabilities—including additional time on tests—at twice the rate of those in other communities.

- Wealthier students are more likely to gain admission to gifted programs, with higher socioeconomic status benefiting white and Asian students more than Black and Hispanic students.

Wealthier families are also in a better position to augment the education that schools provide for their children, and they appear to be taking advantage of that capacity (Pew Research Center, 2015):

- Just over half of parents from low-income households said affordable and high-quality after-school programs are hard to find, compared to less than a third of parents from wealthy households.

- Only 60 percent of parents with a low income reported that their children participated in sports; scouts; lessons in music, dance, or art; or other outside-of-school activities, compared to over 80 percent of parents with a high income.

- Just 7 percent of children from families with a low average income attend summer camp, compared to nearly 40 percent of children from families with a high income.

The wealthiest Americans can also take advantage of tax breaks to direct millions of dollars to support the development of the schools and educational programs that they believe are best. Those private contributions to public education have been growing, as well. From 1995 to 2010, the number of community foundations and nonprofit groups linked to local public schools jumped from 3,500 to 11,500. One report noted that in Coronado, California, where median family income is almost $100,000, local groups raised more than $1,500 per student for their public schools; in nearby San Diego, where median family income is less than $65,000, local funds raised amounted to $19.57 per student (Maciag, 2018). Wealthier families unhappy with their local education officials and other politicians can also make substantial contributions to support the candidates and policies of their choice—or choose to finance their own campaigns.

The coronavirus pandemic has made this cascade of inequality visible again. Even before the pandemic, and even in an advanced economy like the United States, access to online and technology-based learning was already highly inequitable:

- Fifteen percent of households with school-aged children had no high-speed internet connection at home, but that percentage increased to almost a third of households that earned less than $30,000, compared to about 6 percent of households earning more than $75,000; over 35 percent of Native American students and 20 percent of Black and Latinx students, compared to 12 percent of white students, had no internet access at home.

- One in five thirteen-to-seventeen-year-olds said they had trouble completing homework assignments because they lacked a reliable computer or internet service, with Black teenagers and those from low-income households more likely to report these challenges (Auxier & Anderson, 2020; Laurens, 2020).

- A further indicator of challenges with household internet access was that some 25 percent of Hispanic adults and 23 percent of Black adults were "smartphone only" internet users—meaning they lacked traditional broadband service at home but did own a smartphone. By comparison, 12 percent of white adults fell into this category. Black, Hispanic, and lower-income smartphone users were about twice as likely as white ones to have canceled or cut off service because of the expense (Perrin & Turner, 2019).

Predictably, as soon as schools started closing their doors and turning to distance learning to slow the spread of the virus, inequities in access to online learning spiraled into a series of challenges that further impeded learning outcomes for the most underserved students:

- Teachers in schools with the largest percentages of students from low-income households reported that, during the initial school closures, almost one-third of their students weren't logging in or making contact. This was almost *three times* as many students as in schools with the *lowest* percentages of students from low-income households (Herold, 2020).

- Only about one-third of districts with the largest percentages of students from low-income households reported that they were able to provide online learning opportunities to all students, compared to *almost 75 percent* of districts with the *smallest* percentages of students from low-income households.

These inequities compounded: these underserved students were also more likely to have lost their access to needed resources and supports such as school meals, and many were living in communities where the economic fallout and job losses were most severe and where rates of hospitalization and death were the highest. In contrast, many wealthier families and individuals had the capacity and flexibility to work from home or to simply pick up and move to places where they felt safer.

The Bottom Line

Equity in education means that all students have the resources, connections, and support to reach the same outcomes. It's blatantly unfair and unjust when students encounter substantially different educational opportunities because of factors beyond their control, such as where they were born, their racial and cultural heritage, or how much money their parents make. Educators in the United States and in other parts of the world can't end racial, economic, and linguistic segregation, nor can they address all the societal factors that contribute to systemic racism and discrimination in their communities, but we won't reach our goals for a more equitable society unless educators address the inequitable opportunities that students from so many different backgrounds face in schools today.

Learning with Purpose   3

When I talk with my students about the learning experiences they're designing in my course on school change, we keep coming back to one key question: "What is education for?" That question always reminds me of a fifth-grader's response in an interview a colleague of mine conducted. The interview probed students' "practical intelligence" for school and their understanding of how to navigate the educational process. The interview proceeded normally, with the fifth-grader gradually opening up more and more about her experiences. Then my colleague got to the final question. My colleague looked across the table at her young interviewee and asked, "So, why do you go to school?" A stricken look came across the young girl's face, and she quickly exclaimed, "But I thought *you* knew!"

What Are Schools For?

Too often, the default justification for telling children they need to spend a substantial portion of their waking hours in a school (which usually translates into sitting in a classroom, at a desk, listening to someone talk) centers on enabling them to develop basic academic skills so they can get into college and get a good job (which, in some cases at least, also involves spending a substantial portion of their waking hours sitting at a desk, listening to people talk).

But even if one accepts this simple logic and ignores the many other reasons to improve education and make it more equitable, it's not clear how to prepare students for the jobs that they might take on after spending so many years in school. Educational stories often cite a statistic that 65 percent of the jobs students will encounter when they graduate will be new, never having existed when they started elementary school. But a BBC program (Sander, 2017) couldn't find a source for that statistic and estimated that substantially less than a third of those jobs would be "new" (in the process raising questions about what "new" means). Even if we could predict what jobs might be out there after college or what skills and knowledge those jobs might require, it's difficult to know which jobs might provide the right fit for each of us: Which ones might attract our interest or offer an opportunity for personal and professional fulfillment?

Even though my oldest two children are now young adults, it's still difficult to know what they might end up doing. Just two years away from graduation, Clara is majoring in psychology, in part because she doesn't yet know what she'd like to do, and psychology seems like one way to leave her options open. When Hannah entered her senior year, she was majoring in geology, an interest she picked up in high school. But her interest in education grew quickly, and she applied for and was accepted to teach science in Mozambique through the Peace Corps after she graduated. With the coronavirus pandemic and the uncertainty over lockdowns and travel restrictions, however, neither Hannah nor Clara knows for sure whether they'll be able to carry out their plans. Clara at least knows that she has two more years of college. Because all Peace Corps deployments have been delayed for at least a year, Hannah will have to see if she can find anything else to do. Even if she does make it to the Peace Corps, what will she do after that? Who knows. Maybe go back to school.

Even my studies in child development; my work in preschool, K–12, and higher education; and my experiences with my two oldest daughters haven't prepared me to support the learning of my youngest daughter, Stella, who just started high school. Even though Stella goes to the same high school her sisters did, we're still trying to figure out how to help her pursue all the dance and drama activities she loves at the same time that she completes her homework and participates in all the required activities that she doesn't care about as much. My wife and I, familiar with every level of schooling and every selection procedure all the way through graduate school, still don't fully understand the course options in her high school and find it difficult to navigate the college process and equip Stella for whatever postsecondary future she might pursue.

The Power of Unanticipated Learning

The differences between Stella's experience with technology and Hannah and Clara's made clear for me the challenges of designing an educational system based on what *might be* required in the future. Those differences emerged a couple of years ago while our whole family waited for a table at a Japanese restaurant. "Twenty minutes," the hostess told us. Stella, who was twelve at the time, didn't yet have her own smartphone and asked to borrow mine. I handed it over, figuring she would play *Candy Crush* or another game to pass the time. The wait stretched on. Forty-five minutes later, the hostess called us to our table; Stella gave me my phone, and I put it in my pocket. Later that night, when I checked my phone, I discovered what Stella had been doing while we waited. She had produced a 1-minute-and-20-second video—complete with titles, credits, 1960s-style lounge music, and a Ken Burns–style camera panning across still photos that showed her looking incomparably bored.

As I reflected on what Stella had accomplished, I realized that she, only six years younger than Hannah and four years younger than Clara, belongs to a different technological generation. As Hannah and Clara grew up, we sat on the couch in our living room watching videos on TV together. "Interactive" meant singing along and dancing with music videos from Hap Palmer or trying to solve the mysteries laid out in *Blue's Clues*.

By the time Stella came along, she could watch videos on an iPad almost anywhere we went. But she could also make videos with it. She watched how-to videos of kids her own age who used Rainbow Loom to make bracelets and explained each step along the way. Then Stella would videotape herself making her own constructions, producing her own how-to videos and explaining what she was doing for the camera and an unseen audience. Even though she never posted the videos for others to watch, she engaged in a highly reflective and metacognitive activity that I expect benefited her in numerous ways, including preparing her for her waiting-to-be-seated production.

Of course, watching that iPad and making those videos in her own room was a more solitary activity than the videos her sisters watched with us in front of the TV. Stella also got a smartphone at a much younger age than her sisters did, and now the amount of time she spends on that device and on platforms like Snapchat, TikTok, and Instagram also contribute to challenges for development we can't entirely predict.

How does an educational system plan for things like this?

The Education We Need for a Future We Can't Predict

What has happened in the past gives us some clues about what might happen in the future, but not that many. The difficulties of planning for the future reflect the fact that both our children and the society around us are changing. Under these circumstances, as a parent, I try as best I can to pay attention to my children, to who they are and who they might want to be. I try to help them develop the skills, expertise, dispositions, and agency to take advantage of the opportunities around them and to expose and address whatever challenges they face.

As an educator, I try to pay attention to the past and use my understanding of educational systems, their histories and inequities, to inform my efforts to improve our current one. At the same time, this uncertainty about the future leaves me deeply unsatisfied with a "the ends justify the means" education focused largely on academic achievement as the pathway to a college degree and a job that may or may not exist.

What kind of education do we need? Education involves learning foundational knowledge and skills, but it can go so much further: supporting the development of engaged, thoughtful, responsible, collaborative citizens; fostering personal agency, creativity, deep understanding, empathy . . . with so many possibilities, no single list will suffice to guide educational designs. No single set of educational goals can meet the needs and interests of every child or the emerging needs and opportunities of every community, and no set of educational goals should be restricted solely to academic outcomes.

> No single set of educational goals can meet the needs and interests of every child or the emerging needs and opportunities of every community, and no set of educational goals should be restricted solely to academic outcomes.

The Bottom Line

Debates over exactly which skills and qualities should serve as the focus for education will continue. But even if we continue to disagree about exactly how much different skills matter, perhaps we can agree that basic skills and a strict academic focus aren't enough. Rather than trying to predict the unpredictable, we can strive to agree that education needs to be designed both for today and for tomorrow, both for individual students and for society as a whole. To me, "for today" means ensuring that children are developing foundational knowledge and skills at the same time that they're developing social and emotional skills, their own personal interests and strengths, and a commitment to support their communities and the common good. "For tomorrow" means designing education so that children can develop the meaning and purpose in life that can help them navigate the opportunities and challenges that will enable them to lead fulfilling lives. The education we need for both today and tomorrow has to be responsive, flexible, and forward-looking: ready for the next generation, not the last.

KEY IDEAS FROM PART 1

The chapters in this part of the book set the foundation and establish the rationale for both improving schools and transforming education entirely. They provide information that educators can use to make the arguments to support their own efforts to improve schools and to create new educational opportunities. They help explain why every effort to improve schools today also depends on making a long-term commitment to change our school systems and the inequitable opportunities and outcomes they perpetuate.

These chapters are also designed to encourage educators to take basic either/or questions in education and turn them on their heads. I often get questions about homework, such as "Are students spending too much time on it?" In answering, I often respond with a different set of questions: "What is homework for?" and "Why do we have it?" In the process, I hope to expose that even if we could answer the "homework" question definitively, it would hardly help address the issues that really matter:

- Are students capable, healthy, and engaged?
- Are their educational experiences worthwhile?
- Are students spending their time well overall?

These broader questions require thinking about how we balance all the different values, interests, and purposes that inform education, and that sets the stage for working together to transform it.

Taking into account so many different needs and goals necessitates entirely different kinds of educational approaches. It requires approaches that provide many paths and possibilities. It depends on recognizing the fact that not everyone will reach the same academic benchmarks and developmental milestones in the same way or at the same time, but that those differences are no excuse for inequality. It means eradicating the institutional practices that systemically disadvantage students based on where they live and their racial and ethnic backgrounds and creating conditions that make it possible for every student—whoever they are and wherever they live—to craft responsible and satisfying lives. All of that demands flexible, responsive educational systems. That flexibility can come from supporting the development of skills, abilities, and dispositions that go far beyond a focus on academic achievement and by ensuring that powerful learning opportunities extend far beyond the limits of the school day, the academic year, and twelve years of formal education. Planning for education in the future requires more than having a vision or a set of goals; it depends on creating unanticipated opportunities and preparing to adapt.

KEY QUESTIONS TO ASK TO ESTABLISH THE RATIONALE FOR CHANGE

- In what ways have schools and educational opportunities in your community improved?
  - For whom have they improved?
  - What factors contribute to those improvements and to their benefits for some students but not others?
  - Who has been left out and why?

- What patterns are there in access to educational opportunities and in outcomes based on race, class, and gender?

- How are those inequitable opportunities connected across students' educational experiences?

- What strengths and interests does each student demonstrate?

- Where, when, and how can schools, educational programs, and communities foster those strengths and interests?

Why Don't Schools Change?

The many reasons for both improving and transforming schools have inspired educators around the world to develop new learning experiences, new schools, and new supports for education. At the same time, predictable challenges make it difficult for these initiatives to take hold and reach large numbers of students. As David Tyack and Larry Cuban explain it, many of those challenges stem from the difficulties of changing what they call "the grammar of schooling" (Tyack & Cuban, 1995). The "grammar of schooling"—a metaphor based on the immutable rules that govern language use—consists of the enduring structures and practices associated with conventional schools. It reflects the facts that schooling in the United States and all over the world often takes place within a series of common constraints:

- "Egg crate" buildings that separate students into different grades and classrooms

- Classrooms where individual teachers do most of the talking, in "teacher-directed" instruction

- Class periods that cover a wide range of topics in standard subjects (like the national language; mathematics; history/social studies; and the sciences)

- Schedules punctuated by measures of outcomes based primarily on grades and test scores

Each structure and practice builds on the others, further limiting flexibility and tightening the grip of the grammar of schooling.

In the next two chapters, I explore three key features of the grammar of schooling that help explain when and how schools can change:

- Many of the conventional practices and structures of schooling have changed, but they evolved slowly and incrementally (see "The Possibilities of Incremental Improvement" in Chapter 4).

- Key beliefs about schools and schooling, along with "turbulent" and frequently changing conditions in education and society, exert a conservative force that helps maintain the grammar of schooling and perpetuate inequitable opportunities (see "'Real School' and 'Real Learning'" and "Turbulent Conditions" in Chapter 5).

- Some efforts to create more unconventional educational approaches can take hold in "niches"—in a particular geographic area or among a particular subset of students and schools—and in concert with changing values and conditions in society (see "Improving in 'Niches'" in Chapter 5).

These key features of the grammar of schooling come together in the first fundamental principle that can guide school-improvement efforts in the future.

PRINCIPLE #1

Improvement initiatives are most likely to take off when their goals, capacity demands, and values fit the common needs, existing capabilities, and prevailing conditions in the schools and communities they're supposed to help.

This principle, along with the others introduced in this section and explored throughout the book, provide critical guidelines that can help educators design improvement efforts and make decisions about when and under what conditions to try to create innovative and unconventional learning experiences. They can be used to expose the places and times where the grammar of schooling can be challenged and changed and to identify adaptations that can improve educational-reform efforts that are falling short.

Altogether, the principles and examples in the next two chapters suggest that educators are more likely to create more effective, equitable, and meaningful educational experiences by coming to terms with the grammar of schooling than by trying to transcend it. We can rail against the forces that make it difficult to change schools radically and quickly. Or we can take advantage of what we've learned about the challenges of changing schools and build on them. That doesn't mean learning to live with injustice or settling for the status quo. It means strategically and continuously charting a path forward. The Norwegians have a saying: "Don't fight the snow." If you live in Norway, it's going to snow. By studying the wintry conditions and exploiting the possibilities they provide, you can learn to ski.

Educators are more likely to create more effective, equitable, and meaningful educational experiences by coming to terms with the grammar of schooling than by trying to transcend it.

The "Grammar of Schooling" Always Pushes Back

4

From the standpoint of history, the grammar of schooling itself developed relatively recently. In the United States, over the course of the 19th century, education advocates like Horace Mann in Massachusetts established systems of free public education that drew on a Prussian model consisting of eight years of compulsory schooling, as well as a curriculum divided into discrete subjects. By the beginning of the 20th century, that model expanded as the features of the egg crate school meshed well with needs, demands, and values that came along with the industrial revolution. Almost 100 years later, in the early part of my career, as I worked to help schools improve, I learned, over and over again, why it can be so difficult to change that conventional model.

The Possibilities of Incremental Improvement

I learned about several key aspects of the persistence of the grammar of schooling when I joined the Carnegie Foundation for the Advancement of Teaching in 1996. Early in the 1900s, the Carnegie Foundation for the Advancement of Teaching helped popularize the use of what came to be called the "Carnegie Unit": a standard measure for graduation from high school and admission to college. That standard consisted of a course of five periods weekly throughout the academic year, with fourteen of these units (in other words, fourteen high-school courses) serving as the minimum amount of preparation needed for students to go on to college.

Why did the Carnegie Unit take off? For one thing, this standardized measure solved a problem for both colleges and schools. Colleges developed a standardized way of determining which students were prepared for college by using the number of Carnegie Units as a criterion for admission. In turn, by offering the appropriate number of Carnegie Units, high schools could claim that their students were prepared for college.

In addition to meeting key needs of colleges, high schools, and powerful "elites" (like Andrew Carnegie and many college presidents), the Carnegie Unit brought the kind of standardization and organization to schooling characteristic of efforts to promote efficiency in many factories and other aspects of the rapidly industrializing society. The Carnegie Unit easily fit into school schedules and curricula that were already divided into classes based on major disciplines. Teachers didn't have to change their instruction much or develop new capabilities; they could continue to deliver instruction while standing in front of rows of students seated at desks.

Although many aspects of this basic "age-graded" school model persist, the conventional model of schooling continued to evolve, with new developments meeting emerging needs, values, and capabilities. Kindergartens, for example, now a central feature of public schools across the United States, emerged slowly—in 1900, only 7 percent of five-year-olds were enrolled in kindergarten, but by 1970 that figure reached 60 percent; by

THE CARNEGIE FOUNDATION FOR THE ADVANCEMENT OF TEACHING (USA)

Industrialist Andrew Carnegie (1835–1919) established the Carnegie Foundation for the Advancement of Teaching in 1905 to "do and perform all things necessary to encourage, uphold, and dignify the profession of the teacher and the cause of higher education." The Carnegie Foundation has helped shape K–12 and higher education in the United States by contributing to a number of important developments:

- A pension fund to attract and retain faculty at colleges and universities (later spun out to create TIAA, now one of the largest pension funds in the nation)

- The Carnegie Unit

- The Flexner Report, which led to the reorganization of medical education

- The Graduate Record Examination and the Educational Testing Service

More recently, under presidents Ernest Boyer, Lee Shulman, and then Tony Bryk, the Carnegie Foundation pioneered work on the Scholarship of Teaching and Learning (Boyer, 1990; Hatch, 2005; Shulman, 2004) and the development of improvement science in education (Bryk, 2020; Bryk et al., 2015).

2000, it was over 85 percent (NCES, 2020). Several factors enabled kindergartens to take hold in many communities:

- Kindergartens *fit the changing needs and values* of a rapidly industrializing society by: helping parents who needed a place for their young children to go during the day; helping educators and schools who wanted their students to arrive in first grade "ready" for school; and helping well-connected activists and reformers who embraced kindergartens as a vehicle for supporting poor children.

- Many communities also *had the capabilities* to put kindergartens in place: they could be staffed without extensive new training programs and drew on readily available materials, such as play equipment, books, and art supplies.

- Kindergartens could be "added on" to serve as the first step in graded schools without disrupting the predominant structures and practices of those schools.

In short, kindergartens matched the existing infrastructure of facilities, materials, and expertise that supported the development of the conventional grammar of schooling.

Along the way, in a reciprocal process that Tyack and Cuban (1995) refer to as "schools changing reforms," kindergartens adapted. They emerged as a kind of hybrid that retained some of the qualities of the "children's garden" that reformers championed, but instruction and practices in kindergartens also came to look more like those in the other elementary grades. That process of adaptation, in turn, made it easier for kindergartens to spread.

The Challenges of Radical Change

Despite the well-known persistence of the grammar of schooling, improvement efforts regularly underestimate the importance of the fit between the goals, capacity demands, and values of the changes proposed and the common needs, existing capabilities, and prevailing conditions. In the United States in particular, reform proposals often assume that with the "right" knowledge, the "right" ideas, or the "right" people, conventional schools can be transformed.

I learned that lesson as a member of the ATLAS Communities Project—a partnership among four of the leading educational-reform organizations in the 1990s. Funding from a competition to design "break-the-mold" schools launched ATLAS, along with a handful of other "design teams," in 1991. The original request for proposal put out by the New American Schools Development Corporation (NASDC) made clear their belief that educators already knew what to do, declaring: "These 'new' schools do not need to be created from the ground up. Years of experience with school reform have generated valuable lessons about what works and what does not work" (Kearns & Anderson, 1996, p. 11). In our proposal, we at ATLAS echoed that optimism by stating that the four partner organizations "have spawned a set of well-known and effective educational innovations. Collectively, we have over 80 years of experience in school reform and are working with over 800 schools around the country. Certainly, the expertise for launching an educational revolution exists in the traditions, personnel, and visions of our organizations."

To build on that experience, ATLAS sought to draw together all the knowledge and resources developed by the four organizations at the time. Ted Sizer, president of the Coalition of Essential Schools, described our role in "bottom-up" fashion as key suppliers and supporters of local school-design efforts. He characterized our work as akin to loading a moving van with all the resources that our four organizations had developed and delivering those resources to different communities. Educators and community members could then make their own decisions about how to use the resources to create educational pathways that matched their local needs and visions.

Despite the optimism, creating the comprehensive design—and loading that van—turned out to be particularly difficult. Ultimately, ATLAS did create a K–12 design, a set of resources, and a team of coaches that worked with schools in Gorham, Maine; Prince George's County, Maryland; and

THE ATLAS COMMUNITIES PROJECT (USA)

ATLAS (short for Authentic Teaching and Learning and Assessment for All Students) grew out of a partnership between Harvard Project Zero, the School Development Program, Education Development Center, and the Coalition of Essential Schools.

ATLAS's proposal envisioned different communities using the resources of those organizations to create

- a unique "pathway" of elementary, middle, and high schools,

- with students developing "habits of mind, heart, and work,"

- in interdisciplinary learning experiences focused on "authentic" issues of significance within and outside schools.

ATLAS was one of eleven design teams originally funded by NASDC. Several, including Success for All and Expeditionary Learning (now EL Education), have gone on to develop large networks of schools.

Norfolk, Virginia. Ironically, however, rather than a merger of the four organizations, ATLAS spun out as a separate "support provider," one of many "intermediary organizations" that emerged during that era to help schools improve. ATLAS, like the four partners and many of these emerging organizations, experienced occasional successes but never achieved the wide impact imagined in our original proposal.

Those difficulties could've been predicted from the start. Like many efforts to support fundamental changes in conventional schooling, ATLAS sought to promote practices such as personalized, student-centered, and deeper learning; project and inquiry-based instruction; and portfolio assessments. Many reformers embraced those ideas, but these "reforms" didn't meet the immediate felt needs or the expectations of many students, teachers, and parents. These new practices required new skills, new beliefs about children's development, and new ways of working in schools where limited time, ingrained patterns of activity, and rigid work structures already constrained teaching and learning.

Complicating matters further, the ATLAS philosophy and design clashed with the demands and expectations embedded in the design competition itself. In particular, ATLAS had to provide quarterly reports on the production of forty-four "deliverables," including things like the production of a curriculum with "world-class" standards in English, history, geography, science, and mathematics—reinforcing the same old subject-based divisions ingrained in the grammar of schooling. Yet ATLAS sought to foster interdisciplinary approaches to learning that didn't follow those traditional divisions and embraced support for all aspects of development, not just academic development. In other words, ATLAS was being asked to break the mold while still conforming to many of the conventional structures of schooling.

Under those conditions, the evaluation of all the design teams suggested that teams like ATLAS, those that made more ambitious attempts to break the mold, had the most difficulty getting off the ground and getting their designs into practice. Those designs that matched schools' current beliefs and practices developed and expanded more quickly (Berends et al., 2002).

What It Really Takes to Improve

I learned numerous lessons in working with my colleagues in ATLAS, but one stood out: even with eighty years of experience working in schools—and the efforts of countless teachers, administrators, and researchers I consider among the smartest and most dedicated educators I've ever met—we didn't know enough. All the work the four organizations had already done—all the materials and resources and expertise we had developed—was insufficient. We didn't have all the resources and expertise required to address instruction for every subject or all students, particularly emergent bilinguals and students with different abilities and learning needs; we didn't have the local knowledge needed to make adaptations to different circumstances; and we didn't have experience coordinating the work of four organizations or in crafting a comprehensive approach. Even in areas where we had considerable expertise, it was hard to find the right people and resources at the "right" time, and, in many cases, basic differences in beliefs and assumptions meant we disagreed about what was "right" (Hatch, 1998a, 2001; Hatch & White, 2002).

Rather than seeing these as problems that can be "solved," through my experience with ATLAS, I learned that these are enduring challenges that should be anticipated. I learned that it's far better to assume that we don't have all the knowledge we need and that there's always more work to do. But as with so many lessons described in this book, there is a flipside: we may not know enough, but we can draw on what we've learned to make our improvement efforts more effective. We can look squarely at the educational problems in our communities, identify those we have the best chance to address, and develop a realistic sense of what it will really take for improvements to take off and take hold.

Beliefs Endure, but Times Change 5

The basic principle of developing educational practices that fit the needs, demands, and values of particular communities helps explain how the conventional model of schooling has developed; unfortunately, once established, the basic structures and practices of conventional schools are very difficult to change. As I discovered, early innovations like the Carnegie Unit, created to transform education at the beginning of the 20th century, served as major stumbling blocks in ATLAS's attempt to break the mold of conventional schooling at the end of the 20th century.

These conventional structures and practices reflect "sunk investments"—investments of time, money, and other resources—that make changing schools costly as well as challenging. On top of that, underlying beliefs, differences in values, and changing conditions undermine educators' and educational systems' attempts to make the long-term investments that can contribute to widespread changes. All of these factors increase the pressure to maintain conventional schools, perpetuate inequitable opportunities, and reinforce a focus on narrow measures of academic achievement.

"Real School" and "Real Learning"

Efforts to improve schools have to take into account conceptions of what "real schools" and "real learning" look like. Sociologist Mary Metz

Critical Factors That Help Explain Why Schools Don't Change (Quickly or Dramatically)

- *Limited and uneven infrastructure to support teaching and learning*

- *Entrenched beliefs about "real school" and "real learning"*

- *Differences in values, beliefs, and views of "what works"*

- *The interconnections between education and many other aspects of society*

- *The turbulence of the environment*

(1989) has shown that conceptions of real school help explain the resistance that many educators, parents, and students display in the face of a variety of reform efforts. Conceptions of real school generally associate learning with superficial features, such as students sitting quietly in rows while teachers talk, or with taking and passing multiple-choice tests. Students could be learning in these instances, but there's no guarantee that what they might be learning will lead to meaningful developments and further positive outcomes. Conversely, activities that don't conform to expectations about real school—with students moving around, or working in small groups, or engaging in individual or community-based projects outside their schools—raise concerns that students aren't learning and might not be getting the preparation they need to pass exams, get into college, or obtain jobs.

The many discussions and critiques of the remote learning that schools switched to in response to the coronavirus outbreak surfaced many of these same concerns. On the one hand, schools that simply tried to recreate online what had been happening inside their walls could make it look like students were still learning (at least if those students signed on and stayed online). On the other hand, schools that tried to adjust by providing students and parents with resources and support for more self-directed activities, more videos to watch, or more virtual field trips or other virtual experiences immediately raised questions about whether students were really learning what they needed to learn. However, what students took away from online learning had very little to do with how closely those experiences mirrored the schedule and activities of school. Instead, many parents quickly learned that factors like the ability to connect with and engage students quickly, the clarity of communications and instructions, and the level of support and resources provided mattered much more than what "school" *looked* like.

Confronting these beliefs about what school and learning "should" look like remains particularly critical from the standpoint of equity, because the beliefs that equate real school with traditional course arrangements and conventional academic instruction grow out of school practices and structures that reflect many of the same racist views of ability and intelligence embraced by a number of influential psychologists early in the 20th century. Those views contributed to the sorting of students from different racial and ethnic backgrounds into different schools, classes, and tracks in ways that continue to create and perpetuate inequitable educational opportunities (Oakes et al., 2018; Resnick & Hall, 1998).

Real Differences in Values

At the same time that there are pervasive and problematic beliefs about what real schools look like, the different needs, interests, values, and perspectives of all the individuals and groups involved in education— and the reality of inequitable access to social, economic, and political power—make it difficult to develop broadly shared agreements about what *should* change. Crucially, some "improvements" may solve problems and meet felt needs of some of those involved in education but not others. Policymakers, politicians, and funders play a central role in shaping educational-improvement efforts, but these "policy elites"— overwhelmingly white, male, and wealthy—have different needs and concerns than do the students and educators on the ground in classrooms and schools (Tyack & Cuban, 1995). Further, education leaders and politicians receive publicity and rewards for generating initiatives that promise fast improvements, not for sustaining others' initiatives. At the same time, the knowledge that many leaders and their "new" initiatives turn over relatively quickly discourages educators on the ground from embracing those new initiatives.

Differences in basic values also make it hard to come to agreement on how changes should be made and who should make them. In the United States in particular, critical differences revolve around the appropriate role for government in local affairs. On the one hand, reform proposals that focus on school choice and on giving communities, schools, principals, and teachers autonomy highlight the belief that education should be controlled largely at the local level (considered a "Jeffersonian" perspective). On the other hand, reform proposals that concentrate on creating common learning standards and other universal expectations reflect a belief that centralized authorities like the federal government have a prominent role to play in overseeing and supporting the development of education (a "Hamiltonian" perspective).

These predictable and enduring differences in basic values, needs, and perspectives are exacerbated by the number of organizations and people involved in education; by the interconnections between school systems and other government and societal institutions; and by the segregation and inequality throughout society. The necessity for school-improvement efforts to fit with prevailing needs, values, and capabilities among all the different actors and sectors of society makes it hard to challenge the status quo, particularly when systemic racism and racist beliefs about children, learning, and schooling remain so prevalent.

Adding to the difficulties of meeting the needs of many different people and groups is the fact that, in some ways and for some students, conventional schools work. The current school system benefits many white, wealthy, elite students and families who have always been able to navigate the system, but it also supports the success of increasing numbers of students of color, poor students, and other students who have been systematically and historically disadvantaged. Furthermore, conventional schools meet the needs of many parents and caregivers who depend on public schools to provide meals and other social and health-related services. Schools also make it possible for many parents to go to work by providing a place for children to go during the day and the working week (needs highlighted during the school closures caused by the pandemic). Higher-education institutions rely on schools to get the information they need to recruit and admit students who meet their qualifications, and many employers rely on the graduates that schools and colleges produce. These "successes" encourage resistance from those who have always benefited, which generates a tremendous conservative force not to disturb the many functions that schools continue to serve.

Turbulent Conditions

The difficulty in meeting multiple needs and dealing with conflicting beliefs and values contributes to "policy churn"—a regular stream of new policies and initiatives—and a swinging of the pendulum back and forth between different approaches to improvement. In addition to these policy changes, basic conditions change constantly as populations grow and shrink; the economy rises and falls; new technologies come and go; and life and work change along with them.

In *Managing to Change* (2009a), I chronicled these turbulent conditions and their effects on schools in California at the end of the 20th century when I lived in Palo Alto, in the heart of Silicon Valley. Changing conditions at that time included large increases in the percentage of Latinx students and the percentage of emergent bilinguals; drastic fluctuations in school funding; the explosion of the internet; and the dot-com bubble. Changing policies included a major push to establish statewide standards, new policies limiting bilingual education, and several shifts in the tests used to measure schools and the consequences attached to those results.

After the turn of the century, when I moved to New York City, I encountered another dizzying set of local and national reforms. I tried to keep up, but I could barely catalog, let alone comprehend, the daily impact of the constantly changing educational conditions on schools, teachers, and students. From 2002 to 2012, billionaire mayor Michael Bloomberg's administration made a whole series of dramatic policy shifts, including granting principals autonomy and instituting a new "progress report" to hold them accountable (Childress & Clayton, 2012; Kelleher, 2014); but then the next mayor, Bill de Blasio, reversed many of Bloomberg's initiatives. Over that same period, significant policy changes at the state and national level included the following:

- Passage of No Child Left Behind (NCLB) legislation requiring annual testing in English and math in Grades 3 through 8

- Establishment of the federal Race to the Top (RTTT) program, which encouraged states to adopt higher standards and new approaches to teacher and principal evaluation

- Implementation of the Common Core Learning Standards, along with new Common Core–aligned assessments

- Passage of the Every Student Succeeds Act, which replaced the requirements of NCLB with more discretion for states around testing, evaluation, and treatment of failing schools

Meanwhile, student populations continued to change, and technologies shifted from a focus on platform-based to cloud-based computing and from desktop computers to mobile devices. And all these changes took place in the context of the terrorist attacks on 9/11, the economic meltdown of 2008, and Hurricane Sandy in 2012.

These turbulent conditions contribute to a basic dilemma of organizational development: (Garud et al., 1997; Herriott et al., 1985). In education in particular, many existing structures and incentives favor efficiency and short-term improvement over long-term learning and transformation. On an individual level, this encourages teachers and students to concentrate on the development of routine skills that don't build deeper and more adaptive expertise. On an organizational level, it encourages schools and related organizations to concentrate on making existing operations and routines more efficient in order to increase performance on short-term indicators of success, such as annual test scores.

Policy churn and a turbulent environment exacerbate the challenges for organizational and individual learning, because they make it difficult to predict what will happen in the future. In turbulent conditions, it feels reasonable to focus on increasing the efficiency of current practices that seem to be working rather than to invest in exploring new ideas. Such "exploitation" of conventional, successful practices can lead to incremental improvements, but it can also leave the organization unprepared to deal with changing conditions and discourage organizations from taking the kinds of risks that can lead to new discoveries and transformative changes (Levitt & March, 1988; March, 1991).

Improving in "Niches"

Despite these conditions that reinforce conventional schooling, recent developments such as kindergartens prove that some initiatives do take off and may spread across systems over time. As David Cohen and Jal Mehta (2017) explain, some new developments meet the needs, capabilities, and values in a particular "niche": in a particular geographic area or among a particular group of students and schools. For example, the Advanced Placement (AP) program began in the United States in the 1950s in response to the concerns of elite high schools and colleges that some advanced high-school students had to repeat coursework at the college level. To address the concerns, AP developed a series of college-level course materials and exams. Students who took and passed the approved courses and exams could then qualify for advanced standing in college. Although the program began slowly, it found its niche with the many students and their families, as well as those schools and colleges, who shared the desire for more differentiated and challenging preparation for advanced study.

AP courses introduced more advanced materials and assessments by drawing explicitly on existing capabilities and taking advantage

> The demands for increasing efficiency and improving performance in the short term are substantially different from those needed for making and sustaining radical changes over the long term.

of the college course materials and the expertise of faculty teaching those courses to support the adoption of the program. In addition, AP didn't require changes in the predominant forms of teacher-centered instruction and didn't challenge many of the other basic structures of the grammar of schooling. As a consequence, instead of an "add-on" like kindergarten, AP took hold in some schools as a kind of "plug-in" that fit within the typical course structures, subjects, schedules, and college entrance requirements that continue to reflect the influence of the Carnegie Unit.

Beyond AP, a host of schools, programs, and learning experiences in the United States and around the world have found a niche for their own unconventional approaches (Leadbeater, 2014; Winthrop, 2018). In Finland, in 2016, Saku Tuominen established HundrED to find and showcase promising educational innovations around the world. Tuominen and his colleagues began by identifying 100 Finnish educational innovations that they documented and shared online; in 2017, they expanded this catalog with a list of 100 global innovations from Afghanistan to Venezuela and many places in between; and they've continued to produce a new list every year. In the United States, the Christensen Institute (founded by Clayton Christensen, known for his work on disruptive innovation) compiled a list of more than 200 schools that have been nominated as "innovative" schools, with many pursuing unconventional approaches such as experiential learning, socio-emotional learning, blended learning, and incorporating "wrap-around" services for students. The Christensen Institute and HundrED's catalogs of educational innovations are just

Collections of "Innovations" in Education

- The catalog of innovations, HundrED.org (https:// hundred.org/en/innovations)

- The index of innovative schools, the Canopy Project, Christensen Institute (https:// www.christenseninstitute .org/canopy-project)

- Database of educational innovations in the developing world, Center for Education Innovations (https://www.education innovations.org)

- *Leapfrogging Inequality* (Winthrop, 2018) includes excerpts from and analyses of a Global Catalog of Education Innovations (https://www.brookings.edu/ book/leapfrogging- inequality-2)

- Ashoka Changemaker Schools in the United States and around the world (https://www.ashoka.org/ en-us/program/ashoka- changemaker-schools)

- The Innovators Directory from WISE and the Qatar Foundation (https://www .wise-qatar.org/innovators- directory) two of the resources that highlight the many promising educational developments taking place globally.

Many of these alternative schools and programs, however, found their niche in what can be considered the "margins" of schooling: places where children are learning and developing in ways that can support successful life outcomes but that aren't determined by the current demands of conventional schooling. As Hagel and colleagues (2014) describe it, the hope is that these "marginal" conditions will provide a supportive context for the development of new educational practices and activities:

> Innovation can exist at the edges of every organization, whether in a particular department, set of students, or physical location. Focus on these areas where change is blossoming rather than despair about the immovable core and leverage external resources from the surrounding ecosystem of tools and organizations for support.
>
> (p. 27)

At the same time that these marginal or alternative settings can produce more favorable conditions for changing conventional educational practices, succeeding in a niche doesn't necessarily mean that spreading into the conventional system will be any easier. In part, these difficulties reflect the fact that conditions on the margins may be more supportive of alternative educational approaches than are conditions in the system as a whole. To move out of the margins and succeed at scale, any new approach, ultimately, has to meet the needs and demands of those who are already being served by mainstream schools. In short, in order to spread, niche reforms still have to respond and adapt to the pressures and expectations of the grammar of schooling that are embedded not only in most schools, but also in the vast network of interconnected institutions and organizations that support schools. Even with a more radical funder or greater freedom to "innovate," the grammar of schooling can't be ignored. It's like an invisible force that always pushes back. That's the force that helps explain why, as Tyack and Cuban note, the Carnegie Unit and kindergarten took off across an entire system of schooling, but many efforts to create more student-centered, project-based, personalized, and deeper learning experiences in countless reform efforts like ATLAS have not.

KEY IDEAS FROM PART 2

Why don't schools change? This question comes with a sense of exasperation. Given all that we've learned about how children develop, it should be obvious that it makes little sense to sequester them in classrooms and tether them to desks just to listen to instructions from adults. From this perspective, we already know enough about what's best for children to toss out this antiquated system and replace it with one that places students at the center, fosters agency as well as academics, and supports social and emotional development, responsibility, and purpose.

What holds us back? The frustration with the slow pace of improvement often leads to blaming everyone involved with a lack of commitment and political will. Certainly, changing conventional schools demands political will, commitment, and courage, but as Dr. Comer and the School Development Program have argued, blaming others can erode the common commitment needed to transform education for all. Instead, they focus on unpacking the many reasons why we behave the way we do and then working to develop the relationships and common bonds that can forge a new consensus (Comer, 1988).

With understanding comes possibility. Like the Norwegians who excel in the snow, we can build on what we've learned about the difficulties of changing schools and recognize the possibilities in incremental improvement. We can seek out the "high-leverage" opportunities that can help schools become much more effective, efficient, and equitable than they have been in the past. Recognizing that incremental changes are more likely to sustain the conventional model of schooling than overturn it, however, we can also take advantage of the possibilities for developing new products, new services, new practices, and new approaches to learning in niches that fit the needs of particular groups and communities. Rather than despairing when many of these niche developments don't spread or scale, we can strive to sustain and deepen them; we can take advantage of the adaptations and hybrids that result and explore new possibilities for education that we couldn't have anticipated from the start. These developments can expand our visions and expectations about when and where learning can take place.

KEY QUESTIONS FOR IDENTIFYING THE STRENGTHS AND WEAKNESSES OF IMPROVEMENT EFFORTS

- How widely shared is the "problem" that policies, programs, and improvement initiatives are supposed to address?

- What has to change in order for an initiative to take hold and have an impact in schools and classrooms?

- To what extent do teachers, administrators, schools, and their local communities have the resources and capabilities they need to make those changes and have that impact?

- How consistent are the key ideas and practices of the initiative with the sociocultural, technological, political, and economic trends in society?

How Can Schools Improve?

In Parts 1 and 2, I argue that schools do change, and schools have improved in some ways and for some students. However, schools change slowly, over decades and centuries and in concert with changes in society. The slow pace of educational change is understandable: it reflects a convergence of factors that support the incremental development of more efficient and conventional practices and structures on a large scale but allows for the emergence of more radical "innovations" on the margins of schooling and in niches with amenable conditions.

This reality reflects the second principle of school improvement.

PRINCIPLE #2

The more complicated and demanding the changes are, the more difficult the initiatives will be to put in place.

As policies and reform initiatives get more complicated, the likelihood of successful implementation drops. As the demands for time, money, and resources increase, and the need to change everyday behaviors and beliefs grows, the prospects diminish. We haven't learned from our mistakes, however. Many of the major reform initiatives over the past thirty years have continued to be too big and too expansive—promising extensive and complicated changes across many schools and communities regardless of context and conditions.

The efforts to transform teacher evaluation that took off with the Obama administration's Race to the Top program in 2009 provide a case in point.

RACE TO THE TOP (RTTT) AND TEACHER EVALUATION

Between 2009 and 2012, the RTTT program allocated over $5 billion for grants to states that produced approved plans for educational reform. Those plans had to address issues in six areas, including teacher evaluation (U.S. Department of Education, 2009).

Criteria for judging the plans for teacher evaluation included whether states proposed to

1. establish clear approaches to measuring student achievement growth for individual students;

2. design and implement rigorous, transparent, and fair evaluation systems for teachers;

3. differentiate effectiveness using multiple rating categories that take student achievement growth into account as a significant factor and are designed with teacher involvement;

4. conduct annual evaluations that include timely and constructive feedback and provide teachers with data on student achievement growth for their students, classes, and schools; and

5. use evaluations to inform decisions about staff development, compensation, promotion, tenure, and certification, as well as removal of ineffective teachers.

On one level, the basic "logic" of these teacher evaluation reforms seem fairly straightforward:

If we create better estimates of teacher quality and create more stringent evaluation systems . . .

> **then** education leaders can provide better feedback to teachers, remove ineffective teachers, and reward more effective teachers . . .

> > and student learning/outcomes will improve.

However, asking critical questions about the fit between these reforms and the needs and capabilities of those on the ground unpacks exactly what has to happen to achieve these results. In the process, the complications and predictable difficulties quickly become apparent:

- New instruments have to be created, criteria agreed upon, new observations and assessments deployed, and trainings developed.

- Principals/observers have to have time for training and to carry out observations/assessments.

- Principals and other observers have to be able to give meaningful feedback.

- Teachers need to be able to change their instruction in ways that will yield measurable improvements on available assessments of student performance.

At the school and classroom level, these new procedures, observation criteria, and feedback mechanisms have to be developed for *every teacher, at every level, in every subject*, and these developments are supposed to take place *in every single school and district covered by the new policy*.

In addition to highlighting the enormity of the task, this analysis exposes critical practical and logistical issues. In this case, the new evaluation procedures rely to a large extent on measuring growth of student learning on standardized tests. Yet the policy covers many teachers who don't teach "tested subjects" (social studies/history, biology, the arts and music, languages, technology, etc.) and doesn't address the many abilities that standardized tests can't assess.

Even if all the logistical and practical problems could be taken into account, effective implementation still requires administrators and teachers to develop new skills and knowledge: administrators have to improve their ability to observe instruction and to provide meaningful feedback (in many different subjects/levels); teachers have to know how to use that feedback to make appropriate changes in their instruction. Even if administrators and teachers can develop these new capabilities, using the results of new evaluation procedures to sanction or reward individual teachers conflicts with the prevailing attitudes, beliefs, and norms of behavior in many schools (Cohen et al., 2018; Hess, 2013; McShane, 2018; Pressman & Wildavsky, 1984; Wilson, 1978).

These circumstances made effective implementation highly unlikely. Predictably, many schools and districts altered some aspects of their evaluation policies without making substantial changes in their approach and without improving outcomes. Some states added new expectations for multiple observations of teachers, and more than half of all states ended up requiring annual summative feedback. Nonetheless, a report on the effectiveness of the teacher evaluation reforms noted that "no fewer than 30 states have recently withdrawn at least one of the evaluation reforms that they adopted during a flurry of national activity between 2009 and 2015," and many states have rolled back the toughest accountability demands (Walsh & Ross, 2019, para. 2). New Mexico, for example, instituted a student-growth score that accounted for 50 percent of a teacher's overall evaluation but subsequently dropped that requirement after more than a quarter of the state's teachers were labeled as "minimally effective" or "ineffective." As one account of the changes put it: "Educators (including highly rated teachers) hated the system, with some burning their evaluations in protest in front of the state education department's headquarters" (Will, 2019, para. 13).

Certainly, some broad policy changes can help provide resources and create conditions that support incremental improvements in teacher evaluation and student learning. But teacher-evaluation reform in the United States is just one example of the ways in which too many of those policies promise too much and deliver too little.

The next two chapters take up this issue that many reform initiatives are "too big" by outlining key strategies for making concrete improvements in teaching and learning in specific situations and contexts. This critical work on the ground fuels incremental improvements and creates opportunities for new learning experiences to emerge and take hold.

From Common Concerns to High-Leverage Problems

6

Where should improvement efforts start? With so many needs and so many issues facing schools and educators, finding one place to initiate improvement efforts seems like an overwhelming task. Focusing on "high-leverage problems" can help us sort through the possibilities.

- High-leverage problems concentrate on issues *widely recognized* as central to the development of more equitable educational opportunities and outcomes.

- They present opportunities for *visible improvements* in relatively short periods of time.

- They establish a foundation for *long-term, sustained, systemic efforts* that improve teaching and learning.

Addressing high-leverage problems depends on developing a keen sense of what matters to people and what matters in an organization. It requires careful analysis of multiple problems and continuous reflection on the process of addressing them. It relies on a powerful repertoire of strategies that meet the specific demands of different situations and on developing new practices and resources when necessary. Altogether, these steps can lead to the "quick wins" that help propel organizational and social changes in many sectors.

Identifying Common Needs and Concerns

Working with community organizers in Texas in the 1990s taught me the power and value of starting school-improvement efforts by identifying shared, practical interests and concerns. My work in Texas began when Ernesto Cortes Jr. invited Howard Gardner, several of my colleagues, and me to work with the Alliance Schools—a partnership of schools and community organizations throughout Texas and the southwestern United States. As part of that work, I went to house meetings, schools, and organizing seminars in El Paso, Austin, Dallas, Fort Worth, Houston, San Antonio, and the Rio Grande Valley. On several occasions, I joined in "summits" at convention centers that felt like educational conferences, political caucuses, and revival meetings all at once. In all those visits, I heard remarkable stories of schools where substantial improvements were made in programs, structures, and students' test scores over just a few years. One of the most powerful stories I heard concerned Morningside Middle School in Fort Worth (recounted in detail by Dennis Shirley in his 1997 book *Community Organizing for Urban School Reform*). When Odessa Ravin was appointed as Morningside's new principal in 1985, the situation could hardly have been worse. Morningside had the lowest average test scores of any public middle school in the area; the school was dangerous—the previous principal sustained a broken jaw while trying to stop a fight; a liquor store on the corner sold alcohol to minors; drugs were sold openly on the street. But things *did* get worse. On her first day of school, smoke

ALLIANCE SCHOOLS (TEXAS)

Ernesto Cortes Jr. and his colleagues at the Texas Industrial Areas Foundation created the Alliance Schools to bring together community-based organizations, parents, and educators to improve their neighborhoods and schools. Their approach to school improvement built on key principles and tools of community organizing:

- Surfacing common interests and building relationships

- Developing local leaders

- Studying and identifying opportunities for change

- Taking collaborative, coordinated public action

These strategies help develop the social connections and political power needed to address inequities in low-income communities (Cortes, 2011; Mediratta et al., 2009). Following this approach, the Alliance Schools grew into a network of more than 100 schools in Texas and the Southwest in the 1990s and 2000s.

and burning embers greeted Ravin when she arrived: her office had been firebombed the previous night. Despite the challenges, just two years later, the school's average test scores rose to third-highest among Fort Worth's middle schools.

This was far from an isolated case; educators, parents, and community organizers from across Texas told me similar stories. After a successful campaign to establish a health clinic at the Zavala Elementary School in Austin, school and community members banded together to pursue funding to create a Young Scientists Program—an initiative providing hands-on learning experiences in science that prepared dozens of students for entrance into the district's magnet program for advanced students. At the Ysleta Elementary School in El Paso, school and community members got the city to install a traffic light at a busy intersection that endangered students trying to cross the street to get to school. That success spawned a whole series of improvement efforts at the school. Among those initiatives, the creation of a new after-school program at Ysleta inspired a district-wide after-school initiative, generating new educational opportunities across El Paso.

These successful initiatives all followed a similar pattern that reflects basic principles of community organizing (Warren et al., 2011). In each case, efforts began as principals, parents, and community members used one-on-one meetings, neighborhood walks, and other activities to surface common concerns and build relationships. In neighborhood walks, for example, school and community members went from door to door, church to church, and business to business talking to as many people in the surrounding area as they could. In those conversations and other one-on-one meetings, educational and community leaders asked a small set of questions—and listened carefully—to learn what concerned and motivated their colleagues and neighbors and what might lead them to action. Asking open-ended questions—"Can you tell me about your school? Can you tell me about your neighborhood?"—rather than questions with yes or no answers—"Is your school a good school?"—helped surface concerns and identify shared issues and common interests that could connect the members of their community.

At Morningside, Principal Ravin and her colleagues used a neighborhood walk and one-on-one conversations to identify common concerns about the safety and environment around the school. Then they got to work. They convinced the city to force the closure of the liquor store. They garnered additional resources for the library and then established an after-school program so that students had a safe place to go at the end of the day. Although Morningside's initial work took place largely outside the school, it helped build relationships and a sense of hope among school staff that inspired efforts to increase time for professional development and try out instructional interventions as well.

Through the work of Ravin and her colleagues in the Alliance Schools, I learned that the identification of common interests and key practical concerns can set in motion a constellation of activities that support improvements of all kinds (Hatch, 1998b). It serves as a catalyst for improving the physical conditions and resources available; the attitudes and expectations within the school and the community; and the formal and informal learning opportunities for children and adults both inside and outside school.

Community-organizing efforts play a particularly crucial role in making improvements in schools like Morningside when the problems created by systemic disadvantages seem particularly intractable. These efforts build relationships among individuals and establish a core constituency of leaders and a collective power that supports the launch of new initiatives. Visible signs of improvement—closed liquor stores, new traffic lights, new playgrounds, new programs, improved test scores—demonstrate what's possible and inspire new initiatives that raise expectations even higher.

From Common Concerns to High-Leverage Problems

How can educators take advantage of the power and principles of community organizing to create more equitable and effective learning opportunities? Identifying "high-leverage problems" in schooling provides one way to incorporate some of the lessons of community organizing directly into schools. First, community-organizing approaches reduce the complexity of initiatives, thanks to another of the principles of school improvement.

PRINCIPLE #3

When problems are widely shared among the stakeholders involved, initiatives that address those problems are more likely to be seen as worth pursuing.

Drawing on common concerns increases the chance that those involved will see the initiatives as worth pursuing—a key factor in inspiring the people on the ground to do what the initiative requires. Consequently, educators may not have to spend as much time getting initial buy-in or explaining what they want to do or what significance it might have. Working on problems and issues that many people recognize also highlights their common interests and facilitates the personal connections central to collaborative endeavors.

High-Leverage Problems and Foundational Skills

A wide range of community concerns can serve as a productive base for school-improvement efforts; however, work on high-leverage problems ultimately has to have a positive impact on the "instructional core" and the work that students and teachers do together on the content that serves as the focus of learning goals (see Figure 6.1). Given the conservative force of the grammar of conventional schooling and the long-term nature of many aspects of learning, however, quick wins in classrooms are hard to come by. Nonetheless, even complex academic challenges can serve as high-leverage problems. In South Africa, Wordworks' Ready Steady Read Write program targets critical issues for kindergarten and first-grade students who have fallen behind. Beginning in Cape Town in 2005, Wordworks quickly demonstrated, as founder Shelley O'Carroll explained, that "with a weekly lesson for an hour you can make good progress." With that success, Wordworks gradually expanded, and in the 2019–2020 school year it worked with more than 110 sites to implement the Ready Steady program in Cape Town and the surrounding area.

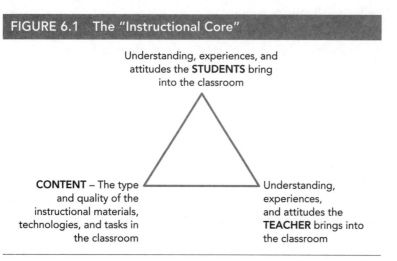

FIGURE 6.1 The "Instructional Core"

Understanding, experiences, and attitudes the **STUDENTS** bring into the classroom

CONTENT – The type and quality of the instructional materials, technologies, and tasks in the classroom

Understanding, experiences, and attitudes the **TEACHER** brings into the classroom

Source: Based on City et al., 2009.

WORDWORKS (SOUTH AFRICA)

Wordworks is a nonprofit organization in South Africa that focuses on early language and literacy development. Wordworks' multipronged strategy relies on addressing critical issues at different developmental levels in the first eight years of children's lives to help establish a strong foundation for literacy learning:

- Working with parents to increase support for literacy learning at home for infants and toddlers

- Providing resources and training for preschool and kindergarten teachers

- Training volunteers to assist students in elementary school

- Offering free online materials, games, and books in a variety of languages to support home and school learning

Now operating in four provinces in South Africa, Wordworks programs reach almost 25,000 students each year.

Ready Steady Read Write took off for a number of reasons. First, the program addressed a clearly recognized but unaddressed need: thousands of students, particularly Black students, from many of the poorest townships weren't learning to read in their first years of school. "Students coming into our system were underprepared and there were no compensatory programs and no remediation to address the issues," reflected O'Carroll. In fact, available programs at the time often began two or three years after students started school in first grade (the first year of mandatory schooling in South Africa at that point). As O'Carroll explained: "There are a lot of interventions for students who can afford them. For kids who really need it, there is very little capacity in the system. So that made grade 1 a critical point at which students were already starting to make it or fall behind."

Second, despite the overwhelming need and the number of students who required support, O'Carroll knew that the problems could be addressed. As an educational psychologist who had studied reading and worked with a number of reading interventions in the United Kingdom, she had experience with a variety of resources, strategies, and expertise that had already created high-quality content and classroom activities; she just had to figure out a way to adapt those materials for South African students and classrooms. To accomplish that goal, O'Carroll drew initially on approaches that got students back on track quickly by providing intense, short-term, and early interventions. In the classrooms in South Africa, however, O'Carroll found that many of the students had fallen much farther behind than their peers in the United States and United Kingdom for whom the short-term interventions had been designed. O'Carroll noted that, in addition to the lack of preschool and kindergarten experience, many of her students had so little exposure to reading and writing in any language that "a few kids knew a few letters and a few kids knew nothing." O'Carroll quickly made adjustments to develop an approach that incorporated much more explicit work on phonemic awareness and phonics into experiences with reading and writing. "It was a mixture of taking what had been done and what was useful in other programs," O'Carroll explained, "and looking at the reality of the levels of the kids in South Africa."

Third, O'Carroll recognized the need for across-the-board improvements in teaching and learning, but she chose to focus on a specific group of students with whom she believed she could make a difference. "Until we get the system fixed here in terms of daily classroom teaching," O'Carroll reflected, "a compensatory program like this is not going to give us the change we need." But she went on to point out that though the program isn't a cure-all and doesn't focus on students who are struggling the most, "anyone from the 25th percentile up to just below average and average students can benefit."

Programs like Wordworks and the Alliance Schools—and others, such as Pratham in India (Dutt et al., 2016)—show that thoughtful, comprehensive interventions can provide the content and activities so central to a strong instructional core and to enabling many students to learn to read and to develop other foundational academic skills. The dramatic improvements that students make in these demonstrations expose the barriers that undermine their abilities to develop in the ways and at rates that the conventional schools demand. From O'Carroll's perspective, these approaches work for students because "pure disadvantage" holds students back. Inequality denies them the basic conditions—decent physical surroundings, adequate resources, positive attitudes, high expectations, and appropriate learning opportunities—that support healthy development. Removing those barriers, improving basic conditions, and providing powerful activities creates a slingshot effect that enables children to learn when learning seems impossible.

From High-Leverage Problems to Systemic Improvement

Despite the evidence that students in many parts of the world can make significant improvements in developing foundational skills, those developments don't guarantee the achievement of other educational outcomes. Initial efforts to focus on high-leverage problems need to be harnessed to launch more comprehensive and systemic efforts.

Inequitable educational opportunities and outcomes present challenges so big and so complex that they may seem intractable and overwhelming. But even these complex problems can be unpacked by exploring how those problems affect different groups of students and by looking for the root causes in particular contexts to launch a cycle of improvement efforts (Bryk et al., 2015). In *Solving Disproportionality and Achieving Equity* (2017), Eddie Fergus uses the root cause process specifically to zero in on common issues in schools that contribute to inequitable outcomes and that can serve as a productive basis for systematic district-wide improvement efforts. Fergus focuses on major challenges, such as the overrepresentation of Black and Latinx students in special education and their underrepresentation in higher-level classes, and shows how to break these problems down into chunks. By looking at data related to the nature and quality of instructional supports, the intervention services provided, and the predominant cultural beliefs, schools and districts can identify critical barriers and begin to address them. To sort through the root causes, the same logic used to approach high-leverage problems—identifying common concerns, focusing on opportunities to make visible progress and building the capacity to sustain long-term work—provides a means of developing a coordinated and comprehensive response.

In Passaic, New Jersey, Pablo Muñoz and his colleagues, members of the New Jersey Network of Superintendents, developed a comprehensive, district-wide improvement strategy by identifying a whole series of instructional and operational issues that contributed to a critical challenge that affected their students as well as many others around the world: *even some students who graduate from high school are not prepared for success at the next level of postsecondary education.* Muñoz recognized the extent of the problem shortly after being hired by the school district as superintendent in 2013. Through a systematic analysis of the district's graduation data, assistant superintendent Rachel Goldberg noted that Passaic had a lower graduation rate than similar districts in the state. Even among those students who graduated, many didn't meet the requirements for enrolling in postsecondary education (or they were required to take remedial courses when they did enroll) (Hatch & Roegman, 2017). This work was originally published in an article published in the January 2019 issue of Phi Delta Kappan magazine.

As Goldberg reported, many students discovered this problem only after they had graduated, when they walked down the street from the high school and tried to enroll in the local community college. Upon arrival, they were told they had to take the Accuplacer test. Many American colleges use the Accuplacer to identify entering students who they believe aren't yet prepared for college-level work and need to take remedial courses. (The College Board produces the Accuplacer, along with the PSAT, the SAT, and Advanced Placement exams that many colleges and universities rely on to make admissions decisions.)

Few of Passaic's students had heard of the Accuplacer before they attempted to enroll. As Goldberg described it:

> They walk in. They register, and the college says "You have to take the Accuplacer," and the students say "Oh, what's that?" and the college says "It's a placement exam." And the student says "Okay, when do I take it?" The student has no idea the Accuplacer even exists, they have no idea about the content, and they have no preparation to take it.

THE NEW JERSEY NETWORK OF SUPERINTENDENTS (USA)

Established in 2008, the New Jersey Network of Superintendents (NJNS) brings together a group of superintendents and district leaders pursuing systemic strategies to create more equitable opportunities and outcomes.

The NJNS's strategy focuses on several related activities:

- The development of a district-wide plan for achieving specific equity goals for Black, Latinx, and other historically disadvantaged students

- Monthly meetings in which members engage in "courageous conversations" about race (Singleton, 2014); share their progress on their equity goals; get feedback on their evolving efforts; and identify and address common challenges

- Equity visits in which members observe classes in a host district, conduct interviews with staff and students, and share reflections (Roegman et al., 2019)

Under these circumstances, many Passaic students failed the test: in the fall of 2015, only 22 percent of Passaic's seniors scored high enough in ELA and math to reach the Accuplacer's category of "Qualified for high school graduation." The mismatch had particularly significant consequences for further learning opportunities for Passaic's almost entirely low-income and Latinx students—many of whom were first-generation college students. Affected students had to take postsecondary remedial courses, which had the effect of increasing costs, significantly lengthening their path to graduation, and increasing their odds of dropping out entirely (Bailey, 2009).

At the same time, Muñoz, Goldberg, and their colleagues saw an opportunity: the district already had a small group of students participating in programs that allowed them to gain college credits while in high school. The challenge and the opportunity highlighted a common concern—increasing graduation rates—that resonated with the board, students and their families, district staff, and community members; but the findings also pointed to a pathway to visible improvements that could jump-start the work—reducing postsecondary remediation rates and expanding the number of students getting college credits while still in high school.

Seizing the opportunity, in 2015, Muñoz, Goldberg, and their colleagues announced a district-wide focus on ensuring that all students had the opportunity to graduate high school with at least fifteen college credits and/or a career certification. "What we're doing is trying to change the game," Goldberg said. To do that, the district carefully reviewed how some students were already meeting these new criteria and examined the hurdles and barriers that prevented many other students from getting to graduation and postsecondary success. That review revealed the particular needs and opportunities of different groups of students:

- Those already taking college-level courses

- Those who met or were near to meeting requirements for college-level coursework but weren't pursuing those courses

- Those who needed more supports to succeed in college-level work

- Those farthest "off-track" and least likely to graduate and go on to either postsecondary education or a job

Muñoz, Goldberg, and their colleagues then developed a series of initiatives to respond to many of those specific needs, including the following:

- Identifying and eliminating a slew of prerequisites and inconsistent policies and expectations that kept many students from accessing the courses that could lead to college credit ("Historically," Goldberg explained, "these prerequisites automatically took out of consideration the large number of students who were not already in an honors class and whittled the eligible pool down to tiny groups of students.")

- Expanding programs and courses in the district that already offered college-level credits (e.g., Advanced Placement courses) so that more students could benefit from them

- Partnering with local community colleges to increase the number of on-site college courses Passaic high-school students could take during the summer and to enable some students to take and get credit for college courses as part of their regular high-school coursework during the school year

- Amending its graduation policy to require students to take the SAT, the ACT, or an equivalent college entrance exam to graduate from high school; adding a requirement that all sophomores and juniors take the PSAT and all juniors take the SAT; and beginning to administer the Accuplacer to all juniors and seniors (with the district paying for any student who couldn't afford the fees)

- Creating an intensive SAT support course and after-school and summer-school interventions designed specifically to meet the needs of students identified by the assessments as "off track" for graduation

With these developments, the district was able to get information about their students' level of preparation for college work while still in high school, identify students who already qualified for higher-level or college-level classes and help them enroll, and develop and target support to meet the needs of those who weren't yet eligible.

Although there are no easy fixes, these developments contributed to several improvements: the number of students taking dual enrollment (college-credit-bearing) courses in Passaic High School skyrocketed from 263 in the 2014–2015 school year to more than 1,600 in 2019–2020, and the number of students taking at least one AP exam went from about 90 students in 2013–2014 to more than 800 in 2018–2019. Numerous other steps have to be taken, however. Even as the number of students getting at least one score of 3 or higher on AP exams grew from 35 in 2013–2014 to 254 in 2018–2019, the majority of AP test-takers are still not achieving at that level. Nonetheless, the first steps taken by the district have helped create a much more efficient and coordinated set of high-school courses and requirements. Those developments have contributed to visible improvements in access to higher-level courses and have helped build the capacities and momentum needed to strengthen instruction for all students.

Crucially, the system-wide work in Passaic isn't unique. Other schools and districts around the country have systematically eliminated barriers and increased access to higher-level classes, including several other members of the NJNS. Freehold Regional High School District has a totally different population from Passaic; almost 85 percent of the students are white, and only about 5 percent are eligible for free or reduced-price lunch. When Charles Sampson arrived as superintendent in 2011, the district already had relatively high average test scores and graduation rates. Nonetheless, Sampson and his colleagues created a metric, which they called the Freehold Regional Opportunity Index, to track the extent to which students from different backgrounds were underrepresented or overrepresented in particular programs, such as enrollment in AP classes and in specialized magnet programs (Sampson et al., 2019). That index showed everyone in the district that their Black and Latinx students were significantly underrepresented in AP and higher-level courses and overrepresented in lower-level courses.

In response, Sampson, like Muñoz, developed a set of coordinated interventions: eliminating lower-level courses, dispensing with teacher recommendations as a gatekeeper for higher-level courses, developing more intensive support for students who previously weren't taking the higher-level classes, and working with guidance counselors to encourage and enable those students to choose those higher-level classes. With those developments, by 2019, the number of Black students taking AP courses grew by over 100 percent and the number of Latinx students taking those courses increased by over 300 percent.

Looking for Leverage: Finding Productive Problems

As with any "solution," effectively using high-leverage problems also depends on recognizing the downsides—the side effects that can work against the same long-term goals and purposes that identifying high-leverage problems was supposed to achieve. In this case, focusing on problems that many people share may leave out the most underserved communities, who face unusual conditions and challenges. By looking for the quick wins, work on high-leverage problems also leads to a focus on increasing the efficiency of conventional approaches rather than making more fundamental and potentially controversial changes that may be needed in the long term.

Short-term goals—such as improving test scores, in particular—can lead to practices that undermine the pursuit of other valued educational purposes (Damon, 2008; Koretz, 2017). Consequently, educators need to think carefully and strategically about which problems are high-leverage and when to address them.

From this lens, the broad changes to teacher-evaluation policies pursued in the United States (discussed earlier in this chapter) weren't "high-leverage." For one thing, although these changes responded to a problem emphasized by policymakers and school leaders who were concerned about reports that almost all teachers were given satisfactory evaluation ratings (Weisberg et al., 2009), "fixing" teacher evaluation didn't appear to be at the top of the list of concerns for many teachers, parents, students, teachers' unions, or other major stakeholder groups. Thus, one of the many other issues to be addressed would provide a much better foundation for improvement. For example, a high rate of chronic absences—when students are absent for more than 10 percent of all school days in an academic year—meets many of the criteria for a high-leverage problem:

1. *Many people recognize the problem with chronic school absence.* Missing school and time to learn creates disruptions and problems for students, teachers, parents, and administrators.

2. *Chronic absences matter for student learning.* Across the United States, more than 6 million students (13 percent) missed at least three weeks of school each year, and research has linked chronic absenteeism to both lower academic performance and higher dropout rates (Balfanz & Byrnes, 2012; Gottfried, 2019).

3. *Addressing chronic absenteeism has special significance for children who have been historically underserved.* An analysis of data from the 2015–2016 school year showed that Native American and Pacific Islander students were over 50 percent more likely to be chronically absent than their white peers, while Black students were 40 percent more likely, and Hispanic students were 17 percent more likely. About 25 percent of students with disabilities were chronically absent, and absenteeism was a particularly profound problem for students experiencing homelessness (Balfanz, 2016; U.S. Department of Education, 2019).

4. *Chronic absence can be addressed.* Research demonstrates that a variety of interventions—including the use of "success mentors"

in New York City, early warning systems that track attendance in cities like Baltimore, and delivery of text-message nudges and reminders for students and parents (Bergman & Chan, 2019; Chang et al., 2014; Jacob & Lovett, 2017; Rogers & Feller, 2018; Sparks, 2010)—have shown promise.

With some success, addressing common concerns, such as chronic absences, can serve as an on-ramp into broader improvement efforts that address issues of teaching and learning directly.

Solving Problems and Developing Micro-Innovations 7

Ambitions for big, rapid changes in education fuel a fascination with educational innovations. The term "innovation" often brings to mind groundbreaking developments that disrupt entire industries or change the course of history—the printing press, the steam engine, the mobile phone. A focus on developing major innovations in education, however, often overlooks the importance of the "micro-innovations" needed to improve teaching and learning in specific contexts and conditions.

Micro-innovations yield practices and products that are new to the contexts in which they're developed. Micro-innovations provide another way of reducing the complexity of improvement initiatives by concentrating on specific challenges and opportunities in different contexts, in both instruction and school operations.

My approach to micro-innovations grows out of the work of Nelson Goodman, a highly influential philosopher whose students included Noam Chomsky, as well as my own adviser, Howard Gardner. Goodman's seminal work included addressing enduring questions like "What is art?" Rather than answering that question directly, Goodman changed the question to ask "*When* is art?" In the process, he shifted from trying to define what did and didn't count as art to talking about the symptoms of art. That shift led to discussions about

> Micro-innovations provide another way of reducing the complexity of improvement initiatives by concentrating on specific challenges and opportunities in different contexts.

when and under what conditions a product, an event, or an experience might be considered "art."

In the same way, shifting from thinking of "innovations" as a singular category—either something is "innovative" or it's not—to thinking about the "symptoms" of innovation highlights that relatively small adjustments and adaptations are worth paying attention to. Symptoms of innovation include the extent to which something departs from convention and the extent to which it changes or transforms related activities within particular contexts. For example, even smartphones still retain some of the features of the landline phones that preceded them, but their mobility and wireless connectivity are new and make possible all kinds of activities (texting, surfing the internet, using apps, etc.) that change the ways people behave and interact. From this perspective, a product or practice may be innovative in some ways but conventional in others; or, a practice or product that's common or conventional in one context might be innovative in others (Christensen et al., 2010, 2015; Lagorio-Chafkin, 2013). In either case, making "small" changes and producing micro-innovations in different settings are central to addressing the on-the-ground problems and opportunities that contribute to incremental improvements. Over time, these micro-developments can accumulate to create new and unanticipated opportunities for systemic improvements in learning on a large scale.

Micro-Innovations for Teaching and Learning

Like high-leverage problems, micro-innovations are needed at every level and in every aspect of education, but they have to reach the instructional core and the day-to-day work of teaching and learning in order to have an impact on student outcomes.

A visit to eduLab—a workshop space within the Academy of Singapore Teachers—helped open my eyes to the many critical developments in classrooms that could be considered micro-innovations. eduLab funded a number of projects initiated by teachers to develop new resources and practices in their classrooms. In one case, a chemistry teacher noted that many of his upper-secondary-school students struggled to remember the key terms so essential to learning in their introductory chemistry course. In response, the teacher developed a card game that gave the students an opportunity to explore the rules that governed the use of the terms. The teacher then worked with staff from eduLab and researchers from the National Institute of Education to carry out a comparative study that demonstrated the benefits of the game. Designs for an app were then developed that enhanced the game with visualizations and that provided feedback on students' performances that teachers could use to inform their instruction. Finally, eduLab worked with local start-up developers to build the app, *wRite Formula*, which was made freely available both on iTunes and through Google Play (Ixora Studios, 2017).

Micro-innovations that address these kinds of "problems of practice" in teaching and learning are central to enabling students to develop critical skills and key concepts across the curriculum. Developing number sense in mathematics, for example, plays a critical role in mathematics learning for students of all ages. Number sense refers to the understanding of numbers and mathematical operations and the ability to use that understanding in flexible ways to solve mathematical problems: for example, recognizing that $3 + 3 + 3$ and 3×3 are related operations.

Jo Boaler, a well-known mathematics expert and founder of the Youcubed approach to learning in mathematics, stresses that the development of number sense can actually be inhibited by typical teaching methods that focus on rote memorization and speedy recall. She notes that PISA test data from 13 million fifteen-year-olds across the world show that the lowest-achieving students often focus on memorization and tend to believe that memorizing is important when studying for mathematics (Boaler & Zoido, 2016). Changing

EDULAB (SINGAPORE)

From 2011 to 2017, eduLab funded a wide variety of projects proposed by teachers throughout Singapore. These projects were designed to foster the development of "ground-level" innovations that supported student-centered instructional practices and focused on "21st century competencies." To accomplish this goal, eduLab administrated a request-for-proposals process for projects that had several features:

- Teachers played key roles in designing and testing the innovation, developing materials, and conducting school-based evaluations.

- The innovations had to leverage information and communication technologies.

- The projects had to have wide, sustainable adoption as a key outcome.

To facilitate the work, eduLab helped connect teachers and schools with researchers at the National Institute of Education and with educational technology companies. Completed projects were also published on the eduLab website, and many were shared as part of workshops at the Academy of Singapore Teachers.

instructional practices that are reinforced by such common but problematic beliefs about memorization presents significant challenges. As Boaler points out, however, educators have devised a variety of specific activities that can help students at different levels develop their number sense without falling back on rote memorization. Among them, Boaler describes a "math cards" activity that she and her colleagues developed. The cards show different representations and operations—such as numbers (6), number sentences (3 × 2 = 6, 2 × 3 = 6), dice, and dominos. Students lay out a set of cards and then are asked to identify all those that show the same answer and then to explain how they know which ones are equivalent. The activity provides an innovative twist on the familiar and conventional design of flash cards and turns a problematic activity that demands quick recall into a new opportunity to explore the relationships between different mathematical operations (Boaler, 2015).

Even in the absence of sustained professional development to help teachers learn new ways to teach mathematics, micro-innovations like Youcubed's math cards activity provide teachers with tools that help them shift from practices that emphasize rote learning to activities that can support the development of deeper understanding and more student-centered learning.

Expanding the Power of Educators

In addition to developing high-quality content and powerful pedagogical practices, developing a powerful, professional teaching force serves as another crucial means of strengthening the instructional core. Nonetheless, there are few shortcuts to achieving that critical goal. As important as it may be to increase the capacity of the teaching force in the long term, it's very difficult to make substantial improvements in the teacher pipeline or increase the number of effective teachers in the short term. In contrast, providing educators with a combination of powerful tools, coaching, and professional development programs can have catalytic effects on learning, even in relatively short periods of time.

Teaching Matters' Jumpstart to Reading program grew directly out of an effort to develop tools to address a critical problem in many of Teaching Matters' partner schools: despite success with some kindergarteners, others (labeled "pre-emergent" readers on the reading assessments) entered school unable to read and made virtually no progress over the course of their kindergarten year. Working together with the teachers in their schools, Teaching Matters developed an approach and a set of tools that made it easier to integrate the use of several different widely recognized, research-based strategies for teaching reading into a much shorter period of time. As Lynette Guastaferro, CEO of Teaching Matters, described it, "Teachers were telling us 'Oh my, I used to spend 15 minutes working on just one of these strategies, and now I understand how to get all of these strategies into a 15-minute period.'" In the process, the teachers were developing their capacity for differentiating instruction and for providing comprehensive support for their students.

Notably, this approach builds on the assessments and books that schools and teachers are already using. The innovation comes from the fact that the three-month program creates what Guastaferro described as a "standard work process" that enables teachers to teach reading in a much more efficient, consistent, and powerful way. The term "standard work process" comes from work on continuous improvement and refers to the development of standard protocols, such as those for hand-washing in hospitals, which the Carnegie Foundation for the Advancement of Teaching and others have adapted for work in education (Bryk et al., 2015). With these developments, Jumpstart classrooms experienced a 21 percent increase in the number of students reading at or above grade level.

Another micro-innovation—peer tutoring—provides an entirely different approach to expanding the educator workforce for organizations like the Kliptown Youth Program and IkamvaYouth after-school programs in South Africa. Although creating pairs and groups of students to facilitate peer-based learning isn't new, each of these organizations developed its own adaptations by taking advantage of local resources and expertise in its local settings. At the Kliptown Youth Program, peer

TEACHING MATTERS (NEW YORK CITY)

Teaching Matters has been working with teachers and schools in New York City for more than twenty-five years. Many of its programs, including Jumpstart to Reading and Early Reading Matters, aim to address the limited preparation many teachers receive, particularly for teaching reading.

Jumpstart's approach has several critical components:

- Twelve days of targeted on-site professional development and coaching

- A "data tracker" to help teachers visualize and identify their students' needs

- A data-management system with access to a variety of resources

- A tool to support instructional planning and formative assessment

KLIPTOWN YOUTH PROGRAM (SOUTH AFRICA)

Established in 2007, the Kliptown Youth Program (KYP) provides after-school tutoring programs and related services for children in Kliptown, the oldest township of its kind in Soweto, just outside Johannesburg. Over the years, KYP has developed a combined approach to tutoring:

• Tutoring for primary-school students by trained members of the community

• Tutoring for high-school students, who work with teachers two afternoons a week and in peer-tutoring groups the other days of the week

Over 80 percent of the KYP students pass their Grade 12 exams, compared to about one in three students in Kliptown more broadly.

tutoring complements instruction and support from local teachers who join the program twice a week. The peer tutoring I observed involved groups of four or five high-school students from the same school, who worked together on their schoolwork with an older volunteer who served as a tutor and facilitated interactions among the whole group. The tutor let the students decide what to focus on and encouraged different students to take the lead. Thulani Madondo, executive director and one of the founders of the program, explained that they adopted this peer approach after they found it difficult to find enough local teachers whose approach suited the after-school setting. "When you work with some teachers," Madondo explained, "they are used to the teaching system of standing in front of the class, and even when it's time to do one-on-one mentoring with the students, they often struggle." In fact, the teachers often brought their own teacher-directed lesson plans, and Madondo continued, "We were chasing a lot of kids away because they had homework already and we were giving them new lessons and lessons that weren't always aligned to what they were doing in school." Adopting the combined approach to staffing both solved the problem of finding enough effective teachers and had a number of other benefits, including reducing costs, distinguishing their after-school activities from "regular" school classes, and enabling the program to meet students' needs more effectively and efficiently.

Micro-Innovations Across the System

Finding teachers constitutes just one of the many related issues that demand creative local solutions. Addressing the cascade of specific, local micro-problems can add up to form systemic approaches to improving learning across a number of sites. In the case of the Citizens Foundation (TCF), critical early discoveries related to both staffing and transportation launched an approach that now encompasses a network of more than fifteen hundred schools in Pakistan. The founders of the Citizens Foundation—six friends in Karachi—began their work in 1995 when they confronted an immense problem: Pakistan had, and continues to have, one of the largest populations of out-of-school youths, including nearly 60 percent of girls out of school by sixth grade (Human Rights Watch, 2018; Naviwala, 2017). To address that problem, the founders set a goal that even they described as "an impossible target": to open a thousand new schools in areas with particularly high concentrations of out-of-school youth. As one of the founders stated, "If the goal is large enough and big enough, that's really something that people should take seriously" (Citizens Foundation, 2018).

To tackle that challenge and to reach as many out-of-school children as possible, TCF founders first looked for neighborhoods and communities that didn't have access to government schools. Second, they sought to put small schools in those neighborhoods to meet the children where they were, rather than require them to travel to a

THE CITIZENS FOUNDATION (PAKISTAN)

The Citizens Foundation (TCF) built its first five schools in 1996. Although many of these schools were established in neighborhoods that had limited electricity, water, and sanitation, TCF didn't want to build "poor schools for poor children." Building on the background and expertise of one of the founders, who was an architect, TCF sought to design schools that would become landmarks in the community. Over time, TCF schools have come to feature

- an all-female staff,

- a welcoming learning environment,

- small class sizes, and

- relatively low costs (roughly $12 per month).

By 2014, TCF reached its initial goal of opening a thousand schools, and in 2016 it continued to expand by shifting from a focus on starting private schools to co-funding and operating government schools across Pakistan.

large school that served several communities. Those choices, however, led to two more stumbling blocks. First, many of the prospective parents reported that they didn't trust their daughters with male teachers. To address those concerns, TCF adopted one of its most unique features by choosing to hire an all-female staff of teachers and principals. That choice, in turn, created a second problem: since there were few educated adults in the surrounding communities, it was hard to find enough qualified women to staff the schools. Adding to the challenges, they couldn't hire many women from surrounding areas, because mobility restrictions and safety issues made it difficult for women to travel on their own. So TCF bought its own fleet of vans and hired its own drivers to get the staff to its schools and into the classrooms safely every day. That approach to transportation served as a micro-innovation by bringing a new practice and new routines to those neighborhoods and catalyzing the development of new educational opportunities. That straightforward solution also demonstrated that "innovation" doesn't necessarily require new, "disruptive" technologies; innovative problem-solving involves creative uses of the resources at hand and rethinking the possibilities in the immediate environment.

Over time, TCF's approach to hiring and transportation has continued to evolve. Today, in 2020, a fleet of 800 vans takes staff members to TCF schools all across the country while a GPS system tracks their routes, speed, and fuel consumption. As it has become easier to find qualified local staff, TCF has also discovered that those "local hires" tend to stay on longer and can be more effective in the long run. Under these circumstances, the vans are being phased out in some areas—but TCF could never have gotten to this point without that initial solution to the transportation problem.

Another series of small-scale innovations supported the development and expansion of IkamvaYouth's after-school programs. Joy Olivier and Makhosi Gogwana founded IkamvaYouth in 2002 in response to what they learned working together on a research project reviewing the results of South Africa's twelfth-grade matriculation exams. Olivier and Gogwana were so shocked by what they found, they thought there was something wrong with the data: "The number of Black students in the entire Western Cape Province with scores eligible to go into studying math or engineering or anything that required a decent math result," Olivier lamented, "the number that came out of a whole province, was what should have come out of about five schools."

When Olivier and Gogwana compared their own school experiences, the results were even more striking. "Makhosi and I had gone to extremely opposite types of schools," Olivier told me. "I went to

IKAMVAYOUTH (SOUTH AFRICA)

Since 2003, IkamvaYouth has developed an after-school program with seventeen branches across five regions of South Africa. Ikamva Youth provides

- academic tutoring and homework help,
- counseling, and
- college and career guidance and mentoring.

There are no academic requirements, and participation is free, but students must meet attendance requirements. In 2019, IkamvaYouth served 2,500 learners, with over 85 percent of graduates passing their matriculation exams and almost half achieving high enough scores to qualify for university (IkamvaYouth, 2019).

a school where everybody went on to university, and Makhosi didn't know anyone else in his school who went to university. And after he got into university, he experienced this weird situation where he got a scholarship to study, but no one had told him what a Bachelor's of Arts was, and he was trying to navigate the use of the scholarship and to access tertiary education but without any help and totally in the dark. And because he was tenacious and didn't let it go, he managed to get into what he thought was a Fine Arts Degree program even though his specialty was geography and environmental sciences."

Together Olivier and Gogwana concluded that the missing ingredients for the students at Gogwana's school were "information, support and the expectation that they will go on to study further." With that as their inspiration, Gogwana called up the principal of his old high school and told the principal that they wanted to come to tutor students on Saturdays; he and Olivier gathered a bunch of friends, started going to the school every week, and worked with whoever showed up. "Our first cohort (who matriculated in 2005) got some amazing results," Olivier marveled. "One-hundred-percent matriculation pass rate (for the sixty students who took the exams), 60 percent got into university, which we weren't really expecting. It was radical. We got some kids into top programs at top institutions." All at a school that, only a few years before, had had only one student out of the entire student body go on to university.

In order to sustain the program, IkamvaYouth had to figure out how to develop a steady supply of tutors who understood the high school curriculum and the national matriculation exams. One unanticipated solution to that problem came from the first group of program graduates: as a way to "pay it forward," they offered to become tutors, and the IkamvaYouth peer-tutoring model was born.

In order to expand that model to additional sites, IkamvaYouth had to find a steady supply of high-school graduates who had passed their matriculation exams, including the alumni of their own program. To address this challenge, the program has tried to open new branches in areas in close proximity to universities. At the same time, the program also had to deal with the challenge that even volunteering comes with costs that many of the program graduates and university students they relied on couldn't afford. As a consequence, as Olivier explained, that meant that IkamvaYouth had to find ways to defray the local costs that volunteers incurred in transportation, mobile phone usage, and development of materials and activities. With the example set by the first group of graduates, however, IkamvaYouth has managed to continue to find a steady supply of capable tutors, with almost 35 percent of those volunteers being program alumni (IkamvaYouth, 2019).

Micro-Innovations Beyond the Classroom

The cascade of issues involved in dismantling inequitable opportunities in and beyond K–12 schooling demonstrates the need for micro-innovations that address operational as well as instructional issues and that administrators as well as teachers can use. For instance, the Freehold Regional Opportunity Index that Sampson and his colleagues created (see Chapter 6) served as a micro-innovation that enabled them to make visible the need to increase access to higher-level courses and to track their progress in doing so.

In instances like these, addressing operational issues can serve as high-leverage problems that can then provide a foundation for deeper, longer-term work on instruction. New Visions for Public Schools, leader of a network of schools in New York City, tackled a long-standing and seemingly intractable operational problem that many of its high-school principals faced. For years in New York City, administrators had great difficulty getting critical information about their students' progress. As *Chalkbeat* described it, "The city's school-data systems are not typically known for being user friendly" (Wall, 2015, para. 12). As a consequence, high-school administrators often found themselves printing out individual students' transcripts to manually compare them to state graduation requirements. Under these circumstances, many high-school leaders didn't know whether their students had enrolled in the courses they needed to take to prepare for the New York State

NEW VISIONS FOR PUBLIC SCHOOLS (NEW YORK CITY)

Established in New York City in 1989 as an after-school program that engaged students in community service, by 1993 New Visions was developing public/private partnerships to create new small schools throughout New York City. Since that time, New Visions has established 134 new public schools and worked with hundreds more with a wide range of instructional philosophies but a common focus on continuous improvement and students' achievement. New Visions has grown to provide a wide variety of programs and resources:

- An urban teacher preparation "residency" program for both public schools and charter schools

- A two-year master's program for school and district leaders

- Curriculum and resources including data tools for educators, students, parents, and educators to track progress toward graduation

Regents exams required for graduation, nor did the administrators know who had failed the exams and needed to retake them. Even some efforts by the NYC Department of Education to pull together this information for the principals weren't sent out until a few weeks before students were supposed to graduate.

New Visions' current president, Mark Dunetz, experienced the same problems as the founding principal of a new small high school, the Academy for Careers in Television and Film. After he joined New Visions, Dunetz and his colleagues set to work to determine how to track students' progress using Google Sheets and other low-cost or open-source applications. The success of the micro-innovations they developed—a set of software applications and tools that allowed principals to visualize and monitor course-taking and exams—surprised even Dunetz:

> We see the development of those tools as a very powerful mechanism for changing behavior. . . . That's become a core part of our strategy and it's become tremendously successful at shifting practice at scale very quickly around very high-stakes things, like what constitutes a meaningful graduation plan and what are the smartest strategies for sitting and preparing students for Regents exams.

The principals responded so enthusiastically that New Visions put these tools together into a comprehensive data portal. That success, in turn, encouraged the NYC Department of Education to make that portal available to all high schools system-wide. Reflecting the growing interest, New Visions eventually developed a unit of about thirty people to create and support these kinds of tools. Among others, Teaching Matters has used some of the data tools as part of its Jumpstart program to support teachers' and students' success in early reading.

An Abundance of Needs and Possibilities

There are countless challenges in education; but there are also educators all around the world who are working to address those challenges. Even under the pressure of the school closures occasioned by the coronavirus pandemic, educators have quickly developed workarounds and micro-innovations in their own practice. At Wordworks, they created literacy activities for parents and families to do at home and established a free data connection to make it possible for anyone with a mobile device to download the materials for free. At IkamvaYouth, they leveraged the communication app WhatsApp to create a new online platform where students and tutors could interact and share questions and responses. Along with the platform, they established a new weekly schedule that rotated students through two-hour blocks devoted to each subject.

Whether they're designed to respond to the school closures or more long-standing issues, these new resources and approaches aren't meant to work in every context. But they illustrate the wide variety of issues that are being addressed—and have to be addressed—to provide much more equitable and powerful opportunities for learning of all kinds:

- *Distribution of books.* For children who live in communities with few bookstores and libraries, book-vending machines and programs like Reach Out and Read (offering books through pediatric offices) have developed new ways to increase the distribution and use of high-quality, diverse, and age-appropriate reading materials (Barshay, 2020; Neuman & Knapczyk, 2020).

- *Support for play, games, and recreational activities.* Organizations like Right to Play, Playworks, and Asphalt Green have created a variety of ways to expand opportunities for play, exercise, and sports in communities with little access to equipment and facilities.

- *Transportation to school.* Ride-hailing apps provide new ways for children to get to school, potentially cutting costs and freeing up funding for other uses.

- *Access to counseling.* The Rajaleidja network (the Pathfinder Program) in Estonia, and organizations like the College Advising Corps in the United States, have found ways to offer free educational counseling services and to connect students with resources and people who can help them navigate the educational process and the path to higher education (Innove, n.d.; Whitmire, 2019).

- *Support for social networks.* By developing strategies to map students' connections to one another, to educators, and to other adults and sources of support, programs like iCouldBe and the Making Caring Common Project are enabling students to strengthen their relationships and expand their access to mentors and educational opportunities (Charania & Freeland Fisher, 2020; Freeland Fisher, 2018).

- *Assessments that make learning visible.* The New York Performance Standards Consortium; the New York City Mastery Collaborative; the Mastery Transcript Consortium; LRNG; the Connected Learning Alliance; and entire states, such as Rhode Island, are creating new ways to track, reflect on, and share students' progress. In the process, they're inventing new assessments, transcripts, certificates, "playlists" (learning pathways), and micro-credentials or "badges" that can support more differentiated learning and more project-, apprenticeship-, and competency-based learning experiences.

- *Assistance in getting through college.* The Dell Young Scholars and Young Leaders programs in South Africa and the United States have developed a small set of critical resources—including a laptop, credits for textbook purchases, and a "swipe card" providing small amounts of cash for urgent needs—that have helped increase completion rates for students who were provided with college scholarships (Sweeten-Lopez, 2017).

These new solutions can't transform instruction on their own, but it would be impossible for learning opportunities to improve substantially without these kinds of inventions and a more flexible, strategic, and comprehensive approach to addressing the many critical issues that constrain learning both inside and outside the classroom.

KEY IDEAS FROM PART 3

The complexities of the challenges that educators face offer a number of angles of approach for identifying high-leverage problems and a host of needs for micro-innovations, but no one solution or innovation will address every need. Like community-organizing efforts, pursuing concerns many people share offers one promising way to get started. But educators have to navigate many different interests in order to surface critical concerns and bring communities together to pursue them. By breaking complex problems down, educators can balance the interests of different groups with the severity of the challenges faced and the capacity for making visible progress in a cost-effective way.

To that end, as in Passaic, New Jersey (see Chapter 6), it's critical to look carefully to see whom each issue affects, how they're affected, and how extensive and comprehensive the changes need to be. For example, interventions need to be adapted to meet the needs of groups at many different performance levels:

- Exceeding a specific set of expectations
- Meeting expectations
- On the threshold of meeting expectations (either just above or just below the standard)
- Not meeting expectations
- Far below expectations

Wordworks doesn't try to be the solution for every student; Teaching Matters' interventions may work particularly well for kindergarten and first-grade students who are having trouble learning to read but not for those with dyslexia or other learning challenges; and eduLab's chemistry app and New Visions' administrative tools may not help every educator or apply across all contexts. But all of these developments add to the infrastructure of materials, expertise, and relationships that can meet a wide variety of needs; and that success builds the confidence, energy, and capacity to go on to address other problems. Initial successes, and even "small" innovations, can encourage communities to take on more difficult issues, build capacities where few existed before, and foster the mindsets and movements that can lead to long-term improvements.

KEY QUESTIONS TO ASK TO IDENTIFY HIGH-LEVERAGE PROBLEMS

- *Does the focal issue matter?*
  - Does it matter for students' lives, their learning, and their education?
  - Is there some evidence that addressing the issue can have a positive impact on students' educational opportunities and learning in the long term?

- Can it help address the disadvantages faced particularly by Black students, indigenous students, students of color, and other historically underserved students?

- *Is it common?*
  - To what extent is the issue shared?
  - Whom does the issue affect, and how are they affected?

- *Is it practical?*
  - Are there some practical steps that could be taken to address it?
  - Are there capabilities—people, resources, relationships—to draw on to take those steps?
  - Is it cost-effective, and is there a way to pay for it?

How Can Education Change?

Pursuing high-leverage problems and developing micro-innovations often work precisely because they don't require significant changes to the activities and expectations of students and teachers in the classroom; but that's also why working on high-leverage problems and concentrating on the micro-innovations that contribute to incremental improvements will never be enough to transform the conditions and structures that reinforce a narrow focus on basic skills and sustain inequitable educational opportunities. At the same time, the many alternative approaches that emerge even as the basic grammar of schooling persists demonstrate the possibilities that come with another principle of school improvement.

PRINCIPLE #4

The demands and pressures of conventional schooling make it easier to transform learning experiences in niches rather than across entire school systems.

"Niches of possibility" are places within and outside schools where more powerful learning experiences can take root. Too often, however, reformers believe these successful alternatives—whether they include magnet schools, charter schools, after-school programs, or programs that take place outside school entirely—demonstrate promising ways to change entire school systems. That logic suggests that

If a school model, program, practice, technology, or other resource can work in one setting . . .

> **then,** with the right support, it can be "scaled up" across many different settings and circumstances.

This logic rests on the idea that any success derives from the qualities of the model, program, or practice—on the "innovation" itself. That assumption, however, ignores the ways improvements depend on the inter-relationship between those new models, programs, and practices and the conditions in which they develop. This assumption and the related focus on "scaling up" highlight another way that many improvement initiatives are too big: in addition to being too complicated, they're also too general. Like the teacher-evaluation reforms pursued in the United States, they often aim to work for many groups across multiple contexts.

These broad, general efforts to work across contexts fail to take into account the "affordances" of different settings that make some kinds of behaviors and activities possible while limiting others. The psychologist James J. Gibson (1977) introduced the term to describe the functions or possibilities that objects and environments provide or "afford": the affordances of cups include that they can be grasped; they can hold liquid; and they can be used for drinking. The psychologist Donald Norman (2013) adds to the original definition by highlighting that the perceived affordances of an object are those that are visible, but some affordances may not be recognized right away and may only be discovered over time. Correspondingly, manufactured objects often lend themselves to uses for which they were never explicitly designed, and eventually, those who use cups for drinking may find out they can be turned into effective paperweights or dangerous projectiles.

Norms and conventions also influence the choices people make about what to do with particular objects and in particular settings. Norms include common routines and practices that guide everyday behavior in different cultural and social settings. Norms and routines related to cooking, eating, and drinking (for example) all shape what people eat, whom they eat with, when they eat, what they do in preparing food and during mealtimes, and how they use different utensils. Although individuals or groups may defy expectations and behave in unconventional ways, policies and regulations promote and discourage certain kinds of behavior by stipulating which kinds of activities are legally disallowed, even if the environment affords the opportunity to pursue them. Although it's possible to defy conventions and disregard regulations, social pressure and legal consequences punish those who do so.

Constraints, affordances, norms, conventions, and regulations in education create both challenges and opportunities for improving schools:

- The design of school buildings with separate classrooms and long hallways makes it difficult to promote collaboration among teachers and students.

- Multiple-choice tests afford standardization and quick machine-grading, but they also promote a focus on fact- and recall-based questions.

- Putting a blackboard (or whiteboard or screen) at the front of every classroom facing rows of desks privileges teacher-directed instruction.

- The conventional styles of conversation and patterns of interaction in schools privilege those of dominant cultural groups, often creating a mismatch that inhibits learning and contributes to negative perceptions of students from different racial, cultural, and linguistic backgrounds (Heath, 1983).

- Compelling schools to track progress in student outcomes by using annual tests in reading and math (as in NCLB) made it possible to visualize disparities in educational opportunities based on students' racial and ethnic backgrounds, but it discouraged teachers and schools from spending time on other valued subjects and other aspects of development.

Characteristics That Shape Learning Opportunities

Philosophers have long debated the distinctions between the terms used to describe the characteristics of different settings that influence behavior, but in common use the key differences relate to what's physically, perceptually, and legally possible. By understanding these different characteristics, educators can determine where students and teachers are most likely to be able to successfully pursue more and less conventional learning opportunities.

Constraints: The physical limitations that restrict movement and behavior

Affordances: The actions and activities possible within a given setting; the functions that the environment offers or "affords" and that users can perceive and take advantage of

Norms and conventions: The accepted and expected patterns of "normal" behavior and social interaction

Policies, laws, and regulations: Legal stipulations and requirements that govern behavior and activity

Exactly how the characteristics of each educational setting influence instruction varies. Elective courses and courses in subjects like music, the arts, and physical education provide teachers with more flexibility in terms of choice of subject matter and instructional approach when there are no high-stakes standardized tests required for evaluating students' performance across schools. The policies and regulations that govern magnet schools and charter schools relieve them of some of the requirements demanded of other public schools, and private schools evade some of the legal restrictions that govern all public schools. Despite such increased flexibility, instruction in these alternatives still has to contend with the conventions of the grammar of schooling and the demands of college entrance and employment, and the conventional expectations of "real school" still shape perceptions of what effective instruction looks like. Although many of the policies and regulations that govern schooling and instruction during the regular school day don't apply after the school day ends, students, parents, and schools often want after-school programs to provide homework assistance or tutoring to help students improve their grades or prepare for standardized tests.

The varied ways that all the constraints, affordances, norms and conventions, and policies and regulations converge in a particular situation make it particularly difficult for any one general approach to address critical issues across contexts. At the same time, understanding how all these factors come together in particular schools, educational settings, and communities creates opportunities for pursuing unconventional approaches to teaching and learning. Those approaches may not fit into every school or school system, but, with a focus on finding and creating the right conditions, it's possible to imagine how a number of alternatives can help transform the system, even if no single initiative can do it on its own.

The next two chapters draw from some programs working "outside" schools, as well as those striving to work into the school day, to explore the specific conditions that support the development of alternative educational opportunities. By understanding these niche conditions and the affordances for learning they provide, educators can find places where they can challenge the boundaries of contemporary schools and create examples and "visions of the possible" that exceed conventional expectations.

The Conditions
for Learning   8

How often do students get to create a twenty-foot-long creature of indeterminate shape that they can pedal around a lake? Or a "Pipe Tree"—a "fully functioning, human-operated pipe organ" nestled among (and shaped like) the trees in the forest? Brian Cohen, Danny Kahn, and an ambitious group of staff engage students in these kinds of outsized, collaborative art installations and "learning productions" on a regular basis at the Beam Center in Brooklyn, New York. They even found a niche for this unusual approach to project-based learning in several New York City public schools. Finding their niche in school settings that supported their unconventional approach, however, took almost ten years.

Cohen and Kahn, former music producers, developed their large-scale approach to project-based learning far beyond the pressures of the grammar of schooling in a summer camp in New Hampshire. Launched in the summer of 2005, the idea for Beam summer camp came from Cohen's own camp experiences, but their approach to the production process emerged out of their work in the record business. "As record company people," Cohen explained, "our whole lives revolved around talent and cultivation and management and respect, so what we came up with was this idea of let's find a talented individual or collective of individuals to design a project that could then become the pretext for everything that happens at camp."

THE BEAM CENTER (BROOKLYN, NEW YORK)

The Beam Center, headquartered in Red Hook, Brooklyn, "builds communities of making and learning" that engage youths in building large-scale learning productions. Beam's programs have developed over time to include:

- A summer camp in New Hampshire

- After-school, summer, and weekend programs for youths

- Partnerships with schools in New York City to integrate multidisciplinary, hands-on projects into students' courses and school experiences

- Workshops for teachers and apprenticeships for students

- FabLabs that give students and teachers access to materials and equipment for advanced digital fabrication

By 2019, Beam was working with twenty-nine public schools in New York City, equipping seventeen with FabLabs.

These monumental and technically challenging productions made the joy of accomplishing something "bigger and better" than the campers could have imagined a central goal. "All we were worried about was getting the project done and getting it done well," Cohen explained, "because of the way kids felt when it was done." He added, "If it's a little harder than the abilities of anyone who works there, then everyone is in it together, to achieve it, no matter what level you're at—whether camp counselor or director—It's like, how are we going to do this?" Like the possibilities for visible progress that make working on high-leverage problems powerful, the Beam productions also came together quickly—in a matter of weeks—and provided a tangible indicator of what everyone could accomplish.

Cohen and Kahn concentrated initially on creating a joyful, rewarding camp experience. Yet, over time, they uncovered affordances of the camp experience and the work on the large-scale art installations that opened up unanticipated developmental and educational opportunities that they then tried to refine. First and foremost, Kahn explained, "our lens is camp: it's twenty-four hours a day." Living and working together twenty-four hours a day created opportunities to develop relationships and trust among campers and staff and to embrace every possibility for learning and development wherever and whenever it occurred. In particular, Cohen and Kahn came to see the inclusion of an expert—the artist or architect who designed the production—as a key ingredient. The expert lent authenticity to the endeavor, provided professional insight to guide the process, and brought what they called a "creative stardom" that inspired campers. The work on the production also put campers into daily work with artisans and other "domain experts," allowed them to use real materials and sophisticated equipment, and enabled them to develop woodworking, digital programming, and other skills. The productions themselves afforded opportunities for participants to do things they had never done before, and the need to get everything done by a real, public deadline tested everyone's motivation, commitment, and character.

Plugging Into Schools

Beam's evolution as a camp, in a setting far from the demands of the regular school day, provided Cohen and Kahn with a crucial opportunity to identify some of the key characteristics that made their learning productions so successful. The camp experience also gave them time to develop the infrastructure of materials, staff, and connections with key suppliers and experts that allowed them to create a more organized and efficient set of learning experiences. From the beginning, however, Cohen and Kahn envisioned bringing the "magic of camp" and large-scale learning productions to students in schools.

Doing so meant finding a place within the school day where the conditions meshed with their understanding of the demands and possibilities of their approach. That meant directly confronting the fact that most conventional schools and classrooms discourage the pursuit of Beam's large-scale learning productions:

- *Division into subject-based courses*—A schedule divided into subject-based, age-graded courses makes it difficult to find a place for students to pursue interdisciplinary projects in heterogeneous groups with a range of developmental levels.

- *Demands for "coverage"*—Requirements to meet standards, pass tests, and meet other outcomes discourage work on projects that don't focus on those requirements.

- *Lack of time*—The schedule and demands for coverage provide little opportunity for students to engage in three-week-long projects or for teachers to plan and collaborate.

- *Limited access to expertise and resources*—Even when teachers and students do find the time to develop large-scale, collaborative projects, those projects often depend on the support of experts and the use of tools, materials, and other resources not often found inside schools.

- *Conflicting expectations*—Assumptions about what learning should look like in "real school" versus in camps and other "extracurricular" settings contribute to predictable resistance even when time and resources are available.

With all these challenges, it took time, some trial and error, reflection, and adaptations to find a place for Beam learning productions in schools. Just trying to run a camp program at a Brooklyn elementary school one summer exposed the conventional pressures they faced. Even though the school wasn't in session, Beam's summer staff found that their camp experience felt much more like school than they had intended. They discovered the source of the problem when they noticed that, during transitions between classrooms and before going outside or to the cafeteria, staffers instinctively lined up all the students in the hallway and tried to keep them quiet, falling back on a familiar, conventional school routine. They then realized that they themselves contributed to that problem by reflexively splitting the campers up into small groups and assigning those groups to separate classrooms, creating a level of rigidity and isolation totally different from the camp experience. In contrast, at camp, groups worked out in the open; campers and counselors could often see one another, collaborate, and flow freely from one activity and one group to another without a fixed schedule. Once the Beam staff recognized these issues, they shifted the groups to working outside and in the cafeteria, settings where the affordances were much more conducive to developing relaxed, informal, and collaborative learning activities.

When Cohen and Kahn looked for a place to bring the Beam productions into the regular school day, they found a home at Brooklyn International High School. Brooklyn International's specialized nature and unusual student population offered a more hospitable context for their approach than a conventional school. Brooklyn International joins twenty-seven other international schools from around the United States in a network designed to serve the needs of recently arrived immigrant students who have spent less than four years in schools in the United States. Cohen described Brooklyn International as the perfect setting for Beam's approach: the students were already organized into heterogeneous groups—mixed by age, grade, academic ability, prior schooling, native language, and linguistic proficiency—and those groups studied in interdisciplinary courses with an emphasis on student-centered learning, the arts, and technology.

The school's participation in the New York Performance Standards Consortium helped create a context for Brooklyn International's alternative approach. The consortium, established in 1990, pursued waivers from New York State regulations in order to allow their students to avoid mandated state testing and to skip most of the Regents exams required for graduation (only the exam in English Language is required). Instead, Consortium schools like Brooklyn International have developed their own graduation requirements, based largely on a portfolio of performance-based tasks and presentations. With these accommodations, Brooklyn International occupies a setting "on the margins" of the public school system—relieved of some of the pressures that sustain the grammar of schooling.

Even in a more flexible and supportive setting, it took some time to find the best place to locate Beam productions within the regular school day. At first, Beam productions were offered as elective courses. This arrangement gave Beam full control over the class, but Cohen, Kahn, and their colleagues found themselves operating largely independently, unable to collaborate with other teachers or to make connections to other aspects of students' school experiences. Over time, Beam staff discovered that the productions were more successful when "co-designed" with teachers in the school. To make the productions work, the teachers and Beam staff split up the responsibilities. The teachers took on the role of pedagogical and curricular experts who figured out how to connect the productions to the scope and sequence of learning goals that their courses demanded. The Beam staff served a role similar to the artists and "domain experts" in camp, with expertise in design and in using the tools and resources needed to develop the productions. In one collaboration with an English and physics teacher, students produced a Digital Poetry Machine: a wall of magnetic laser-cut wood words that could be arranged into short poems and posted to Twitter. In the process, students documented their problem-solving strategies and the skills they were developing. Cohen explained that this integration into regular coursework made it easier for Beam to contribute to the development of the community so essential to the camp experience: "By being part of the [regular] school day," he reported, "the work we do in the classroom becomes the core of a new kind of school community. Instead of the regular stratifications—teachers, students, administrators, high-achieving students, low-achieving students—now you have a blending of roles, an accessible forum for achievement, an incentive for all to be learning, and a common aspiration."

These interdisciplinary productions, integrated into Brooklyn International's core curriculum, took off. The productions engaged all kinds of learners; they energized teachers; and they provided big, visible, public signs of success for the students, the teachers, the school, and Beam. Like other approaches that found a way to both challenge and fit into the grammar of schooling, several factors help explain why the Beam approach was able to take off at Brooklyn International:

- The productions *met a clear need* that educators, students, and parents all experienced: the need to engage students who speak many different languages, with widely varying backgrounds and levels of educational experiences and achievement. The evidence that the productions were engaging to students was visible to everyone almost immediately, and, within a matter of weeks, the evidence of accomplishment and related sense of pride and efficacy was on clear display in the celebrations that accompanied the public unveiling of the end products.

- Cohen and Kahn were able to use their connections and experience as music producers to marshal the resources, find the experts, and make the connections that provided under-resourced and overburdened teachers and schools with the *infrastructure and capacity* to produce work of a scale and quality that many never thought they could produce on their own within a typical classroom setting.

- Like Advanced Placement courses, the production work could "plug into" the basic structures of the school and, in this case, fit into established courses that already supported heterogeneous grouping and interdisciplinary, project-based work; it didn't require large-scale changes in the structures or instructional practices of the school as a whole.

Like work on high-leverage problems, the visible successes at Brooklyn International helped lay the foundation for expanding and deepening Beam's work in other schools in the city, many of which shared some of the characteristics of Brooklyn International: schools with specialized populations or specific themes and approaches consistent with Beam's hands-on, interdisciplinary projects.

Further enhancing those efforts to expand, even though Beam's approach conflicted with basic expectations about real school, it meshed well with both the philosophies of schools like Brooklyn International and *the values and trends* (or "zeitgeist") after the turn of the 21st century. Cohen reflected, "Although we didn't know it, we were participating in the zeitgeist of maker culture, technology-inspired culture." The growing interest in technology and maker culture meant that many organizations—including the New York City Department of Education, philanthropists, and local businesses—wanted to support efforts to prepare students for a digital future and to integrate STEM and real-world learning experiences into schools.

Beam capitalized on the growing demand for sophisticated resources to pursue learning productions and the opportunities for funding in order to create an entirely new initiative: the development of "FabLabs." First established at Brooklyn International in 2016, FabLabs function as a kind of "maker space" Beam describes as an "advanced digital fabrication laboratory." FabLabs include equipment like basic shop tools, laser cutters, electronics equipment, 3-D printers, computers, and design software. Facilitating their development, FabLabs can fit into any conventional school that can find classroom space. That arrangement, like Boaler's math cards (see Chapter 7), takes advantage of conventional routines and practices that make it easy for schools and teachers to integrate the use of resources centers, such as libraries and computer labs, into typical schedules and coursework. All these factors helped Beam turn a single camp in New Hampshire into a sophisticated approach to project-based learning and a model for maker spaces in a growing network of schools in the largest public school district in the United States.

Finding the Right Fit

The successes of Beam and many other alternative programs, both inside and outside school, inspires the hope that unconventional approaches can spread across all schools. This hope hinges on a belief that these approaches can overcome inhospitable conditions by reaching a tipping point, a point of contagion after which new ideas or practices cascade across different settings. But learning how to expand strategically and effectively depends on recognizing that successful programs like Beam, Wordworks (Chapter 6), and IkamvaYouth (Chapter 7) fit better in some settings than others. From this perspective, the goal shifts from scaling up a particular model to finding the right fit: understanding the educational affordances in different settings, identifying approaches that might prosper under those conditions, and making adaptations and adjustments over time.

THE LEARNING COMMUNITY PROJECT (LCP) (MEXICO)

The Learning Community Project's peer-tutoring approach developed in a handful of multi-grade elementary and middle schools between 2004 and 2008 in rural Mexico (Cámara, 2007). The approach encompasses several critical elements:

- Students choose one of many curriculum topics and then engage in an individual inquiry at their own pace.

- Adult tutors, who have studied these topics in their own network, provide support.

- Students demonstrate their mastery of the topics in public presentations, often including family and community members.

- Students who have mastered topics then serve as tutors for other students interested in that topic.

Through this process, each student's growing knowledge and skill becomes a resource—a fund of knowledge—for the whole community.

Even evidence that programs have spread to hundreds of schools doesn't necessarily signal that this expansion can go on forever. Like the Kliptown Youth Program and IkamvaYouth in Africa, the Learning Community Project (LCP) found a niche for the development of its own approach to peer tutoring in rural schools in Mexico. In the LCP tutorial approach, students become "experts" by studying important topics and then work individually or in small groups to help their peers and their teachers learn these topics. As a consequence, when visitors arrive at an LCP school, they're as likely to see students working independently or tutoring teachers or peers as they are to see teachers tutoring students (Elmore & International Perspectives on Education Reform Group, 2011).

To develop that unconventional pedagogy, LCP took advantage of the "marginal" conditions in a handful of rural schools. As Santiago Rincón-Gallardo has documented, "Small schools located in far-off communities offered ideal conditions for trying out a practice that ran against the grain of conventional schooling" (Rincón-Gallardo, 2016, p. 428):

- Recognition that approaches to education in schools like these were producing significantly lower levels of academic achievement compared to schools in more advantaged areas contributed to a demand for alternatives.

- Many students in these communities missed school for long periods of time to help their parents farming, harvesting, home maintenance, and other activities, creating a shared need for a flexible model that allowed students to move at their own pace.

- Small numbers of students of different ages and teachers working in a common space made it possible to rearrange schedules and create the long blocks of time and flexibility in which students could work alone or together and get support when they needed it.

- The "unconventional" tutoring activities matched some of the values and beliefs about learning reflected in the kinds of modeling, guided practice, and coaching characteristic of the apprenticeships used to learn local crafts.

- The remote locations meant that the schools operated without the same level of supervision or attention that might have discouraged government schools in other places from pursuing these unconventional practices.

Although the LCP approach began slowly in four schools, it grew to include a network of sixty schools by 2009. The success of the approach led the Mexican government to adopt the LCP's tutorial strategy as a central feature of a nationwide school-improvement initiative. That adoption sought to spread the approach to 9,000 schools throughout Mexico (Rincón-Gallardo, 2016). By 2012, schools involved in the project had increased the proportion of students scoring at "good" and "excellent" levels in the national standardized test and contributed to a dramatic increase in students' achievement in regions where it had been adopted.

Despite these large-scale successes, in another example of the turbulence of the policy environment, a new government in 2012 replaced the leaders of the national program and turned their attention to other issues. Under these circumstances, further program implementation has been uneven. The approach continues to show positive results in some schools, particularly in those rural communities where the approach began; but in many other schools Rincón-Gallardo reports that only a mechanistic, prescriptive version of the original pedagogy can be observed. In short, the LCP experience demonstrates what can be accomplished in a (very large) niche with very challenging educational circumstances—a truly remarkable achievement worth celebrating. Yet it also reinforces the difficulties of moving successful practices developed on the margins of schooling to the "core" of conventional schools.

Scaling Into School Systems

Some of the best-known school networks in the United States have reached large numbers of schools. Some of those networks build on conventional practices and structures of schooling, and others challenge them:

- Success for All, established in 1987 with emphases on reading and cooperative learning, demonstrated significant growth over a period of twenty-five years, reaching over a thousand schools by 2012 (Success for All Foundation, 2015).

- KIPP (Knowledge Is Power Program), one of the most successful charter-school operators in terms of test scores and graduation rates, opened its first 2 schools in 1995 and expanded to 242 schools by 2020.

- Success Academy quickly became known for its academic focus, high test scores, and high demands on students and teachers. Launched in 2006, by 2020 Success Academy had expanded to forty-five schools in New York City.

- EL (originally Expeditionary Learning Outward Bound) began, like ATLAS (see Chapter 4), with funding from the New American Schools Development Corporation in 1991. By 2020, it worked with 150 schools dedicated to interdisciplinary "learning expeditions" and a focus on mastery of knowledge and skills, character, and high-quality student work.

- Big Picture Learning (BPL) dispenses with the school day almost entirely, creating internships and mentorship experiences that match high-school students' interests and then organizes a series of educational supports around each student's work in the real world. Initiated with a small group of students in Rhode Island in 1995, by 2020, BPL worked with schools in twenty-five states and in eleven countries, including Kenya, Kazakhstan, and New Zealand.

Yet all these networks have taken years to develop their approaches, and, taken together, they still reach only a small percentage of students.

> Rather than scaling up, the success of efforts to improve and transform learning opportunities depends on "scaling into" those settings and niches in and around the conventional system where they can fit.

The challenge for those who seek to improve and transform schools, then, goes far beyond trying to create a model for education that can be replicated with fidelity across multiple contexts. An overemphasis on replication and fidelity ignores the key lesson that successful reform efforts always involve some level of adaptation. Rather than scaling up, the success of efforts to improve and transform learning opportunities depends on "scaling into" those settings and niches in and around the conventional system where they can fit.

"Scaling into" means that educators need to ask two key questions:

- How much is it possible to stretch the boundaries of conventional schooling?
- What settings will provide the greatest opportunity to push those boundaries?

It means paying attention to the features and affordances of different settings instead of trying to transcend them.

From Possibilities 9
to Practice

The limits of "scaling up" highlight another critical principle of school improvement.

PRINCIPLE #5

The more radical the changes are, the less likely they are to spread and take hold across large numbers of schools.

Rather than lamenting this constraint, we can embrace it. This lesson from both the successes and the failures of efforts to improve schools around the world leads to two complementary strategies that make it possible to improve the schools we have and work toward transforming schooling at the same time:

1. Build an infrastructure of materials, people, and relationships that can spread and sustain improvements in learning in a particular niche.

2. Take advantage of "spandrels"—unanticipated opportunities to develop more powerful learning experiences that emerge as educational improvements evolve.

Together, these two strategies provide concrete ways to support and build on the work of educators on the ground in learning experiences inside and outside of school. These strategies can promote improvements that meet immediate needs at the same time as they spawn new educational possibilities rather than simply reinforce conventional school structures and practices. Like the concept of "leapfrogging," described by Rebecca Winthrop and her colleagues, taking advantage of these unanticipated developments can "accelerate educational progress, perhaps skipping steps, but certainly ending up in a new place altogether" (Winthrop, 2018, pp. 33–34).

Building the Infrastructure for New Forms of Learning

Getting "smaller," more local, and more concrete in addressing educational problems produces the building blocks for a stronger infrastructure for teaching and learning in many different communities. That infrastructure grows as those working inside and outside schools share the materials and expertise they develop. Without that infrastructure, educators and schools are left to their own devices to solve the same problems over and over again.

As Danny Kahn from the Beam Center explained, putting a FabLab into a school (see Chapter 8) can catalyze activity the way that building a soccer field, a gym, or a tennis court can. But taking advantage of the new affordances and opportunities that come with new fields and facilities depends on the available infrastructure of resources, expertise, and relationships:

- *Materials and equipment,* such as soccer balls, basketballs, and tennis balls and racquets
- *People* who can act as coaches, mentors, and models who can help "beginners" take advantage of and use the materials and equipment productively
- *Connections* to coaches, teams, leagues, tournaments, and formal learning opportunities that extend the value of simply providing equipment and putting new facilities in place

Without an infrastructure to support learning, FabLabs, learning productions, and other new developments often get implemented in superficial and symbolic ways: putting a FabLab or a maker space into a school can serve as a signal that a school or community center has "modernized" without substantially improving learning opportunities.

Under these circumstances, FabLabs run the risk of turning into the latest computer rooms, now abandoned and dormant in many schools and communities. Given these challenges, to support the productive use of FabLabs, Beam strives to build an accompanying infrastructure that includes guidance on the proper equipment and setup for the lab; models of projects and activities that can be carried out; coaching and access to professional development opportunities with Beam experts; and connections to Beam's widening network of partner schools, supporters, camps, and other activities. In a similar way, Right to Play and Asphalt Green have demonstrated considerable success by helping many communities and schools that lacked adequate space and facilities develop and expand their infrastructure for play, recreational activities, and informal learning.

In Finland, the success of one program, Mehackit, stemmed from the infrastructure it built to fill a niche for computer programming courses and growing demands for schools to engage students in interdisciplinary projects. Mehackit began in 2014 with a mission to provide children with more equitable access to technology by offering programming workshops at community events, maker fairs, and after-school clubs. However, its founders found that many of the children attending those activities had parents who were already tech-savvy and working in technology-related jobs. To create more equitable access, they wanted to reach a wider group that didn't have that technological advantage. To accomplish that goal, they sought to work within the formal educational system. They found the opportunity with the changes in the Finnish curriculum in 2016. Those changes required schools to provide students with opportunities to learn computer programming and to experience real-world learning that cuts across traditional school subjects (what the Finns called "phenomenon-based" learning).

MEHACKIT (FINLAND)

Mehackit is a social enterprise focused on generating the resources and opportunities to make the development of technological skills more equitable. Since 2014, it has created a wide range of materials and services to carry out that mission:

- Courses for students in areas like robotics, music programming, and the arts that teach students programming and coding

- "Kits" that provide materials to support some of those courses

- Professional development courses and workshops for teachers of a variety of subjects

- Creative technology workshops and community arts projects for museums and other institutions

- Open-source online video tutorials and courses

Many of Mehackit's materials and courses are now freely available online in both Finnish and English and have been used in more than twenty-two countries.

Mehackit took advantage of the curriculum changes by shifting its focus to middle- and high-school students and designing course modules that could be offered by schools around Finland as easily and efficiently as possible. Mehackit supported the modules by creating an online "atelier" with links to open-source resources and to videos that provided models and instructions for students and gave teachers explicit guidance on how to integrate the modules into their classes. The electronics module also came with a kit (literally a briefcase) with the needed materials so that teachers didn't need to gather resources on their own.

Like Beam's FabLabs, these project-based, interdisciplinary modules could fit several key needs in schools. First, the new expectation for schools to implement interdisciplinary learning experiences gave schools an incentive to adopt the kind of modules that Mehackit developed. Second, teaching programming to older, high-school-aged students required sophisticated technical knowledge and skills that relatively few teachers possessed. Third, Mehackit's modules could plug right into the schedule of many upper secondary schools: at that level, students (roughly ages sixteen to eighteen) have to take some fifty compulsory courses, but they can also choose about twenty-five other, elective courses. Under these conditions, Mehackit expanded to work in over 100 secondary schools in Finland and went on to provide courses for schools in the United Kingdom and Sweden as well.

Evolution and Expansion of the Infrastructure for Learning

The infrastructure for learning develops over time as critical decisions and "micro"-solutions enable a program to succeed in a particular context and then adapt to the conditions in others. The evolution of Second Chance—which works with young children in Africa who have never been in primary school or who have dropped out of school for two years or more—illustrates the series of instructional, educational, and operational issues that lie behind developing and expanding that infrastructure even in under-resourced contexts. Second Chance programs cover the content of first, second, and third grade in just ten months, allowing the Second Chance students to catch up to their peers and transition into government schools in third or fourth grade.

To accomplish that goal, Second Chance developed an "active" pedagogical approach in which students work independently and in groups on a variety of learning activities involving language, math, and problem-solving. Nikita Khosla, senior director of the Luminos Fund that now supports the program, observed: "If you walk into a Second Chance classroom in Ethiopia or Liberia, you will see about twenty-five children sitting in groups of five. There will be work on the walls. It might be mud walls, but you will see chart paper stuck to them. You'll see alphabets made out of clay. You'll see children using [a] lot of local materials for math or going outside for nature-based learning." In the process, Second Chance seeks to create a place where children *want* to come to school.

In addition to drawing on local resources to create learning materials, Second Chance discovered it had to find a local source for staff who had the capacity to carry out its approach. Like the Kliptown Youth Program, IkamvaYouth, and the Learning Community Project (Chapters 7–8), Second Chance had to develop an approach that didn't rely on a steady supply of effective teachers. Instead, Second Chance quickly found the solution among the younger adults who lived in the same areas as the Second Chance students. This discovery hinged on recognizing two critical opportunities. First, as an unfortunate consequence of the weak local economy, there was a regular supply of unemployed youths who had at least a tenth-grade education and knew the local language. Second, as Khosla explained, although this group had "zero experience teaching, they have a real hunger for learning, and we've seen they are very open, and they really absorb everything like a sponge."

SECOND CHANCE (ETHIOPIA, LIBERIA, AND LEBANON)

Launched initially as "Speed School" in West Africa by the Legatum Foundation, the Strømme Foundation, and Geneva Global in 2007, Second Chance developed a ten-month curriculum to equip out-of-school children with the skills necessary to enter the government school system. In 2011, Legatum expanded the program to Ethiopia, and then in 2016, Legatum established the Luminos Fund to scale the program (renamed "Second Chance") even further.

Second Chance's approach has evolved to include a number of elements:

- An active-learning pedagogical approach

- The hiring and training of unemployed youths from the local community in Second Chance's active-learning pedagogy

- Partnerships with "Link" government schools to help ease Second Chance students' transition into the public system

- Self-help groups for parents, to encourage them to keep their children enrolled in school

Second Chance has served more than 135,000 children in Ethiopia, Liberia, and Lebanon, with their graduates completing primary school at nearly twice the rate of children in government schools (Akyeampong et al., 2018; Simpson, 2019).

Along with the opportunity came a key local challenge: although the local youths were familiar with the content (Second Chance follows the national curricula that all had been exposed to in their own schooling), most had never encountered anything like Second Chance's active-learning pedagogy. Under these circumstances, Second Chance had to design a low-cost professional development program that local youths could complete in a relatively short time. Ultimately, the approach Second Chance created consisted of twenty-one days of training spread across the ten months of the program. The training focused on the activity-based pedagogy and equipped facilitators to develop their own lessons that linked to the national curriculum, drew on the Second Chance activities, and utilized local materials.

Khosla suggested that two aspects of Second Chance's approach made the "innovation" of hiring local youths work. First, the facilitators could get a job at only slightly below the salary of government teachers and at a good rate, given their qualifications. Second, the facilitators were willing to try the active-learning pedagogy, because it gave them an opportunity to develop positive relationships with the students. "The facilitators talk about how happy and excited the children are, and that motivates them to employ the approach," explained Khosla.

With the success of reaching more than 100,000 out of school children in West Africa and Ethiopia by 2015 (Akyeampong et al., 2018), Second Chance expanded to Liberia. That expansion depended on Second Chance's ability to sustain its active pedagogy and training model at the same time that it created some new practices and supports to adapt its approach to a new, and more impoverished, context. Making those adjustments began with understanding how the affordances and constraints change in different contexts. As Khosla said about Second Chance's work in Liberia, "It's exactly the same program, but, oh my god, the challenges are so different." Those challenges included an out-of-school rate in Liberia of over 50 percent for children of primary-school age (compared to about 35 percent in Ethiopia); an economic growth rate about half that of Ethiopia's; and public spending on education also at about half the rate of Ethiopia's.

Those difficult conditions meant that Second Chance had to adjust to increased costs and more limited resources, but it took some time for the Second Chance staff to recognize all the new constraints that affected their program. As Khosla explained, "In Ethiopia they have a one-and-a-half-hour lunch break where they go home every day to eat lunch and then go back. We thought the same model would work in Liberia, but there's no food." Caitlin Baron, the CEO of the Luminos Fund, continued, "Kids were coming to school so hungry. It was a fool's errand not to address that need, but that means we are delivering rice and beans to mothers who are cooking food." Baron pointed out that this "small" adjustment to their program delivery in Liberia introduced a whole series of problems that had to be solved—where to get the food, how to ensure a consistent supply, how to prepare it—that required establishing a whole new supply chain, with new job responsibilities and added costs. "And there are hundreds of weak points in the chain," lamented Baron. For example, periods for traditional religious practices made it unsafe for children to be out collecting the wood needed to fuel the fires for cooking. With no firewood, students could end up going several days without food unless the staff at Second Chance made the local adjustments—like engaging parents to maintain the fires and prepare the lunches—that enabled the work inside the classroom to continue.

The transportation problems in Liberia also complicated Second Chance's efforts to support its teachers. In Ethiopia, they were able to form professional learning communities that brought facilitators together periodically to share information, reflect on what they were doing, and address common challenges. In Liberia, Khosla explained, "if you have to deviate from the main road, then you are in the bush, and then you are in the bush for at least 10 miles to reach one school." As a consequence, it was extremely difficult to get the facilitators to attend the network meetings crucial to professional development in Ethiopia. The Second Chance leaders solved this problem, as well as a problem of distributing salaries to a widely dispersed staff of facilitators (who needed to be paid once a month, in person, in cash, since they didn't have bank accounts), with one adjustment: they paid the facilitators at the end of the day, after they had attended their monthly network meetings. "It's a good way to ensure they come to the meetings," Khosla noted.

In developing the infrastructure required to be successful in different contexts—whether those contexts were in Liberia, Finland, or New York City—educators like those involved in Second Chance have to be careful not to get caught up in dealing with issues that take them far beyond their "core business" of creating effective learning opportunities. But they also have to be flexible enough to take on the basic practical and logistical issues that no one else will address.

Spandrels: Planning for Unpredictable Opportunities

Looking for niches, addressing micro-issues, and building the infrastructure for learning, in turn, generates unanticipated opportunities for creating new learning experiences.

Looking for niches, addressing micro-issues, and building the infrastructure for learning, in turn, generates unanticipated opportunities for creating new learning experiences. Metaphorically drawing from a debate in evolutionary biology, I call these unintended consequences of a design or plan *spandrels* (Gould & Lewontin, 1979; Sloan Wilson, 2015). Architects and builders use the term *spandrels* to describe the triangular spaces that result when trying to build arches and domes. The evolutionary biologist Stephen Jay Gould used a description of the spandrels of San Marco (the famous cathedral in Venice, aka Saint Mark's Basilica) to make his (widely debated) point that not every characteristic of an organism results from natural selection. He pointed out that the ability of the artists to produce the awe-inspiring decorations of the dome of the cathedral and the spandrels in the arches below it emerged as a by-product of the process of construction and the necessity of producing spandrels to build the dome.

In schools, these unanticipated and unintended consequences emerge as people uncover affordances that support new activities. IkamvaYouth developed its model of hiring recent high-school graduates and program alumni to serve as tutors only after the first group of program graduates told the founders they wanted to volunteer. Beam uncovered the opportunity to develop FabLabs and insert them into schools after spending several years trying to integrate learning productions into the regular classroom. New Visions' success in developing small alternative schools at the turn of the 21st century (see Chapter 7) positioned it to take on the management of a large network of new and existing schools when mayor Michael Bloomberg and schools chancellor Joel Klein required schools across the city to join school support networks. That readiness was particularly crucial, because the funding that New Visions and others had relied on to create new schools was drying up. As Mark Dunetz described the work at the time, by becoming a network provider, New Visions unexpectedly found itself as a kind of "laboratory for doing deep work on the day-to-day of everything happening in schools." In turn, that opportunity to learn from both alternative and conventional schools work has set the stage for New Visions to develop the administrative tools, software, and data portal—the micro-innovations—that now serve as central elements in New Visions' work to support a variety of school-improvement efforts across New York City (Bryk, 2020).

Taking advantage of these "spandrels of opportunity" provides another important way for educators to take into account the pressures and demands of conventional schooling while working over the long term to transform those conventions as well. Navigating those pressures requires a careful balancing act, developing programs and practices that work in one setting and adapting to and taking advantage of the circumstances in others. The evolution of Citizen Schools illustrates what's involved in trying to navigate the demands and opportunities of working in conventional school settings, even for organizations that start their work trying to create new educational opportunities outside the regular school day.

Eric Schwarz, a former journalist, founded Citizen Schools in Boston in 1995 to address the fact that many underrepresented and historically under-served students lacked access to the wide variety of extended learning opportunities that students from high-income backgrounds routinely enjoyed. In order to address this problem, Schwarz and his colleagues created an after-school program that offered apprenticeships one or two days a week in which students from several middle schools worked on activities like publishing a newspaper with volunteer mentors—"citizen teachers"— from related fields. From that beginning in a few after-school programs in Boston, Citizen Schools grew to reach 100,000 students in twenty-eight communities in Massachusetts, New York, and California, working primarily in conventional public schools. That journey reflects a series of hard choices about how closely to connect the activities of the original after-school program with the demands and pressures that students and educators face during the regular school day.

Stephen Jay Gould and Richard Lewontin on the Spandrels of San Marco

"The great central dome of St. Mark's Cathedral in Venice presents in its mosaic design a detailed iconography expressing the mainstays of Christian faith. Three circles of figures radiate out from a central image of Christ: angels, disciples, and virtues. Each circle is divided into quadrants, even though the dome itself is radially symmetrical in structure. Each quadrant meets one of the four spandrels in the arches below the dome. Spandrels—the tapering triangular spaces formed by the intersection of two rounded arches at right angles—are necessary architectural by-products of mounting a dome on rounded arches. Each spandrel contains a design admirably fitted into its tapering space. . . .

"The design is so elaborate, harmonious and purposeful that we are tempted to view it as the starting point of any analysis, as the cause in some sense of the surrounding architecture. But this would invert the proper path of analysis. The system begins with an architectural constraint: the necessary four spandrels and their tapering triangular form. They provide a space in which the mosaicists worked; they set the quadripartite symmetry of the dome above" (Gould & Lewontin, 1979, pp. 581–582).

CITIZEN SCHOOLS (MASSACHUSETTS, NEW YORK, AND CALIFORNIA)

Since 1995, Citizen Schools has developed a series of programs to provide access to mentors and real-world learning opportunities. Those programs have developed through three major iterations:

- An after-school program providing apprenticeships for middle-school students

- An after-school program offering apprenticeships as well as tutoring and homework help

- An extended learning time program, integrating apprenticeships with support for academics during the regular school day.

By 2020, Citizen Schools had also developed project-based STEM learning experiences that partnered science teachers with volunteer mentors and created a network of mentors to support STEM and maker-centered learning opportunities for students.

Even in the beginning, working exclusively after school, Schwarz got enthusiastic feedback from many students and parents, but some of the same parents also raised concerns that there was no corresponding improvement in most students' grades or academic performance. In addition, many principals felt increasing pressure from state and national policies to increase accountability for improving students' performance on annual tests. As Schwarz put it in his book *The Opportunity Equation* (2014), those principals had "less tolerance for our rookie mistakes and seemed in some cases to lose their appetite for the enrichment-based learning we were offering" (p. 63).

In response, Schwarz and his colleagues decided to refine the Citizen Schools model. They wanted to remain focused on apprenticeships, but they chose to make support for academic development a more explicit goal and aspect of the design. They started offering the program on an almost daily basis and devoted much of the increased time to homework and tutoring. The shift appeased many of the concerns and enabled the apprenticeships to continue one or two days a week. To deal with the increased staffing demands, Citizen Schools had to expand significantly, but it was able to do so by building on the growth of AmeriCorps, a federal program that funded volunteers to work with a wide range of not-for-profit volunteer organizations. With the inclusion of more academic support, the grades and test scores of many of Citizen Schools' students improved. As Schwarz explained, "The schools changed us in a good way—they made us better academically."

For the next ten years, Citizen Schools expanded this after-school model in Boston and several other cities, with considerable success. But then in 2006, Citizen Schools seized the opportunity to join the movement to create schools that operated on an extended learning time model. In part, the movement grew out of the success of after-school programs like Citizen Schools, but it also made those after-school activities a regular part of a longer school day. In turn, that meant that Citizen Schools, like Beam and Mehackit, had to find ways to create a fit between their apprenticeship approach and more conventional academic courses. To adapt, Citizen Schools partnered with the Edwards School in Charlestown, Massachusetts. Instead of simply adding its activities onto the end of the regular schedule, Citizen Schools chose to integrate its activities and staff into the regular school day in hopes of having a bigger impact. That involved changing the schedule to accommodate several new learning activities for both staff and students:

- A two-hour "elective/apprenticeship block" four days a week

- A regular sixty-minute "math league" period

- A half-day of professional development for teachers every Friday

To help carry out these changes, Citizen Schools provided the staff for many of the apprenticeships/electives, and Citizen Schools staff also took on responsibility for teaching some academic subjects, particularly math. These changes required further adaptations in Citizen Schools' own staffing and training, as they had to spend more of their time and expertise focused on supporting conventional academic instruction.

The changes provided immediate signs that things were different at the Edwards School, and over the next three years, outcomes began to improve. One improvement was an 80 percent reduction in the gap between students' performance levels in ELA and science on state tests. The school grew in popularity as well. In 2005, only 17 families made the Edwards School their first choice on the application asking which Boston middle school they would like their children to attend; but by 2008 more than 450 families applied to the school (Schwarz, 2014). With that success, Citizen Schools found a way to fit its apprenticeships into schools that adopted the ELT approach, and it continued to expand and develop that model.

Along with that success, however, Citizen Schools has had to contend with another dilemma: the focus on working with schools that pursue an extended learning time approach, and the intensive demands and high costs of the model, has limited its expansion. As Citizen Schools' summary of an independent evaluation put it, despite evidence of positive impact on students, "this model, with its cost and complexity, is not suited to every high need school and market" (McCann, 2016). Those limits mean that it's difficult to imagine spreading that model to address the inequitable access that prevents so many students from participating in the kinds of rich apprenticeships that Citizen Schools set out to make more widely available.

In order to deal with those limits on its extended learning time model, Citizen Schools has launched several new initiatives to find different entry points into conventional schools. One project, Catalyst, seeks to find a niche for project-based STEM activities for middle-school science courses by partnering middle-school science teachers with volunteer experts. Citizen Schools is also working to develop an infrastructure that includes an archive of projects; professional development opportunities for teachers; training for volunteers; and access to a network of company partners that can supply some of the volunteers needed to carry out the projects and apprenticeships in both the extended learning time model and the Catalyst program. Like Beam's FabLabs and Mehackit's online courses, this approach provides almost everything schools need to carry out hands-on, real-world projects during the school day. Although the integration of the Citizen Schools projects into existing courses may not have disrupted all the conventional structures and practices in schools, learning opportunities for students have expanded. Further, one can argue that Citizen Schools has, at least to some extent, "disrupted" conventional views of after-school programs and now provides a new model for learning through apprenticeships and offers an existence proof that such a model can be effective.

Creating the Conditions for Improvement

Creating the micro-innovations that catalyze improvements in learning, and building the infrastructure needed to transform the educational system over the long term, depends on careful attention to the specific conditions and affordances in each setting. Those conditions provide opportunities inside and outside school systems to try out new ideas and to carve out spaces where new practices can be deepened and sustained. Such an approach to the development of new learning opportunities in different sectors and niches suggests a different theory of action—a different "if . . . then . . ." proposition from the model of replication and scale-up reflected in many reform efforts and described at the beginning of Part 4. Instead of focusing on broad approaches to changing instruction across levels, subjects, and contexts, this approach concentrates on learning in particular situations where those instructional approaches might be most relevant and most likely to take hold. The approach reflected in a micro-innovation, such as a game for learning the terms of chemistry, might not be replicated in other subjects or even for other learning goals in chemistry; but developing different tools, materials, and services that focus on other goals and different circumstances gradually builds the infrastructure that teachers and students need to be successful. In this scenario, rather than trying to shift all instruction from teacher-centered to student-centered learning, educators can develop the supports that make more powerful learning possible in a whole series of situations, both inside and outside school. The developments in those niches generate the unanticipated possibilities that can take learning to the next level and into the unpredictable future:

If educators can develop more powerful learning experiences in many different situations and niches . . .

> **then** new possibilities emerge as students encounter more and more opportunities for powerful learning.

Instead of trying to scale one or two "big" innovations across contexts, this approach focuses on multiplying the many micro-innovations that fit into the daily lives and educational experiences of children all over the world.

KEY IDEAS FROM PART 4

Improving the schools we have and transforming education depends on focusing on long-term purposes and goals and on looking out for unanticipated new opportunities at the same time. That means coming to terms with the fact that improvement efforts are always likely to move more slowly than many would like while remaining relentlessly committed to moving ahead. As discussed in Part 2, the niches and subsystems in which educators operate are part of a whole set of interconnected systems—district, state, and federal educational systems, and "quasi-systems" like groups of educational providers, universities, and others—that extend beyond education. The need to fit with prevailing needs, values, and capabilities among all these different actors exerts a stabilizing and conservative force. That conservative force is further strengthened by policy churn and a turbulent environment of unpredictable changes in economic, social, and cultural conditions. The interconnected system, policy churn, and turbulent environment, in turn, help maintain systemic racism and inequitable educational opportunities.

KEY QUESTIONS TO HELP DETERMINE WHEN AND HOW SCHOOLS MIGHT CHANGE

- What's required by the structures, constraints, conventions, regulations, and policies in a school or other setting?
- What capabilities are available to pursue a new approach, and what capabilities need to be developed?
- What are the affordances?
- What's possible in this setting that hasn't yet been tried?
- What other settings can provide relevant information, resources, and expertise for taking a new approach?

Under these circumstances, and certainly in the wake of the chaos and heartbreak caused by the coronavirus, those who seek to change and improve education need to treat the turbulence of the environment and the unpredictability of the opportunities that emerge as a given rather than hoping the environment will remain stable. Although a viral pandemic at some time could've been predicted, it was impossible to predict its precise character or exactly what it would take to contain it. Nonetheless, places like Hong Kong, Taiwan, and Singapore were better prepared to respond than others. They were ready to build on what they'd learned from similar outbreaks and were equipped to adopt and adapt strategies and deploy resources flexibly (Barron, 2020). In Singapore, schools even planned to close for one day a week at one point—just to help prepare students, parents, and teachers in case a surge in coronavirus cases required schools to close again (Teng & Davie, 2020). By preparing for the unpredictable and giving up the dream that we can control conditions, we gain the power to use them to our advantage.

What Does It Take to Change School Systems?

The people who are trying to develop new and innovative schools sometimes describe the problem as one of trying to build a plane while flying it. But the dual demands of improving existing schools and transforming conventional approaches to schooling suggest an even more difficult challenge: we have to figure out how to keep the plane in the air at the same time that we take the whole system apart.

This analogy points to another critical problem with many reform initiatives. In addition to being too big, too complicated, and too general, many reform initiatives are also too small: they fail to take into account all the aspects of the educational system that have to be improved. This challenge reflects another basic principle of school improvement.

PRINCIPLE #6

Large-scale improvements in the practices and structures of schooling depend on building capacity throughout the educational system.

Given my critique of the complicated nature of many large-scale reform efforts, the notion that many are also too small may seem ludicrous; but almost as soon as I got to Finland and Singapore, I could see that many of the stories of Finnish and Singaporean success paint far too simplistic a picture of their educational systems. Those stories concentrate almost exclusively on the fact that these countries have developed a powerful group of teachers. That emphasis contributes to overly narrow policy initiatives in the United States and other countries that concentrate on issues like teacher recruitment and retention but fail to consider the many other steps that need to be taken to build the capacity to support teachers and improve teaching and learning on a large scale.

The focus on the recruitment and retention of teachers begins with the assumption that schools *already* have the capacity to make improvements and educators just need to be motivated to do it. As far back as 1983, *A Nation at Risk*—the report that inspired a surge in educational reform in the United States—championed this perspective. That report contended that the lessons gained from numerous examples of successful schools provided the "raw materials needed to reform our educational system" and argued that they "are waiting to be mobilized through effective leadership" (National Commission on Excellence in Education, 1983, para. 8). Fueled by similar assumptions, many subsequent policies and reform initiatives placed more emphasis on establishing incentives and increasing accountability than on building capacity. As one illustration, the "Desktop Reference" (Office of the Under Secretary, 2002), prepared by the US Department of Education that explained the key provisions of the No Child Left Behind legislation (NCLB) passed in 2001 uses the word "capacity" fourteen times and the word "accountability" seventy times.

These narrow efforts make a bet on individuals to change schools:

If we can find those individuals who are most likely to be successful, and . . .

   if we can provide incentives to encourage them to become teachers and stay in teaching . . .

      then they can overcome the inequitable conditions that make substantial improvements in learning for all students so difficult.

NCLB, for example, included provisions designed to ensure that public schools hired only "highly qualified" teachers in core academic subjects. In this case, the policy logic suggested that replacing unqualified (and presumably less effective teachers) with more qualified teachers could lead to across-the-board increases in student learning. Rather than investing in improving teacher preparation or the development of more powerful curricula, NCLB relied on the existence of an untapped reservoir of "talented" teachers, capable of enabling all of their students to reach much higher standards of academic achievement. Unfortunately, after the enactment of NCLB, the number of qualified teachers increased, but clear signs indicated those numerical changes didn't add up to much. In fact, in some states, such as Minnesota, teachers who already had a full license to teach were simply relabeled as "highly qualified" (Walsh & Snyder, 2004).

It took my visits to Singapore, Finland, and Norway and comparisons with my experiences in the United States for me to recognize that rather than seeing education as a societal project, many US policies like those of NCLB rely on the power of the individual. Faith in individuals doesn't absolve the wider community of the responsibility for ensuring that every child gets the education they need. Balancing those individual and societal contributions is a difficult task, but Singapore, Finland, and Norway demonstrate some alternatives to focusing so heavily on individuals and the rewards and penalties meant to incentivize their behavior.

In the next three chapters, I highlight the ways in which Singapore and Finland have built an expansive infrastructure to support teaching and learning strengthened by deliberate efforts to foster common understanding of the goals and purposes of schooling. Although Norway hasn't invested in building the same kind of instructional infrastructure as Finland and Singapore, Norwegian improvement efforts reveal the power of developing collective responsibility and making education part of a wider commitment to the health and well-being of the entire society.

Capacity-Building 10

There are always reasons to question comparisons between "higher-performing" and "lower-performing" educational systems. Singapore's approach is often dismissed by those who see such explicit governmental control as impossible and unwanted in a decentralized system like that of the United States. The considerable differences in the size and diversity of the population between countries like Finland and the United States also make it difficult to apply any lessons across them. At the same time, the differences and similarities between Singapore and Finland prove instructive. Both have populations just under 6 million, but they differ dramatically in terms of their diversity, geography, cultural traditions, and approach to education. Yet the substantial differences between Singapore and Finland make their common, systemic focus on developing an infrastructure of materials, expertise, and relationships particularly striking.

As I went to schools and talked to educators, researchers, and policymakers, I found that both countries invest significant time and attention in three key components to help schools build the capacity to achieve their educational goals:

- Preparing and supporting teachers (building "human capital")

- Developing high-quality facilities, curricula, assessments, and other resources (building "technical capital")

- Fostering relationships and connections that share resources and expertise and coordinate work across different parts of the educational system (building "social capital")

The available expertise, materials, and relationships form the infrastructure that both sustains the grammar of schooling and provides the foundation for large-scale changes and improvements. That infrastructure supports the "instructional core" and the work that teachers do with students in the classroom, but the educational systems in Singapore and Finland also illustrate the ways that the infrastructure needed to support learning stretches far beyond individual schools and districts (see Figure 10.1). That infrastructure reflects the contributions of a host of people and organizations, both inside and outside the school system, who produce the facilities, materials, preparation programs, and political and public support needed to fund, run, and sustain educational systems. The way that Finland and Singapore support and coordinate these many "outside" influences on schools serves as a critical, but often unrecognized, factor in building a strong infrastructure for teaching and learning.

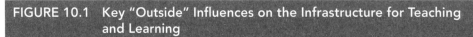

FIGURE 10.1   Key "Outside" Influences on the Infrastructure for Teaching and Learning

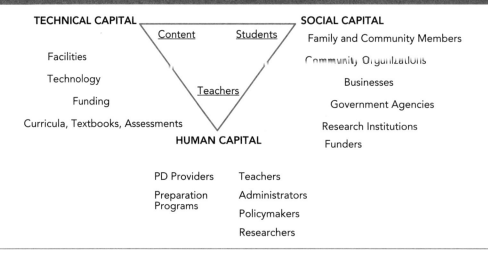

Investing in Expertise and Materials

The investment that both countries make in teachers and teaching were easy to spot. In Finland, I saw it when Karen and I arrived at the school outside Helsinki, where two of our daughters spent the last two weeks of the academic year. The school, like many of those we visited in Finland, looked more like the campus of a high-tech company than the aging buildings surrounded by chain-link fences we were so familiar with in the United States. In Singapore, I saw it on the back of a bus: an advertisement showed a picture of two smiling students, in school uniforms, with the caption "A teacher pays just as much attention to the students at the back. Be a teacher." In both places, that support for teachers went hand in hand with an investment in equipping teachers with high-quality materials and assessments linked to common and clear curriculum frameworks and educational goals.

Investments in Teacher Preparation and High-Quality Materials in Finland

Beyond the gleaming facilities, Clara and Stella's school stood out to us as a "practice school." Practice schools in Finland are regular government schools developed expressly for the purpose of preparing and supporting the learning of prospective teachers. In these schools, experienced "practice teachers" (called "mentor teachers" in many other systems) both lead their own classrooms and supervise student-teachers—co-planning, conducting observations, and reflecting with them. The practice teachers and the practice schools receive additional government funding to pay for the special work they do. The sleek interiors of the building were even designed to support their work, containing teacher lounges and workspaces that included a suite of rooms dedicated specifically to the student-teachers. That suite consisted of their own meeting room; lockers and bookcases for storing materials and resources; a coatroom; and a lunch room.

Student-teachers' clinical experience in practice schools forms just one part of the extensive and rigorous five-year-long master's degree program required of all primary and secondary teachers in Finland. That degree integrates the work in practice schools with university-based coursework and culminates in the production of a thesis with standards similar to those in other disciplines. With these high standards and rigorous expectations, there are no shortcuts or alternate routes, and it takes, on average, five to seven and a half years for candidates to complete their degree and qualify to teach (Hammerness et al., 2017; Sahlberg, 2011).

The statistics also demonstrate that the teachers in Finland feel supported: although the average teacher's salary falls below the OECD average, 92 percent of teachers—the highest rate among all OECD countries—believe the advantages of being a teacher clearly outweigh the disadvantages. Further, more than half of all teachers in Finland, more than twice as many as the OECD average, say that their profession is valued in society (OECD, 2019).

Finnish teachers, like those in Singapore, also benefit from what are generally considered strong textbooks, instructional materials, and assessments that are all linked to a national curriculum framework. Finland's investment in materials includes the development of a variety of high-quality informal and formal assessments. These include diagnostic and classroom-based assessments that elementary teachers can use early in children's school careers to identify those who may need some additional help with academics and to ensure that all students stay on track. In secondary schools, well-known exit exams anchor and focus the system (Graham & Jahnukainen, 2011; Sahlberg, 2011). The National Board of Education in Finland also regularly gives tests to samples of students and schools, providing an overview of national and regional performance in key subjects, such as Finnish and mathematics. Although the National Board doesn't use that information for ranking (and can't, because not all students and schools are assessed), it shares school-level information with the schools that participate and municipal-level data with the municipalities involved. In addition, the National Board makes these sample assessments widely available for free, so that any teacher, school, or municipality that wants to administer these tests can do so. As a consequence, even without national testing, Finnish schools and municipalities have government-paid tools that link directly to the core curriculum that they can use to benchmark their performance against regional and national samples.

Investments in Support for Teachers and High-Quality Materials in Singapore

The bus advertisement encouraging Singaporeans to join the teaching force was one I saw on the first day of my visit to Singapore as I went to talk to colleagues at the National Institute of Education (NIE). NIE is responsible for preparing almost all of Singapore's teachers and school leaders. Like Finland, Singapore has established a teacher-preparation program in order to ensure that all new teachers meet the same high standards. Those programs are offered to both undergraduate and graduate students, and, in general, all new teachers also participate in an induction program at their schools that includes in-service courses and the support of a peer "buddy," an experienced teacher mentor, and a supervisor (usually a head of department) (Goodwin, 2014).

Although Finland invests much more in teacher preparation than professional development opportunities, Singapore makes substantial investments in supporting teachers throughout their careers. Teachers in Singapore can choose the kind of support and the kind of career goals they would like to achieve by pursuing one of three tracks:

- A "Teaching Track," leading to Master Teacher and Principal Master Teacher designations

- A "School Leadership Track," for those interested in becoming principals and superintendents

- A "Senior Specialist Track," where teachers can become "Chief Specialists" with opportunities to develop their knowledge and skills in particular areas

Teachers can also take advantage of a variety of scholarships and study opportunities (including studying at American universities like Teachers College, where a number of Singaporean educators have taken my course on school change).

Singapore accompanies its direct support for teachers with substantial investments in regularly renovating existing schools and building new ones, and the Ministry of Education (MOE) continuously reviews and updates curriculum and assessments aligned to the nation's educational goals. From the very beginning, high-quality textbooks and instructional materials have served as a particularly powerful lever in the development of the Singaporean educational system. In the early days of mass education, Singapore imported the best textbooks and materials from other parts of the world and then in the 1970s began to build its own capacity to produce curricula and textbooks in multiple subjects and in multiple languages. Those efforts were so successful that schools around the world have begun importing Singapore Math, the curriculum Singapore developed in the 1990s.

Rather than standing pat, however, at the turn of the 21st century, the MOE developed a cycle for the review and revision of its curriculum frameworks and related syllabi on a regular basis. Reviews draw on analyses of data on student performance, scans of curricula and assessments in other parts of the world, and changing economic and societal demands. To help teachers keep up with the changes, the three-year review can only change up to 30 percent of the curriculum, with further changes up to 60 percent allowed at the six-year review.

Singapore's educational infrastructure also includes a wide range of formative and summative assessments, surveys, and inspections that schools can use to monitor and improve their performance (Ng & Tan, 2010). Those tools are all connected to a substantial and sophisticated set of high-stakes exams, all of which are aligned and connected to international standards. Those exams include the Primary School Leaving Exam at the end of sixth grade; "O-level" exams at the end of tenth grade; and "A-level" exams for students at the equivalent of twelfth grade, when students are in junior colleges, polytechnics, or secondary schools preparing for either university entrance or the workforce. The "O"- and "A"-level exams were created initially in collaboration with the developers of the same exams in the United Kingdom. Although the Singapore Examination and Assessment Board has taken over the development of those exams so that they better match the demands of the Singaporean educational system, the exams continue to be recognized as internationally equivalent to the UK exams. Although the rewards and consequences for these exams have changed over time, they've exerted a powerful force that focuses the Singaporean educational system on academic achievement and other key goals. For many years, that pressure included public rankings for all secondary schools, based largely on their students' results on the national exams (as well as on their students' performance in the National Physical Fitness Test and the percentage of overweight students in the school) (Ng & Chan, 2008). By 2019, however, Singapore scrapped some exams (including for first- and second graders), rounded off marks (previously, the marks included decimal points), and eliminated public rankings of students by their exam results.

Relationships and Social Networks

In Finland and Singapore, I could see investments in teacher preparation, well-equipped facilities, and high-quality textbooks and assessments in every school I visited; but it was harder to uncover each system's commitment to the development of the relationships that help connect people and organizations and coordinate work across schools and among the different sectors of society. Even with my experiences with Sizer and Dr. Comer and their emphasis on "relationships, relationships, relationships," I couldn't envision the major investment in connecting people and building social networks that brings coherence to these educational systems.

Singapore's systemic approach certainly benefits from the fact that its educational system functions like a highly centralized school district.

At the same time, extensive informal social networks undergird the formal bureaucracy and facilitate the sharing of information and expertise across the system. The MOE's careful and deliberate rotation of many employees throughout different sectors of the educational system supports the development of these informal connections. For example, after several years at a school, teachers and principles are often assigned by the MOE to work in a different kind of school or at a different level or to do a rotation at the MOE or NIE before returning to schools. In the process, individuals meet and get to know a variety of people within the system to whom they can continue to turn for assistance and information; and they gain familiarity with the nature, demands, and future directions of work in different sectors.

Singapore's deliberate management of human resources is also reflected in the government's offer of scholarships to encourage the top students in every cohort to join the teaching force (which is considered a branch of the civil service). The Public Service Commission of Singapore oversees these scholarships for teaching, as well as for other branches of the civil service, as part of its mission to "safeguard the values of integrity, impartiality, and meritocracy" (Public Service Commission Singapore, 2020). These scholarships pay almost all college-related expenses, whether inside or outside Singapore, in return for a commitment from the students to work in a given public-service sector for a set number of years (referred to as a "bond"). In 2020, students who accepted a scholarship for the teaching service could get funds to pay for full tuition and fees for an undergraduate degree, "maintenance and other allowances," return airfare (if they chose to attend a university outside Singapore), and sponsorship for a master's degree if they qualified. Those who chose to use the scholarship to pursue undergraduate education in an English-speaking country agreed to a bond period of six years; those who pursued an undergraduate education in a non-English-speaking country agreed to a bond of five years; and those pursuing undergraduate education in Singapore agreed to a bond of four years (Public Service Commission Singapore, 2020).

Notably, many of the top students who pursue these scholarships are already connected, as they participated together in top-performing schools (with their own strong alumni networks) and scholarship and study-abroad opportunities before they decided to work to devote their early careers to the civil service. Those connections also develop and expand as all teachers and principals go through preparation programs at NIE together. Further supporting connections between policymakers and practitioners, MOE deliberately holds meetings of

MOE directors and other staff in schools and jointly conducts school visits and observations. These kinds of connections provide opportunities for system administrators to learn firsthand what's happening in schools and to get feedback directly from the school level. Although cultivating these informal networks can be seen as a means of controlling and influencing individuals' behavior, it can also help individuals and organizations work together in the pursuit of common aims.

The Finnish system is more decentralized than Singapore's (though not as decentralized as the system in the United States) and is well-known for supporting the autonomy of teachers. Yet comparative studies that highlight Finnish "autonomy" often fail to mention the strong network of formal and informal relationships that help ensure that all educators work together as part of a common enterprise. The Finnish core curriculum—along with the textbooks and materials based upon it—serves as the linchpin of the development of this common enterprise. In contrast to the detailed scope and sequence of topics and skills dictating what should be taught in the Common Core adopted by many American states, the Finnish core curriculum provides a broad "framework" that provides general guidelines for many aspects of schooling, not just curriculum and instruction. The framework, for example, describes the main features of a school's "working culture"; outlines objectives for pupils' behavior; states that parents and guardians should be able to have an influence on local educational objectives; requires the drafting of the local curriculum in collaboration with people involved in municipal social and health services; and specifies that the curriculum developed by municipalities and schools should reflect the underlying values of Finnish basic education ("human rights, equality, democracy, natural diversity, preservation of environmental viability, and the endorsement of multiculturalism"; Finnish National Board of Education, 2004). As a result, the Finnish core curriculum leaves wide latitude for teachers to use their professional judgment at the same time that it helps make sure that curriculum, assessment, teaching preparation, and teaching and learning are aligned and coordinated.

Roughly every ten years since the 1970s, when the Finnish comprehensive educational system was established, Finland has engaged in a curriculum-renewal process to revise that framework. That process brings together a wide range of stakeholders in working groups to examine and reflect on the basic purposes of the Finnish educational system and the progress made toward fulfilling those purposes. These working groups include large numbers of teachers, as well as researchers, school leaders, policymakers, and (in some cases) textbook publishers, who join together in a spirit of trust and collaboration. Notably, many of the members of these other groups have themselves spent time teaching (and, relatedly, going through and graduating from a teacher-education program). Consequently, arguing simply that the Finnish story suggests that teachers should "have autonomy" fails to capture all the support that enables teachers to negotiate and coordinate with others and work together toward common goals.

From "Best Practice" to Comprehensive Support

As a result of the extensive and long-term investments that Singapore and Finland make in human, technical, and social capital, their educational systems support extensive informal social connections among well-prepared educators who share common experiences and rely on a small set of relatively good resources to reach common goals. Although advocates for almost any reform idea can find a correlated "best practice" in some higher-performing system, comparisons of many different high-performing countries reveal that no single approach or policy explains their success. Nonetheless, it's possible to see the investment of many of those systems in some combination of high-quality materials, support for teachers, and support for building individual and organizational relationships around common goals (OECD, 2013; Tucker, 2011).

Coherence and Common Understanding 11

Even the many examples from Singapore and Finland can't capture all the ways in which their higher-achieving educational systems invest in building the human, technical, and social capital in order to enable all students to learn; but they illustrate how much more goes into developing the infrastructure needed to support a powerful education system than many policies in the United States and elsewhere allow. The systemic focus of these "higher performers" became even more and more apparent to me as I learned about the difference between the efforts in the United States to establish the Common Core Learning Standards and the efforts to develop and sustain coherent educational systems in Finland and Singapore (Hatch, 2015).

In the United States, the Common Core was built expressly on the idea that high-performing educational systems like those of Singapore and Finland have national curriculum frameworks that help focus and coordinate teaching and learning across schools. To that end, the Common Core initiative created a set of shared standards in English language arts and mathematics that describe what students should know and be able to do at the end of each grade, from kindergarten to twelfth. The governors and Chief State School Officers from almost every state who spearheaded the design hoped to encourage every state to adopt the standards they released in 2010. Although the number of adopting states has changed over time, as of 2020, forty-one participating states, the District of Columbia, four territories, and schools run by the Department of Defense used the Common Core.

The development and adoption of the Common Core reflects a theory of action that rests on the power of common standards to align work in many different parts of the educational system. This approach takes into account the importance of developing technical and human capital by suggesting that common standards can catalyze the production of new textbooks, curricula, assessments, preparation and professional development programs, and other resources aligned to the new standards; those aligned supports would then help educators across the country develop new skills and expertise and spread new instructional approaches across English and mathematics classrooms, at every level.

Nonetheless, the design and implementation of this approach reflects a mechanical view of alignment that underestimates the complexity of creating a consistent educational approach:

If we can align different parts of the educational system . . .

and facilitate coordination and common focus . . .

then we can increase efficiency and improve performance.

Unfortunately, this approach largely ignores the way the development of productive relationships and social networks among individuals, groups, and organizations in Finland and Singapore support the development of common goals and shared understanding.

What Does Curriculum "Renewal" in Finland Really Entail?

Although I had read about Finland's curriculum-renewal process, I didn't fully understand what it really involved until I dropped Stella off for her first day of school in Helsinki. We were greeted by a substitute teacher, who welcomed Stella and led each of her new classmates to stop by her desk and introduce themselves. The head teacher for the class was out for the day, because she was on one of a number of national committees that were reviewing proposals for the new curriculum framework.

In past revision cycles, there were opportunities to give feedback to the draft curriculum before it was formally adopted. However, the last revision, enacted in 2016, was the most "open" of all. Surveys were sent to all the municipalities, so that they could share their responses to initial drafts; municipalities and schools were encouraged to share and discuss the initial proposals with parents and students; and initial drafts of the curriculum were made available online so that anyone who wanted to could provide feedback that way as well. That feedback came from numerous individuals, as well as from more than 200 different organizations representing many aspects of Finnish society.

As a result, as Anneli Rautiainen, head of the Innovation Center at the Finnish National Agency for Education, explained, "almost everyone can have a say in what children should learn." Furthermore, municipalities and local schools then have considerable autonomy in deciding how to implement any changes. The previous curriculum-renewal process, in 2004, concentrated on the development of the school as a holistic learning environment for students, but the most recent one, in 2016, emphasized the "phenomenon-based" learning and "transversal" competencies that cut across traditional school subjects. Although the new framework doesn't eradicate subject-based teaching, it stipulates that all students should participate each year in a multidisciplinary learning module. Those modules are to be designed locally by teachers, with the expectation that students will be involved in the planning.

Of course, such an open process can be unwieldy, and implementation is likely to vary, but the wide engagement of stakeholders creates social connections that facilitate the sharing of information and knowledge about the changes *long before those changes are actually made*. In fact, the working committees and feedback process for the curriculum renewal enacted in 2016 began in about 2012. That means that those who are involved in supporting the work of teachers and students—such as teacher educators and textbook publishers—are already getting a sense of where the revisions are heading and what kinds of changes they will need to make so that the whole system is "ready" for the introduction of the new local curriculum. In contrast, in the United States, some teachers and other educational stakeholders participated in or reviewed the developing standards, but there was no mechanism for systematically building a wide understanding of the emerging standards during the development process. The Common Core in the United States also never established a large-scale process for engaging those involved in the educational enterprise in revising and improving the Common Core in the future.

Coherence Inside and Outside Schools in Singapore

Curriculum frameworks and strategic investments in the materials, expertise, and relationships needed to advance National Education goals contribute to the development of a coordinated and focused school system in Singapore as well. Singapore's comprehensive approach began with its integrated approach to the development of education and the economy as part of the nation-building process. As Singapore's first prime minister, Lee Kuan Yew, described it:

> Our job was to plan the broad economic objectives and the target periods within which to achieve them. We reviewed these plans regularly and adjusted them as new realities changed the outlook. Infrastructure and the training and education of workers to meet the needs of employers had to be planned years in advance.
>
> (Lee et al., 2008)

This integrated approach gradually built the capacity of Singapore's educational system and contributed to steady improvements over a period of fifty years.

Until my last trip to Singapore, I didn't understand the extent to which this integrated approach reflects the fundamental belief that education doesn't stop at the schoolhouse door and involves all members of society. In fact, the Singaporean government engages in a number of explicit initiatives to connect individuals and organizations that offer learning opportunities outside the school day (in after-school programs and museums, for example) with the work being done inside schools. This work to connect learning opportunities inside and outside schools encompasses a number of components that now play a key part in Singapore's efforts to create a more holistic education that fosters the development of 21st-century skills and learning throughout life:

- *Required "co-curricular" activities.* Every secondary-school student in Singapore has to participate in at least one co-curricular offered by the school—such as physical sports, "uniformed groups" (such as the Boy Scouts and Girl Scouts), visual and performing arts groups, or other club or society. Leaders of co-curriculars give students grades based on a framework that emphasizes "LEAPS": Leadership, Enrichment, Achievement, Participation, and Service

(Ministry of Education Singapore, 2018a, 2018b). (In 1999, the Ministry of Education replaced the term "extra-curricular" activities with "co-curricular" activities to make a statement that these activities are a central aspect of education, not an "add-on" or "extra" option [Sim, 2014].)

- *A master plan for National Outdoor Adventure Education (NOAE).* The NOAE master plan mandates that, beginning in 2020, all secondary students must participate in a five-day outdoor adventure camp. Administered in conjunction with Outward Bound Singapore, the camps immerse students in "authentic and often challenging situations, where they need to work in teams and learn to take responsibility for decisions they make" (Yang, 2016a).

- *Learning journeys.* Learning journeys are "experiential and multidisciplinary learning trips" that students are required to make on a regular basis to learn about key national institutions and heritage sites. Launched by the Ministry of Education in 1998, learning journeys provide experiences that align with curriculum in subjects such as social studies, history, and geography and support the goals of National Education—an explicit program and set of goals enacted in 1997 to help students understand and appreciate Singapore's history, development, and national identity.

- *Outside-of-school educational programming.* Government agencies—particularly the Ministry of Community, Culture and Youth (MCCY) and government support groups like the National Arts Council—provide funding for educational activities that serve the same objectives as Singapore's schools. Offerings include classes, workshops, and Heritage Trails created by museums and other cultural institutions and often sponsored by government agencies like the National Heritage Board. For example, a "Spirit of Saving Lives" Trail winds through the grounds of the Singapore General Hospital and introduces visitors to Singapore's medical history.

- *Edusave accounts.* The Singaporean government creates an Edusave account for every child who is a Singaporean citizen, and it makes annual contributions of between $230 and $290 (as of 2019) to that account during the period the child is in primary and secondary school. Those funds can be used for a variety of other educational resources and enrichment activities, including educational trips overseas. These education funds are in addition to a "baby bonus" cash gift of $8,000 (payable over a period of eighteen months) when each citizen is born, as well as a Child Development Account (CDA) and CDA First Step Grant of $3,000 (Mark, 2019; Ministry of Education Singapore, 2020).

These initiatives build human, technical, and social capital by leveraging the entrepreneurship, knowledge, and resources of people and organizations who work outside of schools (in companies, cultural institutions, and other governmental capacities) and connecting them with students and teachers inside schools. Many of these activities are paid for by the schools or government, but when students are asked to pay, opportunities for financial support are usually made available for those who need it.

All these efforts reflect several of what Pak Tee Ng has called the powerful paradoxes that fuel Singapore's comprehensive approach to education. One is a shift to a "centralized-decentralized" approach to changing the educational system over the past twenty years (Ng, 2017). This approach departs from the tight top-down management Singapore's leaders used to develop the comprehensive school system initially by simultaneously supporting "ground-up" initiatives (what those in the United States might call "grassroots" efforts) and creating a context for focusing on National Education goals that reinforces alignment and promotes coherence across initiatives. It results as well in a system that, like Finland's, emphasizes collective responsibility while also embracing many aspects of accountability that characterize the US and other systems.

In the case of the learning journeys and other co-curricular learning opportunities, the government both (a) provides some funding for government agencies and for private and public organizations to develop resources, expertise, and programs consistent with governmental priorities and (b) funnels government funding to schools for these out-of-school experiences. As a result, the organizations need to pay some attention to the government's priorities, and they still have to rely on schools for ongoing revenue, which means that they also have to respond to the immediate needs of principals and teachers, who are also striving to meet the nation's educational goals.

Government ministries (such as the Ministry of Education), public-private partnerships, and cultural institutions also have advisory or governing boards with members drawn specifically from different sectors. Having board members from different ministries, different industries, academia, and other institutions helps build connections and support cross-sector communication and information sharing. For example, the Ministry of Defence established the S'pore Discovery Centre in 1996 as a museum to showcase the history of Singapore's armed forces; but since that time the Discovery Centre has evolved into a multifaceted "edu-tainment" complex (complete with paintball, a "4D thrill ride," "Crisis Simulation theatre," and a first-run movie theater) that offers a wide range of educational programs, field trips, professional development workshops, and corporate events designed to support Singapore's goals for National Education. Although the Discovery Centre operates under the aegis of the Ministry of Defence, it has a board that includes members from other government agencies, including NEXUS (the Central National Education Office), the Ministry of Education, and other organizations in the public and private sectors.

Support and pressure for achieving national goals also comes from the Singaporean government's focus on customer service and embrace of many of the principles of total quality management and performance management. As a consequence, organizations like the Discovery Centre and the National Gallery of Singapore get feedback from their own surveys, and the agencies that oversee them also get feedback on their work through nationwide surveys such as the National Education Orientation Survey and the Heritage Awareness Index. That means that the S'pore Discovery Centre and the National Gallery have to fulfill their goals in ways that satisfy the government agencies with which they're associated, and they have to respond to the demands of their "customers" and attract students, schools, and families in a competitive marketplace with a wide range of public and private vendors.

Some constraints, however, come along with the close connections between the work inside and outside the educational system. All the organizations that support education outside school face the reality that their programs that are most closely tied to the academic topics in school assessments and high-stakes tests are likely to be the most popular. This is particularly challenging for institutions (such as the Discovery Centre) that focus on National Education, which isn't a tested subject. Of course, any efforts to offer support for students' learning after school also have to compete with the continuing growth and dominance of academic tutoring. It has been estimated that, between 2004 and 2016, spending on tutoring in Singapore almost doubled, from about $650 million to about $1.1 billion (Yang, 2016b).

Not surprisingly, under these conditions, Singapore continues to work to change the basic structures and practices in many classrooms and schools. Although researchers have documented that many teachers have adopted a "hybrid" of traditional and newer instructional practices, in general, instruction continues to reflect the conventional grammar of schooling. As one review of Singapore's educational development explained:

> Notwithstanding multiple reform initiatives to encourage the TSLN's [Thinking Schools, Learning Nation] pedagogical vision, pedagogical practice in Singapore's classrooms has remained largely traditional, directed towards curriculum content delivery and examination performance. There is very little evidence of sustained teaching for higher-order thinking, meaningful use of ICT [Information and Communication Technology], students' constructing knowledge, and interdisciplinary learning.
>
> (Deng & Gopinathan, 2016, p. 458)

Nonetheless, the systemic approach in Singapore means that an extensive, well-resourced, and aligned set of educational opportunities outside of schools surrounds an already focused and coherent public educational system that makes extensive investments in materials, expertise, and relationships. Notably, this connection between learning opportunities inside and outside schools is achieved even though many of those outside opportunities aren't overseen directly by the Ministry of Education. That coherence and coordination benefits from the mix of government funding and competition, the many organizational and personal connections across institutions and sectors, and the constant focus on customer service and feedback.

Beyond Alignment

The extent of interconnections, common understanding, and coherence in educational systems like those of Finland and Singapore serves as a resource—a critical part of the infrastructure and context that support the work of educators in schools. Like the strategies of the community organizers of the Alliance Schools (see Chapter 6), the mechanisms that help bring people together build social capital and collective power, but they function at a system level, not just a neighborhood level.

These societal investments create educational systems with a series of critical, self-reinforcing elements:

- Well-prepared teachers

- A set of productive and aligned textbooks, assessments, and other educational materials

- Support from well-connected groups of teacher educators, researchers, publishers, and policymakers linked by common educational experiences and work in schools

- National curriculum frameworks and processes for the regular review and revision of educational goals and purposes that foster common understanding

In Singapore, those elements extend beyond schools to support the pursuit of National Education goals throughout society.

These comprehensive approaches highlighted, for me, a critical difference between focusing on "alignment" and focusing on "coherence," as well as a critical limitation of "systemic" approaches in the United States, such as the Common Core. Alignment aims to line up different structures and expectations. But those aligned initiatives may be experienced very differently on the ground in schools as they're interpreted and enacted by a host of different people. In order to make initiatives work together, educators need to develop a sense of coherence. Coherence is a state of mind that comes from a common understanding of *how* these different elements fit together (Honig & Hatch, 2004).

> Coherence is a state of mind that comes from a common understanding of *how* these different elements fit together.

In turn, common understanding and coherence grow out of the connections and relationships between people that facilitate the flow of information, resources, and knowledge. Sharing information, knowledge, and resources makes it possible for individuals and groups to coordinate their activities and develop a common sense of what they're supposed to be doing and why. Leaders can then delegate and distribute responsibilities more effectively, and members of schools and districts can then take initiative and act independently in ways that are consistent and reinforcing.

The architects of the Common Core in the United States did draw together some stakeholders to inform the development of the standards, and they invited feedback and made revisions. But there was no mechanism for generating the kind of wider common understanding and coherence that undergird the curriculum frameworks and National Education goals in Finland and Singapore. Under these conditions, it should be no surprise that numerous publishers in the

United States produce many curricula and textbooks that claim to be aligned to the Common Core but actually aren't (Polikoff, 2015).

More than mere adjustments to ensure the system is aligned, the curriculum-renewal process in Finland and the integrated inside/outside approach to education in Singapore serve as an extension of the collective, nation-building efforts that each country has engaged in. Roughly every ten years, curriculum renewal in Finland provides an opportunity for people all across the country to recommit themselves to a national enterprise and to develop the common understanding and sense of coherence that can help them carry it out. In Singapore, the support and pressure of regular exams, tests, assessments, and customer-service surveys; private-public partnerships; cross-sector advisory boards; and strategic, integrated planning for the future all help develop a common understanding of the educational enterprise and its role in sustaining a tiny nation-state into the future.

Collective Responsibility 12

I learned a lot from my experiences in Singapore and Finland, but once I began to understand what was happening in Norway, I realized that I had an unusual opportunity. To my American audiences, it was obvious that the US educational system couldn't be like that of Finland, but when I explained that Norwegian students performed about as well as American students on the PISA tests, they were confused. With so many regional, economic, political, and cultural similarities between Norway and Finland—and, particularly, with Norway's robust oil-based economy—how could Norway's educational performance be *worse* than Finland's? And then after I pointed out that Norway, like the United States, spends much more on education per-student than almost every other country in the world—including Finland—many people, like me, were intrigued.

Over the course of the year I spent in Norway, my fascination grew as I recognized that what I was learning served as a counterpoint to what I had seen in Finland and Singapore. In contrast to these high PISA performers, historically, Norway isn't particularly well-known for the quality of its textbooks, the strength of its curricula, or the effectiveness of its teacher-preparation programs. But with the notable exception of Norway's performance on some of the academically focused international tests, almost everywhere we looked we saw other signs of a successful educational system: low levels of dropouts, high percentages of high-school graduates going on to postsecondary education, high levels of adult literacy, low levels of unemployment, and high levels of health and happiness. What could possibly explain these confounding results?

The more I learned about what was happening in Norway, the more I thought back to the growth of the conventional grammar of schooling in the midst of the industrial revolution and another basic principle.

PRINCIPLE #7

Educational systems and the efforts to improve them reflect the social, cultural, geographic, political, and economic conditions in which those improvement efforts take place.

I knew that the grammar of schooling had emerged along with industrialization, immigration, and new trends in work, life, and culture, but I hadn't always paid as much attention to how those larger forces influence the choices made about when and how to change that grammar. Looking at the improvement efforts in Norway in comparison to those in Singapore, Finland, and the United States highlighted for me the crucial ways that context shapes the choices systems make about schools and how to improve them.

I can clearly recall the moment, four months into our year in Norway, when things began to come together. On December 10, my family and I spent the evening in a large crowd outside, in the cold, in the dark. It was a joyous occasion—the torchlight parade celebrating the awarding of that year's Nobel Peace Prize. The parade concluded with a huge gathering in one of the main public squares. We waited there in a light rain until we caught the barest glimpse of President Obama and First Lady Michelle Obama as they stepped out onto a balcony to wave to the crowds.

The next morning, as I headed to my office at the University of Oslo, the first Norwegian colleague I saw came right over to shake my hand. "Congratulations on your Nobel Peace Prize," he told me. I thought I had misheard him, so I just nodded and thanked him. But then another colleague stopped me to congratulate me as well. "Congratulations on your Peace Prize," she said. This time, I was sure I'd heard her accurately, so I politely tried to correct her:

"Thank you, but it's not *my* Peace Prize," I responded. She smiled, nodding, but I got the sense she didn't believe me. That feeling was reinforced throughout the day, as colleague after colleague shook my hand and congratulated me on "my" Peace Prize. Hearing things like that often enough can get into your head, and it got into mine. My thoughts started to drift—what if I did have some role in that Peace Prize? Perhaps I should accept their congratulations rather than rebuff them? Maybe I could say I was at least partially responsible for this Peace Prize? But then the fantasy ended. I suddenly realized that if I was responsible for this Peace Prize, I was also responsible for everything else that this president—and any other president—had done or would do in the future.

In that moment, I knew that regardless of what I thought, my Norwegian colleagues saw me as responsible for the actions and developments of the society I belonged to. That experience helped me realize how narrow our conceptions of "accountability" are in the United States, and I began to explore an aspect of accountability that's largely overlooked in US policy but that helps explain a lot about what I was learning in Norway: collective responsibility. I came to see collective responsibility, along with coherence and common understanding, as central elements of systemic efforts to support the development of all children and adults.

Trust in Society

Despite believing that our daughters were benefiting tremendously from their school experiences in Norway, we couldn't help worrying at least a little about the lack of testing and grades and whether they were keeping up with their peers back home. Over the course of the year, we learned that we weren't alone in our concerns and that, in fact, there were long-standing issues with tracking the academic progress of students and the weak assessment and evaluation system in use in Norway for both teachers and students.

These issues stemmed from the facts that the Norwegian educational system at the turn of the 21st century focused more on pursuing broader purposes than on achieving specific academic outcomes. The education regulations emphasized three aims (Norwegian Ministry of Education and Research, 2001):

- *Education for all.* Public education should be free, children should have equal access to education, and education should be adapted to individual needs.

- *Integration.* Students of different abilities should be mixed, with integration of pupils with special needs into the ordinary schools.

- *Participation.* Pupils should be encouraged to cooperate in school activities and to be active in the life of the local community; close links should be established between school and home and between school and local community.

In order to fulfill these broad purposes, up until the improvement efforts that began in the early 2000s, the central government focused on specifying what it called the "inputs of education"—such as the curriculum content and the facilities and programs offered—but left it up to educators, schools, and local authorities to decide how to use those resources to fulfill their obligations (Klette, 2002; Skedsmo, 2011). My colleague and host at the University of Oslo, Kirsti Klette, described this approach as a "this you have to deliver" strategy. She contrasted this approach with a "this you have to achieve" approach she viewed as more characteristic of Finland during the same time period.

Correspondingly, the Norwegian educational system didn't develop the kind of regular assessment infrastructure or curriculum-renewal process that Finland had. As my daughters and I discovered, Norway's regulations forbid teachers from giving primary-school students (Grades 1–7) written marks or grades, and students don't "fail" classes or repeat a grade. In Finland, students rarely repeat a grade, but primary-school teachers are legally required to use assessments to identify students who need extra help and to provide the necessary assistance. Norway, like Finland, does have exit exams at the end of lower secondary school (tenth grade) and upper secondary school (twelfth grade), but Norway didn't carry out the kinds of national sampling tests central to the Finnish system, nor did it have the extensive inspection systems used in countries like the Netherlands and England. As far back as 1988, an OECD report noted Norway's lack of interest in "quality assurance." As one Norwegian policymaker I talked to put it, the report essentially said, "Hello, Mr. Minister, how do you know what's going on in your schools?"

The worries about Norwegian educational performance and the limited capacity for quality assurance erupted after the publication of the first PISA test results in 2000. Now referred to simply as "the PISA shock," the publication of Norway's mediocre test results led to a burst of headlines in newspapers and speeches in Parliament about the suddenly discovered poor standing of the Norwegian schools. Adding to the concerns, results of the next rounds of both the TIMSS and PISA tests showed a decline in the performance of Norwegian students.

Following this shock, a broad coalition of conservatives and liberals concluded that improvements had to be made, particularly in Norway's approach to assessment and evaluation. The changes put in place by a conservative-leaning government at the time focused on two key aspects of the efforts to increase accountability reflected in the No Child Left Behind Act (NCLB) in the United States and in new approaches to performance management gaining popularity across the globe:

1. Establish measurable outcomes.

2. Develop the instruments needed to monitor progress toward those outcomes.

To those ends, Norway created new competence aims and an emphasis in every subject on the development of basic skills—including oral and written expression, reading, numeracy, and the use of digital tools—from first grade on. In what came to be called the Knowledge Promotion reforms, Norway also established several new mechanisms for monitoring students' progress, tracking schools' performance, and reviewing the extent to which schools and local authorities provided all their students with an adequate education. These instruments included new national tests in reading, numeracy, and English that were originally proposed for fourth, seventh, and tenth grades; pupil and parent surveys; and a new system—the "Tilsyn"—which generally translates as an inspection of the municipalities' and county governments' compliance with legal requirements. All of these developments sought to generate data and make visible how well schools and municipalities were doing across Norway.

But the Norwegians never adopted a third aspect of accountability: the follow-up mechanisms such as incentives, rewards, and sanctions that policies like NCLB in the United States relied on to motivate people to achieve the desired outcomes. Despite initial proposals from the conservative government at the time to publish test scores and rankings and establish rewards and sanctions to motivate schools to improve, Norway never put those rankings or incentives in place.

Accountability, Answerability, and Responsibility

At first, I was puzzled by what I was learning. From the standpoint of many who advocate for increased accountability as a key vehicle for systemic educational improvement, "failing" to establish follow-up mechanisms seems like a critical lapse—a "bad" choice—likely to undermine the strengthening of accountability that the other reforms were supposed to support. The more I learned about Norwegian society and reflected on experiences like "*my* Nobel Prize," however, the more I could see the Norwegian reforms as a logical extension of policies and practices that have always placed significant emphasis on trust and a collective sense of responsibility for the common good (Tolo et al., 2020).

Over time, I began to see the Norwegians' educational-improvement efforts as suggesting a different way of dealing with the inevitable tensions between two aspects of accountability: answerability and responsibility (Gregory, 2003; Hatch, 2013). Answerability reflects the beliefs that individuals and groups should be accountable for meeting clearly specified and agreed-upon procedures and/or goals. Responsibility reflects the belief that individuals and groups should be held accountable for living up to and upholding norms of conduct and higher purposes that are often ambiguous and difficult to define in advance.

While accountability in the United States has become synonymous with approaches that embrace answerability, in countries like Norway and Finland there's no equivalent for the English word "accountability"; instead, responsibility takes center stage. Part of the challenge policymakers face in addressing both answerability and responsibility lies in a well-known paradox: if members of an organization are answerable only for reaching certain outcomes, then logic suggests they shouldn't be held responsible if their actions to reach those goals are inconsistent with broader, undefined responsibilities or purposes; conversely, if those members are behaving in ways that are consistent with the pursuit of larger purposes, it seems unreasonable to hold them accountable if they don't meet all the specified targets along the way (Harmon, 1995).

These tensions between answerability and responsibility are central to the most fundamental debates over social justice and human rights: if people "do their jobs" or "do what they are told," can they be held responsible if they violate fundamental moral principles? These tensions also underlie critical questions over "bureaucratic" and "professional" accountability. Governments and administrators can establish "bureaucratic" accountability: carefully specifying what needs to be accomplished and establishing consequences for failing to meet those targets. Tightening answerability in this way can increase efficiency but can lead many other valued outcomes to be ignored, and it can undermine the discretion and expert judgment that may be needed to make many decisions. When taken to extremes, this approach can lead to efforts to game the system—such as teaching to the test and reclassifying all teachers as "highly qualified"—that make it look like the goals have been achieved when they haven't. Conversely, emphasizing personal responsibility—trusting individuals, even those who are thoughtful and responsible members of a profession—can increase inconsistencies and inefficiency and provides no guarantee that essential goals will be achieved. In other words, both approaches have "side effects" that compromise basic purposes they're designed to fulfill (de Wolf & Janssens, 2007; Ehren & Visscher, 2008; Koretz, 2003).

Too often, answerability and responsibility are seen as two ends of a continuum: either focus on answerability (and undermine responsibility) or focus on responsibility (and ignore answerability). Along with this polarized view, many policies seem to suggest that there has to be an either/or choice: either strengthen the bureaucratic controls that go along with answerability or leave people alone to exercise their professional responsibility. However, simply leaving individuals and groups alone is not the same thing as supporting the development of individual or collective responsibility. Developing responsibility also involves developing the capacity—the investments, resources, abilities, commitments, and relationships—needed to carry out responsibilities effectively. In short, accountability comes from the capacity to support a balance between answerability and responsibility (see Figure 12.1).

FIGURE 12.1 The Capacity for Accountability

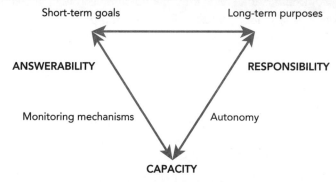

In fact, whereas NCLB and other US policies focused on increasing rewards and sanctions by investing in the apparatus needed to determine whether people were doing what they were being told to do, I began to see the Norwegian reforms as trying to build the capacity for individuals and schools to act responsibly. The challenges around implementing those reforms, however, made clear to me the limits of the educational infrastructure in Norway and just how much work it takes to support collective responsibility, even in a society that values it.

Building the Capacity for Collective Responsibility

The need to develop technical, human, and social capital became apparent to Norwegians as soon as the efforts to develop the new national tests began. With only limited previous use of large-scale tests and assessments, the first implementation of the national tests in Norway in 2004 was judged by experts to be inadequate and unreliable (Elstad et al., 2009). Concerns about the quality of the tests were so serious that some of the initial test results were never released, and the government declared a pause in the national testing—no tests were administered in 2006. During the pause, a new framework, along with a set of quality requirements, was developed by an international group of experts to guide the development of new tests; the test-makers revised the tests substantially and, according to the experts, significantly upgraded the quality. While some argued for a continuation of the pause, the national tests were relaunched in 2007 and continued to grow in technical sophistication and acceptance (Nusche et al., 2011).

The Tilsyn's initial review of local education authorities also revealed the need to develop new systems, routines, and procedures to support communication and information-sharing between schools, school leaders, school owners, and the central government. In fact, the Tilsyn's first report suggested that as many as 70 percent of municipalities surveyed weren't fulfilling the requirements for the evaluation and follow-up of schools (Norwegian Directorate for Education and Training, 2007).

The efforts to strengthen quality assurances also revealed a serious omission: it wasn't clearly specified in the education regulations whom to hold responsible if schools failed to live up to their obligations. In contrast to the United States, where (for the most part) publicly elected school boards are clearly designated as responsible for meeting education requirements laid out in laws and regulations, schools in Norway were run primarily by municipalities or county governments, along with many other local responsibilities, without a clear designation of authority. Therefore, as part of the improvement efforts, policymakers in Norway created new regulations that introduced the term "school owners" to refer to the county and municipal governments, to signal that those political authorities had specific responsibilities for ensuring educational quality for all.

To further address these infrastructure problems, following the Knowledge Promotion reforms of 2006, Norway pursued a wide range of efforts to support the development of human capital and teachers' expertise. These efforts focused particularly on improving teacher preparation. Up until 2010, in a striking contrast to Finland and Singapore, almost all teachers who completed Norwegian teacher-education programs were qualified to teach at almost any level, in any subject, from first grade to tenth grade. After 2010, however, a series of changes included requiring teacher candidates to get a master's degree, with teacher-education programs focused on elementary school (Grades 1–7) or lower secondary school (Grades 5–10) (Norwegian Ministry of Education and Research, 2016). A new emphasis on helping prospective teachers develop relevant subject-matter knowledge at each level was also established.

Educational-improvement efforts in Norway also focused on building social capital by fostering the development of a whole series of local and regional networks, including those bringing together

- municipal and county "school owners," to help them develop a common understanding of their new responsibilities;
- unions, school administrators, local government authorities, and universities and colleges, to discuss issues like assessment and quality assurance both within and across regions; and
- school leaders, teachers, teacher-preparation institutions, and local authorities, to develop their assessment competence.

Taken together, these improvement initiatives had a different emphasis than accountability policies like those of the NCLB legislation in the United States. The Norwegian reforms invested in building the capacity for teachers, school leaders, and schools to fulfill their responsibilities rather than on establishing a complex array of rewards and punishments. These reforms suggest that making improvements isn't simply a matter of motivation—of getting people to do things they've been unwilling to do; instead, this approach treats educators as willing to make improvements if they have the competence to do so, but it recognizes that considerable work needs to be done to build that competence and enable them to carry out their responsibilities and meet new outcomes.

My experiences in Norway showed me that accountability doesn't have to be synonymous with answerability, and accountability policies don't have to be equated with strengthening the rewards and sanctions for particular behaviors or specific outcomes. One can be answerable for pursuing explicit goals and activities and responsible for aspiring to broader purposes, ideals, and expectations. Accordingly, educational-improvement efforts need to build the capacity to balance the strengths and weaknesses of answerability and responsibility and to deal with the effects of neglecting one or the other.

Improvement in a Norwegian Context

Where does Norway fit? How can Norway remain in the middle of the pack on international tests like PISA while simultaneously topping the charts on so many other indicators of success in education, work, and life? Everything I learned about Finland and Singapore suggested that educational high performance depends on comprehensive investments in key aspects of the educational system. And the reforms I studied in Norway suggested that the Norwegians are now making a more systemic effort to develop what was previously a relatively weak overall infrastructure for teaching and learning. Shouldn't those investments translate into significant improvements?

Maybe, but it took Singapore and Finland thirty years or more to develop their systems, and undertaking a massive effort to build the capacity to change and improve schools is a significant challenge, even in a well-resourced context like Norway's. Given that, maybe it's no surprise that since the launch of Norway's 21st-century educational reforms, Norwegian students' performance on PISA tests has been mixed: rising to its highest levels in reading and math and exceeding the OECD average in 2015 but dropping again in 2018.

Nonetheless, the more time I spent in Norway, the more I came to see Norway's educational system as just one part of an expansive and highly developed infrastructure that supports life and work and a much higher level of educational and economic equity than other systems choose to support. Ironically, the extent and success of that overall infrastructure means that Norwegian society can function relatively well without developing a much more expansive infrastructure for teaching and learning.

That perspective on the unique nature and the specific context of the educational system in Norway crystallized at the end of our year there after I talked to two different Norwegian parents. Both parents told me what happened when they raised concerns about the progress their children were making in their elementary schools in Oslo. Although these parents didn't know one another or have children in the same school, they both told similar stories. One parent described going to her daughter's third-grade teacher to share her concerns that her daughter was falling behind other students and needed help, particularly in reading, to catch up. The other parent said he went to see his daughter's second-grade teacher because he thought she wasn't being challenged academically and needed more advanced work. In both cases, the parents reported that the teachers told them the same thing: "Oh, don't worry about that! They'll take care of that in high school."

In short, I learned that the Norwegian educational system is doing about as well as the one in the United States without even trying, *and* the Norwegian system is trying to do something different. With less instructional time, less emphasis on academics, less homework, no written marks, and limited testing, elementary schools in Norway seek to support all aspects of children's development and, especially, to support the development of strong social relationships and a common national identity.

As I reflected on the different choices the Norwegians were making, I also began to see more clearly the way these improvement efforts in Norway, and those in the United States, are shaped by the broader social, economic, and geographic conditions in which they're situated. Norway's decision not to establish rewards and sanctions is consistent with cultural values and societal practices that emphasize responsibility over answerability and may undermine efforts to put more "American-style" accountability in place. In particular, the efforts to emphasize basic skills and introduce more testing into the elementary years in Norway comes into conflict with the values and assumptions underlying extensive parental-leave policies, a limited emphasis on early education, the low levels of homework, and limited instructional time in elementary school that all suggest that childhood should be protected: children should have a chance to be with their families and their peers and to develop socially, emotionally, physically, and artistically, not just academically. Norwegian government policies also treat learning as a lifelong endeavor, by placing much more attention on adult education than the United States does. At the same time, any efforts to use assessments that might publicly differentiate among students or schools have to contend with the prohibitions against the use of any written marks before the end of seventh grade and the concerns about equity and equal treatment for all that are reflected in many aspects of the social welfare system.

The work to create an assessment and inspection infrastructure and strengthen teacher education in Norway has also had to contend with the difficulty of establishing the relationships and the access to information and expertise that all educators and schools in the country need. Those difficulties stem from the demands of a widely dispersed population with many geographically isolated regions and small communities. These communities—particularly those with only one school—are unlikely to have much, if any, administrative structure beyond the school leader, and those municipal leaders are unlikely to have much, if any, expertise in education. Small communities may also have had a hard time getting access to and attracting and retaining teachers. Before the reforms to teacher education, estimates indicated that somewhere between 4 and 12 percent of teachers didn't have a required degree, but those teachers were significantly more likely to teach in small rural communities (Nusche et al., 2011). Furthermore, members of those small schools and communities faced bigger hurdles in developing the kind of personal relationships and networks that could help them carry out the new policies and responsibilities. In particular, they were likely to have to travel much greater distances to connect with experts and others who could help them meet their new assessment responsibilities.

While educators in Finland face some of the same geographical challenges as their peers in Norway, the Norwegian authorities never made the choice that the Finnish authorities did in the 1970s to consolidate control of the educational system or to centralize teacher education in a small number of university-connected programs. Instead, Norway has maintained a host of teacher-education programs around the country that serve those communities. This decision is consistent with other political decisions in Norway designed to provide the services and economic support needed to sustain its widely distributed population. This approach affords opportunities for substantial local control and discretion, but the low population density and challenging geography makes it difficult to form the networks of formal and informal relationships that support collective work in Finland and Singapore. Furthermore, particularly over the last century, Norway hasn't faced the same threats to its borders and sovereignty that have contributed to the consolidation and development of the centralized systems in Finland and Singapore.

At the same time that these conditions constrain educational-improvement efforts in Norway, Norway's high performance on many other measures of education, employment, health, and happiness suggest that the Norwegian educational system is achieving many of the larger goals and purposes of Norwegian society. And Norway has managed to do all this with only recent efforts to develop an infrastructure for assessment and to strengthen teacher education in a country with widely dispersed social networks and few, if any, rewards or consequences for poor performance.

On top of everything else, although concerns about economic performance often motivate efforts to improve education and increase accountability, Norway's oil-based economy continues to be one of the strongest in the world. But the economic support for life, work, and education in Norway is no accident. That support was made possible by the decision to use the profits from the discovery of one of the world's largest offshore oil fields to create one of the largest investment funds in the world, for the benefit of the Norwegian people. By 2017, that fund had grown so large that it owned roughly 1.5 percent of all the shares in the companies listed on stock exchanges all over the world. It became more than two and a half times the size of the entire Norwegian economy, with the equivalent of $185,000 for each person in the country (Fouche, 2017). In other words, many Norwegians may see their high-functioning society and strong economy as reasons to resist the very educational "improvements" that some argue a successful economy requires.

THE NORWEGIAN OIL FUND

The Norge Bank description of the Norwegian Oil Fund highlights its long-term focus: "The fund's role is to ensure that our national wealth lasts for as long as possible."

The Norwegian government has also established a "fiscal rule" that, on average, only 4 percent of the fund's value can be used for the national budget and has adopted an ethical mandate not to invest in companies that produce tobacco, nuclear weapons, or anti-personnel landmines, among other criteria. The fund's website provides a full listing of every one of the 9,000-plus companies and all the properties and bonds in which it's invested, which anyone in Norway—or anywhere else in the world—can peruse at any time.

The Mechanisms That Can Support Education Into the Future

The educational-reform efforts in Norway after the turn of the 21st century sought to build the capacity for both some level of answerability and responsibility: building an assessment and testing infrastructure almost from scratch; strengthening teacher preparation; fostering expertise on testing, assessment, and the use of data to improve students' and schools' performance; and facilitating the connections and social networks that can share information and expertise across widely distributed and largely independent local actors.

In the process, Norway has put many of the mechanisms for defining specific outcomes and determining who's answerable in place, but it hasn't established the specific means for following up and ensuring that those who are answerable meet their objectives. Such a system that moves partway toward answerability may never produce the kind of tight alignment and efficiency that could result in chart-topping performance on international tests, but it may allow for more attention to the capacity-building that supports a focus on the fulfillment of broader purposes—an aim more consistent with Norway's unusual mix of rugged individualism and collective responsibility.

KEY IDEAS FROM PART 5

The contextual nature of educational systems and the larger societal forces that shape improvement efforts help explain why no simple lessons or practices transfer seamlessly from one jurisdiction to another. But it's still possible to learn from different educational systems when considering the broader conditions in which those systems make choices about how to improve schools. From this perspective, Singapore's and Finland's comprehensive approaches to building capacity stand in marked contrast to approaches in the United States that rely largely on individual motivation, alignment, and rewards and consequences.

In Finland and Singapore, teachers

- learn in strong preparation programs, with costs paid largely by the government;

- work in well-equipped schools, with the opportunity to draw from a small set of high-quality curricula and assessments;

- grow in systems that support the development of relationships, sharing of expertise, and development of common understanding and collective commitment to well-articulated learning goals; and

- live in societies that provide a strong social safety net, support for the health of all their citizens, and a high standard of living overall.

In contrast, in countries such as the United States, teachers

- learn in a wide range of preparation programs of varying length, quality, and effectiveness;

- rely on a wide range of materials of varying costs and quality, in which even many curricula and textbooks that claim to be aligned actually aren't;

- work in schools with substantial differences in funding and the quality of facilities;

- participate in highly decentralized and fragmented educational systems, disconnected from other community and government institutions; and

- live in a society with vast differences in standards of living across communities, where many lack access to support for housing, health care, or other social services.

Under these circumstances, it should be no surprise that in the United States, teachers make more of a difference in students' test scores than any other school-related factor. Those results are a reflection of a weak system overall, with massive inequities in the distribution of technical, human, and social capital.

Norway may not have made the historical investments in the development of an infrastructure for teaching and learning that Singapore and Finland did, but its students and teachers live and work in a society where that education forms just one part of a comprehensive societal infrastructure.

In Singapore and Finland, just as in the United States, good and effective teachers drive the educational system. But if we truly want to enable as many students as possible to reach high levels of learning, we have to embrace the fact that powerful education takes more than the efforts of individuals. It takes a system and a society that focuses on the development, health, and well-being of everyone, both inside and outside schools.

KEY QUESTIONS FOR UNDERSTANDING THE STRENGTHS AND WEAKNESSES OF EDUCATIONAL SYSTEMS

- What mechanisms are in place to support common understanding of the goals and purposes of education?

- What are the key elements of the existing infrastructure for the teaching and learning needed to accomplish those goals and purposes?

- To what extent are those key elements accessible, available, and appropriate for each student, particularly students historically left out or disadvantaged by the system?

- What opportunities are there to develop more powerful learning experiences, both inside and outside schools, that challenge conventional structures and practices? What can be done to connect and build on those alternatives?

- What means are available for developing the coordination, coherence, and collective responsibility needed to transform education over the long term?

Conclusion

In 1918, the rapid spread of the Spanish flu led to school closures, quarantines, bans on public gatherings, and requirements to use face masks. With all the developments in medicine and health care, 100 years later, those same social strategies serve as the primary defense against coronavirus. Under these conditions, perhaps it's no surprise that many of the structures and practices of conventional schools also remain the same. Yet even as so much seems to be standing still, the coronavirus demonstrates that the world is changing—for better and worse—in ways we can't control.

That lack of control can be frightening, but it forces us to recognize that we don't have all the answers. It makes educational change and strategies for providing and improving education a constant focus of discussion, particularly for the many parents and families who are suddenly trying to provide some support for teaching and learning at home. In times like these, rather than pitting one approach against another and fighting over inadequate funding and limited resources, we're in a better position than ever before to get beyond zero-sum games and strategies that create opportunities for some and obstacles for others. Even under these difficult circumstances, today we know why it's so hard to change schools and what to do to improve them. We can use that understanding, along with the many inspiring examples of powerful educational programs and practices, to create more efficient, equitable, and effective schools right now at the same time that we strive to transform education in the future. That work depends on

- coming to terms with the predictable obstacles that block major reform initiatives;

- making concrete, specific improvements in classrooms and schools in different contexts;

- finding the niches where students and educators can stretch the conventional boundaries of schooling;

- building a much more extensive infrastructure for supporting the learning and development of every child, both inside and outside school; and

- developing the common understanding and collective responsibility that support the social movements that can sustain us in an unpredictable future.

This improvements-to-movements approach relies on both a concrete focus on critical issues at key developmental stages and a long-term commitment to generate new opportunities to enable all children to lead healthy, productive, responsible, and satisfying lives. This work begins with taking those actions that we already know can create more equitable and effective educational opportunities right now, and it depends on taking advantage of the changing circumstances and conditions today that can create the educational opportunities we'll need tomorrow.

From Improvements to Movements 13

The coronavirus pandemic exposed, again, the extent of inequality that many Black students, indigenous students, students of color, and other historically underserved students face, but it also made visible the fact that many communities already have the capacity to address at least some of these inequities. In New York City, in the first month of the school closure, the Department of Education worked with businesses like Apple and Microsoft to provide almost 500,000 computers and iPads to students who needed them. Although initially some cable/broadband suppliers in New York City cut off some subscribers who couldn't pay their bills, these companies eventually offered free connections (for a limited time) to new subscribers and opened up hotspots around the city for public use (Feiner, 2020). Even in other areas, with more limited digital infrastructure, solutions to many access issues are already available: school buses equipped with Wi-Fi (and sometimes solar power) have been deployed to help students, while other districts have raised the funds to buy or rent cell phone towers (Carter, 2020; Lee, 2020). Given these existing possibilities, one commissioner for the US Federal Communications Commission testified that the connectivity gap could be closed "virtually overnight" with swift action from Congress in response to school closures (Modan, 2020). If it could be done, then it should be done. No need to wait any longer.

Getting students connected to the internet is no panacea for educational challenges—particularly in many parts of the developing world, where almost half of all students don't have a computer at home and over 40 percent lack access to the internet. We also know that even with internet access and online opportunities, significant improvements in students' learning depend on developing more powerful instructional practices and providing better support for educators. Nonetheless, the responses to the coronavirus show that we have the capacity to address some inequitable learning opportunities, and we can take these steps without ever having to challenge the conventional structures and practices of schooling that have blunted so many ambitious educational-reform efforts.

Pursue a Series of High-Leverage Problems

The power of high-leverage problems comes in part from the fact that there are specific steps that can be taken in different contexts to create more effective and equitable schools right now. Building on what we already know, we can identify high-leverage problems in different contexts, and we can put together sequences of powerful initiatives that address key developmental needs, particularly for historically underserved students.

Books, Glasses, Attendance, and Reading

In the case of learning to read in primary schools, unpacking a series of predictable challenges yields a cluster of related strategies that can launch improvement efforts:

1. Make books by authors from a variety of backgrounds freely accessible.

2. Identify children with vision problems, and provide them with glasses.

3. Identify why children are chronically absent, and support regular attendance.

4. Identify children who are struggling to learn to read, and provide targeted interventions.

The logic is simple: when children have access to books, when they can see, when they're in school, and when they receive targeted support if they're struggling, they're much more likely to learn to read. Despite this, many children around the world lack access to the basic resources and support they need to be successful.

Even in the United States, children in high-poverty areas have a much harder time getting books than their peers in middle-income areas do. One study showed that, in a middle-income neighborhood, plentiful bookstores meant there were thirteen books available for every child, but in a community of concentrated poverty, only one age-appropriate book was available for every 300 children (Neuman & Moland, 2016). At the same time, we know that making books and other print materials freely available matters: one recent review of studies identified three different book-giveaway programs (including one sponsored by the country singer Dolly Parton) that promoted more interest in reading and the development of literacy-related skills. That study also showed that the number of books didn't even matter much: a program that gave away just a few books was just as effective as one that gave sixty books to each child over a five-year period (Barshay, 2020).

Producing and distributing books equitably can be challenging, but it can be done. Organizations like Wordworks (see Chapter 6) make printable materials freely available online, along with explicit instructions on how parents and children can create books using whatever materials they have. On top of all that, organizations like EmbraceRace and the Jane Addams Peace Association post lists of books by authors from different racial and cultural backgrounds so that there's no excuse not to provide all children with access to materials that reflect their heritage.

Of course, making books and print materials available in a variety of languages, by authors from a range of backgrounds, is just one step. Children still need to be able to read those books once they get those books into their hands. Nonetheless, 25 percent of school-aged children in the United States have undiagnosed eye problems that inhibit their ability to read, and one in three children haven't had their vision tested in the past two years (if at all) (Sparks & Harwin, 2018); but relatively low-cost programs to test students' vision and get glasses to those who need them do exist (Slavin et al., 2018). In the developing world, it may be complicated to create a supply chain that makes print materials readily available and ensures that every child who needs glasses gets a pair, but it can be done.

In turn, the discussions in Chapter 7 demonstrate that there are available strategies for addressing many issues that make it difficult for young students to attend school on a regular basis. Further, programs like Wordworks, Teaching Matters (Chapter 7), Second Chance (Chapter 9), and numerous others demonstrate different ways to address the specific needs of at least some of the students who experience difficulties. These first steps may not reach every student right away, and any initial success has to be followed by developing educational activities that foster more advanced skills—an even more challenging proposition. Yet all these changes—developing the capacity to provide glasses, to address chronic absences, and to provide targeted support in reading—can be accomplished with relatively little disruption to teachers' and students' everyday work and the conventional practices and structures of schooling. Taking this high-leverage approach to addressing predictable problems builds the capacity and momentum that can lead to more successful and sustained improvement efforts in the future.

Access to College-Level Content, Assessments, and Counseling

For older students, even challenges as difficult as increasing access to college can provide opportunities for high-leverage problems. In particular, low-income and other historically underserved students often "undermatch" by not applying for entrance in programs for which they qualify. One study in North Carolina found that over half of students from low-income families undermatched by attending a less selective college than one to which they could gain access, but only about a quarter of students from high-income families undermatched. Although undermatching has also been associated with decreased odds of graduating from college, successful interventions can have a meaningful effect on these students' long-term life outcomes (Bowen et al., 2009; Chingos, 2014; Hoxby & Avery, 2012).

Illustrating the possibilities, Susan Dynarski and colleagues designed a low-cost intervention at the University of Michigan that focused specifically on increasing the enrollment rates of low-income students who undermatched. This "informational" intervention sent these students a letter that offered a promise of four years of free admission and encouraged them to apply. The researchers found that the students who received this information were more than twice as likely to apply and enroll. Notably, the intervention "closed by half the income gaps in college choice among high-achieving students." Further, it didn't create added costs for the university; it allowed for more efficient and productive uses of funds already dedicated for scholarships (Dynarski et al., 2018).

The issues faced by "threshold" students, such as those who under-match, make particularly good candidates for high-leverage problems because they address systemic inefficiencies as well as implicit and systemic biases that can prevent students from making progress. Developing any comprehensive approach depends on finding the fit between the needs, concerns, and capacities in different communities, but the work of districts like Passaic and Freehold and the other members of the New Jersey Network of Superintendents demonstrates that educators already have it within their power to pursue a coordinated series of interventions that can help increase access to college (Hatch et al., 2019):

- *Offer assessment preparation for all.* Enable all students to take required college entrance tests early in their high-school careers; waive registration fees; and provide free online preparation opportunities for those who need them.

- *Remove barriers for entrance into college-level courses.* Opt all students into college-level courses; establish clear, consistent criteria rather than subjective criteria for students who choose to opt out.

- *Provide targeted, intensive support.* Monitor access and outcomes in college-level courses with disaggregated data to identify students who need additional support; provide targeted interventions to enable those students to get back on and stay on track, rather than demoting them to lower levels.

- *Strengthen supports for navigating the college and career process.* Provide underserved students with access to counselors, mentors, and peers who can help guide them through finding colleges and careers; eliminate fees and complicated forms and procedures for applying for colleges, jobs, and scholarships.

These steps are just the beginning, but they provide a foundation for the long-term work of developing more intensive and effective academic support and addressing directly the low expectations and systemic barriers that Black and Latinx students and students from families with lower incomes face in schools.

Develop New Approaches to Critical Challenges

Micro-innovations serve as the building blocks for addressing high-leverage problems and building the infrastructure for more powerful learning opportunities. Linking innovations can strengthen that infrastructure in almost any context. Imagine teachers supported by access to more powerful materials; a network that connects their students to capable tutors, mentors, and other caring peers and adults; and assessments and information systems that assist them in meeting the needs of all their students.

Drawing on materials like eduLab's *wRite Formula* and the math cards of Jo Boaler's Youcubed approach, teachers can support students' learning in key areas where their students regularly experience difficulty. Putting these materials into the hands of tutors, as well, can amplify teachers' efforts. Tutoring provides one of the most effective means of improving academic achievement, but it comes at a high cost, made more complicated by needs for training and difficulties in finding capable tutors (Hill & Loeb, 2020; Nickow et al., 2020). Nonetheless, approaches like those of the Learning Community Project (Chapter 8), IkamvaYouth (Chapter 7), and the Kliptown Youth Program (Chapter 7) demonstrate productive ways to find, support, and organize tutors and "learning facilitators" even in circumstances where qualified and effective teachers aren't available. In countries like the United States, the examples of Citizen Schools (Chapter 9) and City Year and other AmeriCorps programs demonstrate ways to create a steady supply of tutors and mentors who can support learning both inside and outside schools (Balfanz & Byrnes, 2020). To unlock the power of social networks more broadly, Julia Freeland Fisher, in *Who You Know* (2018), and Marc Freedman, in *How to Live Forever* (2018), describe how to connect students in schools with the many people (including seniors) who can also provide support.

In turn, this growing infrastructure for teaching and learning can be enhanced and surrounded by the development of more effective technologies for adaptive learning and expanding opportunities to link students with online learning resources, tutors, and other allies. New tools and software, like those being developed by New Visions for Public Schools (Chapter 7), can help teachers and administrators keep track of students' progress; surface individual and collective learning problems that need attention; and take care of routine tasks, such as tracking attendance.

Strengthening instruction in critical areas and creating related efficiencies can free the time and mental space that teachers need to connect with individual students, focus on their educational and developmental needs, and differentiate instruction. In this scenario, new learning opportunities are added into the school day over time.

Such an approach shifts the focus from trying to overhaul the entire curriculum in a matter of a year or two to providing the tools and support that enable educators to effect a series of targeted interventions that can transform their practice over time.

Take Small Steps to Make Big Changes

The incremental approach to school improvement relies on a fairly simple series of ideas:

- Enable educators to add more powerful and more efficient learning opportunities into the school day.

- Create time and space in the school year that allows educators to provide more targeted support for academic achievement and for pursuing a broader range of developmental goals.

- Develop "add-ons" and "plug-ins" to the school day that take advantage of the new time and space by fitting into some aspects of the conventional grammar of schooling but extending it as well.

- Establish broader social networks of caring adults who can foster students' learning, both inside and outside school.

Of course, making even incremental changes can be challenging, but changes in society, including crises, can create new demands and opportunities for changes in schools. As devastating as the coronavirus pandemic has been, it has exposed ways to begin to address a critical problem with the design of conventional schools: *schools are designed to house students, not to educate them.*

Conventional schools are a better medium for spreading disease than they are for supporting meaningful learning. Learning depends on healthy, safe conditions for students, educators, and all those who work in schools; but schools cram too many people into too little space, and the typical layout of age-graded classrooms along long hallways limits collaboration, exploration, and engagement with the world. We've made things worse in the United States by leaving buildings in disrepair, particularly in low-income communities, and failing to provide adequate ventilation, air conditioning, or heating. Add on a draconian schedule that leaves very little time for healthy activity—whether it's just to take a break, get some exercise, or get lunch at a reasonable hour with enough time to eat—and then ramp up stress levels with high-stakes tests and exams, for which students have to sit in rows, in silence, for hours, facing a ticking clock.

To address this problem, we can take advantage of some of the same steps that help protect students and staff from a widespread outbreak and create a foundation for much healthier and more powerful educational opportunities in the future.

KEY IDEAS FOR CREATING THE EDUCATION WE NEED

- Address high-leverage problems, and build the capacity and constituency for sustained, long-term work.

- Focus on learning that matters.

- Break down the barriers between—and connect—learning experiences "inside" and "outside" schools.

- Condense schooling and increase learning.

Focus on Learning That Matters

The coronavirus-related school closures, and the inequities in access to online learning they exposed (see Chapter 2), raised concerns about "learning loss" and generated a slew of proposals for counteracting it by adding and intensifying work on academic subjects. That conception of learning loss, however, ignores the mile-wide and inch-deep curriculum and age-graded pacing that make it almost impossible for students to catch up once they're left behind.

To address these issues, we can focus on a small set of key skills and concepts every month and provide educators with the tools to ensure that every child meets those goals. Approaches to such a "less-is-more philosophy" have already been laid out by people like Ted Sizer and the Coalition of Essential Schools. The Teaching for Understanding project (developed by David Perkins and Howard Gardner at Project Zero) and the Understanding by Design approach (from Grant Wiggins and Jay McTighe) also provide a wealth of examples and resources to help educators focus in on the most generative topics and goals.

At the primary-school level around the world, programs like Second Chance in Africa (see Chapter 9) and Pratham's Read India (Dutt et al., 2016) have already demonstrated how children who are out of school or who are being left behind can catch up to their peers in basic skills relatively quickly. Even at the high-school level in the United States, the responses to the school closures demonstrated that some substantial reductions in academic demands can be made. Shortly after schools in the United States went online, the Advanced Placement program slashed its curriculum and produced shorter exams, with 75 percent of the usual content. According to one of the directors of the program, "Psychometricians have identified subsets of questions that have correlations to the questions we won't be asking this year, so that the shorter exam will have high predictive validity, as usual with AP exams." He added that AP has shortened its exams under a number of other emergency conditions, and colleges have always accepted those scores (Hess, 2020).

Break Down the Barriers Between Learning "Inside" and "Outside" Schools

As we remake the school schedule to help stop the spread of the coronavirus, we can stagger schedules to fit students' sleep patterns and development as they get older. We can make sure that students have regular opportunities to take the breaks and get the exercise that we know benefits learning and productivity. As we limit the numbers of people using school facilities at any given time, we can rotate students in and out of schools and expand support for students' learning far beyond school walls. In addition to online learning, we can take advantage of possibilities for education outside on playgrounds, in the natural world, and in gyms, museums, community organizations, and businesses in the surrounding neighborhoods. In the process, we can shift the focus from getting children into schools and embrace the possibilities for supporting students' learning and development wherever and whenever it occurs.

Expand the Power of the Education Workforce

To increase the reach and power of teachers who have been limited largely to working with students in classrooms, we can engage the volunteers and other young people and adults who have the time and the capacity to play positive roles in learning inside and outside schools (National Commission on Social, Emotional, and Academic Development, 2018). The means to fill the demand for this support could come from creating 1 million service jobs (Khazei & Bridgeland, 2020) or other proposals to expand national service, such as the Cultivating Opportunity and Response to the Pandemic through Service (CORPS) Act developed in the US Senate during the pandemic (Ignatius, 2020).

> We can shift the focus from getting children into schools and embrace the possibilities for supporting students' learning and development wherever and whenever it occurs.

Condense Schooling and Increase Learning

All these changes are within our reach right now. They don't require new curricula, massive professional development for teachers, or new technologies. Reimagining education begins with reorienting our priorities, making schools healthy and safe, and focusing first and foremost on students' needs and interests, particularly those of Black, Latinx, and other historically underserved students. If we have to, we can start an incremental "less is more" approach slowly, by dropping the teaching of at least one major topic from every subject every semester and monitoring the results. But as we take these steps and rethink our priorities, a more radical possibility emerges: *condense the school day.*

Instead of extending the school day and requiring students to spend even more time on basic skills, imagine concentrating academic support in a few hours, with educators able to utilize sophisticated materials and coordinate contributions from colleagues with specialized expertise, as well as from volunteer tutors, mentors, and online and offline guides. If we could cut the curriculum in half, in a sense, every day would be a half day, opening up opportunities during the rest of the day for students to

- have lunch;
- get outside;
- participate in a variety of school-based, community-based, and online activities;
- pursue their own educational interests; and
- participate in activities that foster a much wider range of goals for their development and education.

Schools in Norway, Finland, Estonia, and other places already demonstrate that students can thrive and succeed in systems with a shorter school day. And Estonia, with a well-established tradition of publicly supported "hobby schools," provides every school-aged child with funding to participate in at least one after-school activity (e.g., music instruction, astronomy and computer clubs, or sports teams) every week.

More radical approaches to rethinking the school day highlight the limits of every improvement effort that focuses solely on changing what happens in schools (Corson, 2020). These "beyond school" approaches to educational improvement take advantage of the opportunities both inside and outside schools for developing what Jal Mehta and Sarah Fine (2019) suggest might be an alternative grammar of schooling: learning arrangements and practices that can be found in extracurricular activities such as drama clubs, community service projects, and recreation leagues.

Such an approach to rethinking the school day also rejects the tacit assumption that equates education with schooling. As laid out at the beginning of this book, children learn all the time, and that learning goes on throughout life. We can't create much more equitable learning opportunities without addressing the inequitable access to learning opportunities and support wherever learning takes place: inside and outside the classroom, after school, and over the summer.

Whether incremental or radical, these approaches to improvement begin by looking at the educational potential of all the hours children spend inside and outside of schools and then building the infrastructure that enables them to take advantage of the whole day and the whole year in ways that are most productive and personally meaningful. These changes open up conventional schools to allow more unconventional approaches—like those of the Beam Center, Citizen Schools, and others—to take root on a wider basis. This approach shifts from asking how much time children need to focus on school and academic work to asking how can we support children's constructive engagement throughout the day and what role can school play in that process?

The Problems and Possibilities for Improvement in Every System

14

When I describe radical possibilities for reimagining time and schooling, the concerns emerge immediately:

- What will happen if students don't learn all the skills and concepts they need to make progress?

- How do we know which skills and concepts to focus on?

The answers are fairly straightforward:

- Too many students don't learn the concepts and skills they need to make progress right now.

- We don't know, with certainty, what concepts and skills students need to focus on to be successful in the future.

Maintaining the status quo is unacceptable, but how can we plan ahead if unpredictability and lack of certainty are the norm? We have some evidence and ideas about what students need at different stages of development that we can build on. But adaptability and flexibility, responding to students' emerging needs and interests as the conditions and demands in our communities evolve, remains central to meaningful education.

To create adaptable educational systems, beyond the rigidity of school schedules, we have to address two other critical sources of inflexibility. First, the intractability of schooling is reinforced by the narrow focus on a small set of academic goals and benchmarks presumed to lead to college, careers, and economic productivity. In the United States, some of the goals and benchmarks seem clear:

- Learn to read with proficiency by third grade.

- Stay on track for graduation by ninth grade.

- Graduate from high school with high enough test scores to avoid remedial college courses or with qualifications that allow access to appropriate vocational training.

However, run into any of a host of minor or major issues or life events and miss any one of those benchmarks, and the odds of "making it" drop precipitously. Add in the fact that Black and Latinx students, students from low-income families, and other underserved students are much more likely to face those obstacles than are their advantaged peers are, and the road to college seems much more like a winding path than a superhighway. As long as the potential and progress of almost every educational enterprise—whether inside or outside school, whether conventional or radical—continues to be measured in terms of whether it helps students meet these narrow benchmarks and goals, the prospects for change remain limited.

Second, as the coronavirus-related school closures demonstrated, many families around the world depend on schools to look after their children during the adult workday. All of a sudden, essential workers who had to continue to go to their jobs faced a critical need for childcare; many of those ordered to work at home instantly found themselves trying to figure out how to provide homeschooling at the same time that they participated in online meetings and tried to carry out some aspects of their job responsibilities. In my house, we were extremely fortunate that when the school closures hit, Stella was already in tenth grade, Clara and Hannah were in college, and all could work independently. Yet for the twenty-two years that we've had children, Karen's and my ability to work and to write anything has depended on our having the capacity to afford childcare before our daughters started kindergarten and to pay for after-school programs and summer activities once they were in school.

As long as the United States and many other countries need a place to keep most children and young adults between the hours of 8:00 a.m. and 3:00 p.m., even efforts to reinvent education are likely to continue to make schools the "seat of learning." That constraint makes it extremely difficult to change the basic structures and classroom practices that have grown so familiar worldwide. Just as the industrial revolution contributed to the development of the factory model of schooling, it may take another profound change in the relationships between adults and children to finally break down school walls. As long as access to quality childcare and so many other resources and opportunities remains inequitably distributed, the most advantaged parents and their children will continue to have the most flexibility to respond to and benefit from any changes that are made.

Improvement in Context

The ubiquity of the constraints of the narrow goals for schooling and the adult workday help explain why, even in higher-performing systems, educational opportunities remain largely confined to conventional schools and to those who can get access to the path to college or careers. Given these constraints, both more successful and less successful systems have invested heavily in building the infrastructure that supports age-graded egg-crate schools with a focus on traditional subjects and academic achievement on standardized tests. Not only does it take time to change the grammar of schooling, but these "sunk investments" means it costs a lot as well. Like the complexity and costs of making wholesale changes in the production processes and supply chains for established manufacturing products, it takes enormous effort and investment to transform the many materials, relationships, and conditions dedicated to sustaining conventional schools and traditional instructional practices.

Looked at in context, however, both higher-performing educational systems like Singapore's and lower-performing systems like the United States' provide possibilities and challenges for improvement, but they are different. In Singapore, schools are part of

- a relatively small, centralized educational system under the control of a single Ministry of Education,
- in a political system controlled by one party,
- with a robust infrastructure to support all schools,
- in a society recognized as valuing education and as treating teaching as a profession,

- where the government makes deliberate, long-term, strategic connections between education, the economy, health, and other sectors.

Under these conditions, almost all students reach at least basic standards of academic achievement. Students can enter into a wide range of specialized and vocational tracks that provide alternate pathways to graduation and into the working world, and the government has the capacity to make a comprehensive series of incremental improvements over the long term. But the system remains focused on narrow outcomes and on tests and exams in academic subjects sustained by direct connections to economic policy. That tight focus and coordination contributes to high levels of stress and concerns about support for creativity, social and emotional learning, and other aspects of development; reinforces conceptions of "real school"; encourages conformity; and discourages the development of structures and practices that challenge convention.

In contrast, in the United States, schools work with

- decentralized governance structures that cede much of the control for schooling to states and local school districts,

- inequitable distribution of resources,

- limited and inconsistent infrastructure for teaching and learning,

- little support for teaching as a profession,

- weak and often informal connections between institutions and organizations in education and those in other sectors.

All of these factors contribute to highly inequitable educational opportunities that disadvantage students who aren't white and wealthy but still enables many students to reach high levels of achievement and allows for the development of individual creativity and entrepreneurship that countries like Singapore continue to aspire to. This approach encourages the development of many kinds of alternative approaches in niches, but there are few mechanisms for spreading and sustaining those alternatives systemwide.

Steering Toward the Future

Finland offers possibilities for improvement that are somewhere between those in Singapore and those in the United States. In Finland, schools work in a context with

- a well-established social welfare state that connects education, health, and other sectors of society;

- a national curriculum framework and a strong, aligned infrastructure of facilities, materials, assessment, and preparation programs to support teaching and learning;

- widely recognized respect for teachers and teaching; and

- considerable autonomy for schools and teachers at the local level.

Under these conditions, students don't have to pass tests that require them to demonstrate proficiency by third grade; they hardly ever "fail" or have to be held back; and most students reach at least a basic level of educational achievement. Students can enter into a number of academic and vocational tracks in high school, and they even have some opportunities to change tracks if they need or want to. Teachers and schools may develop and pursue new practices in niches, and the roughly ten-year reviews of the curriculum framework provide some opportunities to pursue systemwide changes.

Although teachers, schools, and municipalities in Finland experience considerable autonomy, over time, the educational system has developed the human, technical, and social capital needed to steer a system toward broad education goals without having to rely heavily on rewards or punishments. In the process, Finland supports the development of the collective responsibility that can guide education into an unpredictable future. The US and other educational systems use tests to hold teachers, school leaders, and schools accountable for doing what they're supposed to do. But rather than using assessments to look back to see what was done, educators and system leaders in Finland use assessments to look forward and to see whether people, classes, and schools are headed in the right direction. Such an approach doesn't require data on every single aspect of students', teachers', or schools' performance, but it depends on making sure no one gets too far off course. It means using assessment to look for outliers and listening for signs of trouble, not to check on each individual or make sure everything is done a certain way or in a certain time frame.

At the same time, the more people are involved in coming to a consensus on a common direction, the less likely they are to embrace dramatic or radical changes. As a result, as in Singapore, changes to the educational system in Finland take place slowly and incrementally. Illustrating this challenge, proposals to drop many of the requirements for teaching to be organized by subject and requiring interdisciplinary or "phenomena-based teaching" were discussed but not adopted in the 2004 curriculum-renewal process. Twelve years later, in 2016, the proposals came up again, but only a small step was taken: the new framework included the stipulation that all students should participate each year in a multidisciplinary learning module. The head of the Innovation Centre at the Finnish National Agency of Education, Anneli Rautiainen, described this development as a "nudge" to the system.

As you would find in the United States, some teachers and schools were already poised to take advantage of this nudge and used it to expand their work. In Fiskars, a Finnish community well-known for its artisans and craftspeople, the local school had already expanded the learning environment to include the whole village and offered a variety of interdisciplinary projects, such as glass-blowing and historically based theatre productions, that meet the requirements for the new modules.

At the same time, a host of factors continue to discourage educators and schools from deeply engaging in these experiments or replacing conventional curricula and courses with these modules entirely. For one thing, while the new curriculum framework adds expectations for students to engage in interdisciplinary projects, little, if anything, has been left out of the "old" curriculum. The changes in the national curriculum framework in Finland still try to squeeze more into the conventional curriculum and school day. Finland's textbooks and high-stakes exit exams help align the whole system, but they also serve as constraints, reinforcing the traditional divisions between subjects. Furthermore, with a relatively successful system aligned to a national curriculum and international tests, why would a well-regarded group of autonomous professionals change their pedagogy? Along with teacher autonomy comes a highly independent teaching force that can choose not to change its practice quickly or deeply.

Perhaps most problematic, this commitment to autonomy runs smack up against Finland's deep commitment to equity: if early adopters take off with the interdisciplinary projects but others don't, learning experiences across Finland are likely to become less and less comparable. In fact, people I spoke to in Finland were less concerned about overall decreases in average scores on the PISA tests and much more concerned about inequity as gaps in student outcomes grow. Given this level of autonomy, in a system that many still consider to be "working," with few incentives to change, it should be no surprise that many people both inside and outside the educational system see maintaining the status quo as a sensible way to operate.

Introducing new practices into teacher preparation might support changes in schools over the course of a generation, but Finland's relatively limited focus on professional development and its comparatively weak control of school leaders compared to Singapore means that in Finland, there's no mechanism for spreading new practices quickly across the system. And as we discovered in Norway, any changes have to be made within a context that discourages adding more academic instruction if it interferes with children's opportunities to play and direct their own activities that are also viewed as important developmental experiences. Since the Finnish system is designed to "steer" rather than to penalize, there will be no grading, sanctions, or public humiliation, but there aren't likely to be quick or dramatic changes in conventional practices either.

Between Nudges and Disruption

The different possibilities and challenges for changing schooling in many different contexts help explain why no single approach, program, technology, product, or other resource has produced the disruptive "big bang" that could sweep away the conventional grammar of schooling in the United States or anywhere else. But we can take advantage of the many opportunities to improve schools and learning experiences by paying attention to the affordances of the different systems and the local conditions and circumstances in which those systems operate.

As much as I've learned about the challenges of improving schools on a large scale, perhaps the most important lesson is one of hope: choices matter. In the 1960s, Singapore committed to making comprehensive investments in education an integral part of economic and social development and a central means of bringing together a diverse, multilingual population. In the 1970s, Finland chose to forge a comprehensive public educational system with a focus on equity for all out of a variety of inequitably distributed grammar schools and work-oriented civic schools. In the 1980s and 1990s, Norway made a series of decisions that resulted in the creation of the government investment fund that now supports education, development, and a high standard of living for all for generations to come. With these changes, all three countries chose to provide the societal supports so that those who don't make it through school can get access to health care and other services they need throughout their lives.

All these decisions reflect the final principle of school improvement.

PRINCIPLE #8

The structures and practices of conventional schools are most likely to change in concert with changes in other aspects of society.

In Singapore, Finland, and Norway, leaders responded to changes in the world around them in ways that made it possible for their societies to do things they had never done before, including providing better opportunities for learning and development.

Understandably, many educators shy away from tackling changes that depend on societal, economic, and political issues that are out of their control. But ignoring these larger issues contributes to the problem that many reform initiatives are "too small": they fail to inspire the social movements needed to change conventional schools; they never address the conditions that perpetuate inequitable educational opportunities; and they never reach for the social equality and mutual respect that a truly inclusive and integrated educational system requires.

Big movements grow out of small sparks. Hope comes from the examples I've seen in Texas, New Jersey, New York, Oslo, Helsinki, Singapore, Cape Town, and Johannesburg. These local efforts do more than improve schools; they make connections, build relationships, and bring communities together. They foster common understanding of the goals and purposes of education, build the capacity for improving and transforming schools, and develop the collective responsibility needed to eliminate the biases and barriers that leave so many out.

As I finish writing this book on a humid afternoon in June, Stella is also at home, her high school closed for the rest of the year. In the press and on social media, many are voicing hope that amid the devastation, the pandemic might change schools dramatically. I share the hope—but, given my experiences, I can't assume things will change . . . unless we all choose to change them. Real improvements in school won't come from some invention, from a virus, or from closing schools and somehow starting over. Schools will improve by taking advantage of the opportunities that arise as work and family life change and by making a collective commitment to the health and development of every child and every community.

High-Leverage Leadership

I've argued that everyone has a role to play in building a much stronger, more expansive, and more equitable set of supports for teaching and learning. For teachers and administrators, that role includes carrying out three different kinds of leadership:

- *Managing with*: Working with all the people inside schools to manage day-to-day operations; identify common concerns and high-leverage problems; develop strategic, coordinated plans; and gather relevant information and make adjustments

- *Managing up*: Working with people at "higher" administrative levels and those who provide funding to ensure that they understand the goals, purposes, capacities, and needs of the school

- *Managing out*: Working with people "outside" the school (parents, community members, members of the press, businesses, religious and community organizations, etc.) to develop an inclusive school community and a common understanding of the goals, purposes, capacities, and needs of the school

People in conventional school leadership positions often try to tackle all these responsibilities, but common understanding of purposes and priorities makes it possible to distribute these responsibilities productively so that anyone can play a role in developing and advancing the collective interests of the school community (Hatch, 2009b).

Working with all these constituencies enables schools and other educational organizations to manage and find the fit between the organization's goals, needs, and values and the demands and expectations on the "outside" so central to improving conventional structures and practices. "Bridging"—developing connections with individuals and organizations on the outside—provides access to needed resources and a cadre of advocates who can support and sustain the work on the "inside." Those connections also provide information about how policies and conditions might be changing and, at the same time, provide an avenue for influencing those policies and conditions. Crucially, this work also enables schools and organizations to protect themselves by creating their own niche. Thus, organizations like the Beam Center

(Chapter 8) and Citizen Schools (Chapter 9) can make choices about whether to work within or outside the constraints and demands of the conventional school day. In that sense, a crucial role of leaders lies in deciding who their "allies" are and how to build a constituency that will support them and join with them in developing the collective responsibility for meeting joint interests and goals. In the process, high-leverage leaders manage for today by doing what they can to make incremental improvements right now, and they manage for the future by making sure those improvements position the community to continue on toward broader purposes long after they leave.

To address high-leverage problems and simultaneously embrace niches of disruption, educators have to accept responsibility for enabling all children to learn and recognize that no generic solution will address every child's needs. Pursuing micro-innovations and taking advantage of unanticipated opportunities depends on developing a problem-finding and problem-solving mindset and embracing the fact that there will always be another challenge to tackle and unanticipated problems and possibilities to pursue. That mindset demands a paradoxical mix of confidence and humility: the confidence to move ahead thoughtfully and decisively and the humility to recognize that adjustments will always have to be made. It's a mindset that recognizes that all solutions and all innovations are, at best, partial: they work for some people in some contexts for some time. In this context, a leader's job becomes one of artfully and strategically organizing a series of meaningful improvement efforts in the short term while building the capacity and the constituency for transforming conventional learning opportunities over the long term. Rather than a commander leading troops into battle, this collaborative and distributed approach casts the leader as a conductor, listening for and drawing out the best work of everyone involved in a common enterprise.

By listening for and addressing key concerns in their own communities, educators can create the foundation for the social movements that can shift our perspectives on learning, schools, and education altogether . . .

from a focus on short-term improvements on a narrow set of academic outcomes . . .

to a focus on fulfilling common purposes that support individual and collective development over the long term,

from concentrating on generic solutions to problems across all schools . . .

to developing specific solutions to critical problems in particular communities,

from trying to invent programs and practices to scale up across contexts . . .

to creating niches of possibility in particular conditions that push the boundaries of conventional schooling,

from assuming that good ideas or effective practices will spread rapidly or quickly . . .

to building the infrastructure that enables educators to develop more powerful and equitable learning opportunities and sustain them over time, and

from looking back to see if we did what we said we would do . . .

to looking forward to see if we're headed in the right direction.

We can all work together to build and expand the capacity of schools, school systems, and our local communities to support the work of educators and students. Over time, developing the infrastructure that facilitates more efficient, effective, and equitable learning can contribute to improvements in outcomes and to the emergence of more radical educational approaches in niches. In turn, those improvements and new developments can generate possibilities for education that lie beyond our imagination.

References

Advocacy Institute. (2020). NAEP and students with disabilities. https://www.advocacyinstitute.org/NAEP/NationPerformance2013-15-17.shtml

Akmal, M., & Pritchett, L. (2019). *Learning equity requires more than equality: Learning goals and achievement gaps between the rich and the poor in five developing countries* (Working Paper No. 19/028). Center for Global Development Working Paper Series. https://www.riseprogramme.org/sites/www.riseprogramme.org/files/publications/RISE_WP-028_Equity_Akmal_Pritchett_0.pdf

Akyeampong, A., Delprato, M., Sabates, R., James, Z., Pryor, J., Westbrook, J., Humphreys, S., & Tsegay, H. (2018). Speed School Programme in Ethiopia: Tracking the progress of Speed School students 2011–2017. Research report. Falmer, Brighton, UK: University of Sussex Centre for International Education.

Aldrich, M. W. (2019, October 4). Money over merit? New study says gifted programs favor students from wealthier families. *Chalkbeat.* https://chalkbeat.org/posts/tn/2019/10/04/money-over-merit-new-study-says-gifted-programs-favor-students-from-wealthier-families

Alexander, M. (2012). *The new Jim Crow: Mass incarceration in the age of colorblindness.* New York, NY: The New Press.

America's Promise Alliance. (2019, June 11). *Building a grad nation: Progress and challenge in raising high school graduation rates.* https://www.americaspromise.org/2019-building-grad-nation-report

Annie E. Casey Foundation. (2019, September 24). *Kids in concentrated poverty data snapshot.* https://www.aecf.org/blog/percentage-of-kids-in-concentrated-poverty-worsens-in-10-states-and-puerto

Auxier, B., & Anderson, M. (2020, March 16). As schools close due to the coronavirus, some U.S. students face a digital "homework gap." *Fact Tank, Pew Research Center.* https://www.pewresearch.org/fact-tank/2020/03/16/as-schools-close-due-to-the-coronavirus-some-u-s-students-face-a-digital-homework-gap

Bailey, T. (2009). Challenge and opportunity: Rethinking the role and function of developmental education in community college. *New Directions for Community Colleges* (*145*), 11–30.

Balfanz, R. (2016). Absenteeism matters to schools and students. *Phi Delta Kappan 98* (2), 8–13.

Balfanz, R., & Byrnes, V. (2012). The importance of being in school: A report on absenteeism in the nation's public schools. *The Education Digest, 78*(2), 4–9.

Balfanz, R., & Byrnes, V. (2020, May). Connecting social-emotional development, academic achievement, and on-track outcomes: A multi-district study of grades 3 to 10 students supported by City Year AmeriCorps Members. https://www.cityyear.org/wp-content/uploads/2020/05/EGC_CityYearReport_BalfanzByrnes.pdf

Balonon-Rosen, P. (2016, January 7). Massachusetts education again ranks no. 1 nationally. *Learning Lab.* http://learninglab.legacy.wbur.org/2016/01/07/massachusetts-education-again-ranks-no-1-nationally

Barron, L. (2020, March 13). Coronavirus lessons from Singapore, Taiwan and Hong Kong. *Time.* https://time.com/5802293/coronavirus-covid19-singapore-hong-kong-taiwan

Barshay, J. (2020). Proof Points: The literacy secret that Dolly Parton knows: Free books work. *Hechinger Report.* https://hechingerreport.org/proof-points-the-literacy-secret-that-dolly-parton-knows-free-books-work

Benjamin, R. (2019). *Race after technology: Abolitionist tools for the new Jim Code.* Cambridge, UK: Polity Press.

Berends, M., Bodilly, S., & Nataraj Kirby, S. (2002). *Facing the challenges of whole-school reform: New American Schools after a decade.* Santa Monica, CA: Rand Education.

Bergman, P., & Chan, E. (2019, January). *The impact of text messages to parents on middle and high school student achievement in the United States.* The Abdul Latif Jameel Poverty Action Lab (J-PAL). https://www.povertyactionlab.org/evaluation/impact-text-messages-parents-middle-and-high-school-student-achievement-united-states

Boaler, J. (2015, January 28). Fluency without fear: Research evidence on the best ways to learn math facts. *YouCubed.org.* https://www.youcubed.org/evidence/fluency-without-fear

Boaler, J., & Zoido, P. (2016). Why math education in the U.S. doesn't add up. *Scientific American Mind, 27*(6), 18–19.

Bowen, W. G., Chingos, M. M., & McPherson, M. S. (2009). *Crossing the finish line: Completing college at America's public universities.* Princeton, NJ: Princeton University Press.

Boyer, E. L. (1990). *Scholarship reconsidered: Priorities of the professoriate.* Princeton, NJ: Carnegie Foundation for the Advancement of Teaching.

Bristol, T. (2019, September 3). The value of student-teacher matching: Implications for reauthorization of the Higher Education Act. *Brown Center Chalkboard, Brookings.* https://www.brookings.edu/blog/brown-center-chalkboard/2019/08/26/the-value-of-student-teacher-matching-implications-for-reauthorization-of-the-higher-education-act

Bryk, A. S. (2020). *Improvement in action: Advancing quality in America's schools.* Cambridge, MA: Harvard Education Press.

Bryk, A. S., Gomez, L. M., Grunow, A., & LeMahieu, P. G. (2015). *Learning to improve: How America's schools can get better at getting better.* Cambridge, MA: Harvard Education Press.

Cámara, G. (2007). *Enseñar y aprender con interés: Logros y testimonios en escuelas públicas* [To teach and to learn with interest: Achievements and testimonies in public schools]. Mexico City, Mexico: Siglo XXI.

Carter, W. (2020, March 20). School district buys Internet transmission towers to keep students connected. *Solutions Story Tracker.* https://solutionsu.solutionsjournalism.org/stories/school-district-buys-internet-transmission-towers-to-keep-students-connected

Chang, H., Gomperts, J., & Boissiere, L. (2014, October 7). Chronic absenteeism can devastate K-12 learning. *Education Week.* https://www.edweek.org/ew/articles/2014/10/08/07chang.h34.html

Charania, M., & Freeland Fisher, J. (2020, July). *The missing metrics: Emerging practices for measuring students' relationships and networks.* Cambridge, MA: Christensen Institute. https://staging.whoyouknow.org/wp-content/uploads/2020/07/THE-MISSING-METRICS.pdf

Childress, S., & Clayton, T. (2012). Focusing on results at the New York City Department of Education. In S. Childress (Ed.), *Transforming public education: Cases in education entrepreneurship* (pp. 267–297). Cambridge, MA: Harvard Educational Publishing Group.

Child Trends. (2018). *High school dropout rates.* https://www.childtrends.org/indicators/high-school-dropout-rates

Chingos, M. M. (2014, January 15). Can we fix undermatching in higher ed? Would it matter if we did? *Brown Center Chalkboard, Brookings.* https://www.brookings.edu/research/can-we-fix-undermatching-in-higher-ed-would-it-matter-if-we-did

Christensen, C. M., Horn, M. B., & Johnson, C. W. (2010). *Disrupting class: How disruptive innovation will change the way the world learns* (updated and expanded new ed.). New York, NY: McGraw-Hill.

Christensen, C. M., Raynor, M. E., & McDonald, R. (2015, December). What is disruptive innovation? *Harvard Business Review.* https://hbr.org/2015/12/what-is-disruptive-innovation.

Citizens Foundation. (2018, January 26). What founders say about TCF! [Video file]. https://www.youtube.com/watch?v=UxHeWfW1csY

City, E. A., Elmore, R. F., Fiarman, E., & Teitel, L. (2009). *Instructional rounds in education: A network approach to improving teaching and learning.* Cambridge, MA: Harvard Education Press.

Cohen, D. K., & Ball, D. L. (1999). Instruction, capacity, and improvement. *CPRE Research Reports.* https://repository.upenn.edu/cpre_research reports/8

Cohen, D. K., & Mehta, J. D. (2017). Why reform sometimes succeeds: Understanding the conditions that produce reforms that last. *American Educational Research Journal, 54*(4), 644–690.

Cohen, D. K., Spillane, J. P., & Peurach, D. J. (2018). The dilemmas of educational reform. *Educational Researcher, 47*(3), 204–212. https://doi.org/10.3102/0013189X17743488

Comer, J. P. (1980). *School power: Implications of an intervention project.* New York, NY: Free Press.

Comer, J. P. (1988). Educating poor minority children. *Scientific American, 259,* 42–48.

Comer, J. P. (1989). *Maggie's American dream: The life and times of a Black family.* New York, NY: Penguin Group.

Corson, J. (2020). *Undocumented educations: Everyday educational practices of recently immigrated youth beyond inclusion/exclusion* (Doctoral dissertation). Teachers College, Columbia University, New York, NY.

Cortes, E. (2011). *Metis* and the metrics of success. In R. F. Elmore (Ed.), *I used to think . . . And now I think . . . : Twenty leading educators reflect on the work of school reform.* Cambridge, MA: Harvard Education Press.

Damon, W. (2008). *The path to purpose: Helping our children find their calling in life.* New York, NY: Simon & Schuster.

Davis, B. W., Gooden, M. A., & Micheaux, D. J. (2015). Color-blind leadership: A critical race theory analysis of the ISLLC and ELCC Standards. *Educational Administration Quarterly, 51*(3), 335–371. https://doi.org/10.1177/0013161X15587092

Deng, Z., & Gopinathan, S. (2016). PISA and high performing education systems: Explaining Singapore's education success. *Comparative Education, 52*(4), 449–472. https://discovery.ucl.ac.uk/id/eprint/10089823/1/Deng_Gopinathan%20_2016_Singapore%20PISA%20final_.pdf

de Wolf, I. F., & Janssens, F. J. (2007). Effects and side effects of inspections and accountability in education: An overview of empirical studies. *Oxford Review of Education, 33*(3), 379–396.

Dutt, S. C., Kwauk, C., & Perlman Robinson, J. (2016). *Pratham's Read India Program: Taking small steps toward learning at scale.* Center for Universal Education at Brookings. https://www.brookings.edu/wp-content/uploads/2016/07/FINAL-Read-India-Case-Study.pdf

Dynarski, M. (2018, May 3). Is the high school graduation rate really going up? *Evidence Speaks, Brookings.* https://www.brookings.edu/research/Is-the-high-school-graduation-rate-really-going-up

Dynarski, S., Libassi, C. J., Michelmore, K., & Owen, S. (2018). *Closing the gap: The effect of a targeted, tuition-free promise on college choices of high-achieving, low-income students.* NBER Working Papers 25349. National Bureau of Economic Research.

Economist. (2017, January 7). South Africa has one of the world's worst education systems. *The Economist.* https://www.economist.com/middle-east-and-africa/2017/01/07/south-africa-has-one-of-the-worlds-worst-education-systems

EdBuild. (2019, February). *$23 Billion.* Washington, DC: EdBuild. https://edbuild.org/content/23-billion/full-report.pdf

Ehren, M. C., & Visscher, A. J. (2008). The relationships between school inspections, school characteristics and school improvement. *British Journal of Educational Studies, 56*(2), 205–227.

Elmore, R. F. (2002). Bridging the gap between standards and achievement: The imperative for professional development in education. Washington, D.C.: Albert Shanker Institute.

Elmore, R., & International Perspectives on Education Reform Group. (2011, May 18). What happens when learning breaks out in rural Mexico? *The Futures of School Reform.* http://blogs.edweek.org/edweek/futures_of_reform/2011/05/what_happens_when_learning_breaks_out_in_rural_mexico.html

Elstad, E., Nortvedt, G. A., & Turmo, A. (2009). The Norwegian assessment system: An accountability perspective. *CADMO, 2,* 89–103. https://doi.org/10.3280/CAD2009-002009

Feiner, L. (2020, April 5). How NYC moved the country's largest school district online during the coronavirus pandemic. *CNBC.* https://www.cnbc.com/2020/04/03/how-nyc-public-schools-are-shifting-online-during-the-coronavirus.html

Fergus, E. (2017). *Solving disproportionality and achieving equity: A leader's guide to using data to change hearts and minds.* Thousand Oaks, CA: Corwin.

Finnish National Board of Education. (2004). *Perusopetuksen opetussuunnitelman perusteet 2004* [National Core Curriculum of Basic Education 2004]. https://www.oph.fi/sites/default/files/documents/perusopetuksen-opetussuunnitelman-perusteet_2004.pdf

Fouche, G. (2017, June 2). Factbox: Norway's $960 billion sovereign wealth fund. *Reuters.* https://www.reuters.com/article/us-norway-swf-ceo-factbox/factbox-norways-960-billion-sovereign-wealth-fund-idUSKBN18T283

Freedman, M. (2018). *How to live forever: The enduring power of connecting the generations*. New York, NY: Public Affairs.

Freeland Fisher, J. (with Fisher, D.). (2018). *Who you know: Unlocking innovations that expand students' networks*. San Francisco, CA: Jossey-Bass.

Gardner, H. (1983). *Frames of mind: The theory of multiple intelligences*. New York, NY: BasicBooks.

Gardner, H. E. (2006). *Multiple intelligences: New horizons in theory and practice* (Rev. and updated ed.). New York, NY: BasicBooks.

Garud, R., Nayyar, P. R., & Shapira, Z. B. (1997). *Technological innovation: Oversights and forecasts*. Cambridge, UK: Press Syndicate of the University of Cambridge.

Gibson, J. J. (1977). The theory of affordances. In R. Shaw and J. Bransford (Eds.), *Perceiving, acting, and knowing: Toward an ecological psychology* (pp. 67–82). Hillsdale, NJ: Lawrence Erlbaum Associates.

Goldhaber, D., Lavery, L., & Theobald, R. (2015). Uneven playing field? Assessing the teacher quality gap between advantaged and disadvantaged students. *Educational Researcher, 44*(5), 293–307. https://doi.org/10.3102/0013189X15592622

Goldstein, D., & Patel, J. K. (2019, July 30). Need extra time on tests? It helps to have cash. *The New York Times*. https://www.nytimes.com/2019/07/30/us/extra-time-504-sat-act.html

Gooden, M. A. (2012). What does racism have to do with leadership? Countering the idea of color-blind leadership: A reflection on race and the growing pressures of the urban principalship. *The Journal of Educational Foundations, 26*(1/2), 67–84.

Goodwin, A. L. (2014). Perspectives on high performing education systems in Finland, Hong Kong, China, South Korea and Singapore: What lessons for the US? In S. K. Lee, W. O. Lee, & E. L. Low (Eds.), *Educational policy innovations* (pp. 185–199). Singapore: Springer.

Gottfried, M. A. (2019). Chronic absenteeism in the classroom context: Effects on achievement. *Urban Education, 54*(1), 3–34. https://doi.org/10.1177/0042085915618709

Gould, S. J., & Lewontin, R. C. (1979). The spandrels of San Marco and the Panglossian paradigm: A critique of the adaptationist programme. *Proceedings of the Royal Society of London. Series B. Biological Sciences, 205*(1161), 581–598.

Graham, L. J., & Jahnukainen, M. (2011). Wherefore art thou, inclusion? Analysing the development of inclusive education in New South Wales, Alberta and Finland. *Journal of Education Policy, 26*(2), 263–288.

Gregory, R. (2003). Accountability in modern government. In B. G. Peters & J. Pierre (Eds.), *Handbook of public administration* (pp. 557–568). London, UK: SAGE.

Hagel, J., Brown, J. S., Mathew, R., Wooll, M. & Tsu, W. (2014). *The lifetime learner: A journey through the future of postsecondary education*. Westlake, TX: Deloitte University Press.

Hammerness, K., Ahtiainen, R., & Sahlberg, P. (2017). *Empowered educators in Finland: How high-performing systems shape teaching quality*. New York, NY: John Wiley & Sons.

Hargreaves, A., & Shirley, D. (2009). *The fourth way: The inspiring future for educational change*. Thousand Oaks, CA: Corwin.

Harmon, M. (1995). *Responsibility as paradox: A critique of rational discourse on government*. London, UK: SAGE.

Hatch, T. (1997). Getting specific about multiple intelligences. *Educational Leadership, 54*(6), 26–29.

Hatch, T. (1998a). The differences in theory that matter in the practice of school improvement. *American Educational Research Journal, 35*(1), 3–31.

Hatch, T. (1998b). How community action contributes to achievement. *Educational Leadership, 55*(8), 16–19.

Hatch, T. (2001). What does it take to break the mold? *Teachers College Record, 102*(3), 561–589.

Hatch, T. (with Eiler White, M., Raley, J., Austin, K., Capitelli, S., & Faigenbaum, D.). (2005). *Into the classroom: Developing the scholarship of teaching and learning*. San Francisco, CA: Jossey-Bass.

Hatch, T. (2009a). *Managing to change: How schools can survive (and sometimes thrive) in turbulent times*. New York, NY: Teachers College Press.

Hatch, T. (2009b). The outside-inside connection. *Educational Leadership, 67*(2), 16–21.

Hatch, T. (2013). Beneath the surface of accountability: Answerability, responsibility and capacity building in recent educational reforms in Norway. *Journal of Educational Change, 14*(1), 1–15.

Hatch, T. (2015). Connections, coherence, and common understanding in the Common Core. In J. A. Supovitz & J. P. Spillane (Eds.), *Challenging* standards: Navigating conflict and building capacity in the era of the Common Core (pp. 103–112). Lanham, MD: Rowman & Littlefield.

Hatch, T., & Gardner, H. (1993). Finding cognition in the classroom: An expanded view of human intelligence. In G. Salomon (Ed.), *Distributed cognitions: Psychological and educational considerations* (pp. 164–187). Cambridge, UK: Cambridge University Press.

Hatch, T., & Roegman, R. (2017). Equity goals and equity visits: Leaders in a superintendent network jointly study each other's diverse schools to pursue high-leverage academic goals. *School Administrator*. http://my.aasa.org/AASA/Resources/SAMag/2017/Nov17/HatchRoegman.aspx

Hatch, T., Roegman, R., & Allen, D. (2019). Creating equitable outcomes in a segregated state. *Phi Delta Kappan, 100*(5), 19–24.

Hatch, T., & White, N. (2002). The raw materials of reform: Rethinking the knowledge of school improvement. *Journal of Educational Change, 3*(2), 117–134.

Heasley, S. (2019, January 30). Graduation rate for students with disabilities shows improvement. *Disability Scoop*. https://www.disabilityscoop.com/2019/01/30/graduation-rate-shows-improvement/25962

Heath, S. B. (1983). *Ways with words: Language, life, and work in communities and classrooms*. Cambridge, UK: Cambridge University Press.

Herold, B. (2020, April 10). The disparities in remote learning under coronavirus (in charts). *Education Week*. https://www.edweek.org/ew/articles/2020/04/10/the-disparities-in-remote-learning-under-coronavirus.html

Herriott, S. R., Levinthal, D., & March, J. G. (1985). Learning from experience in organizations. *The American Economic Review, 75*(2), 298–302.

Hess, F. M. (2013). The missing half of school reform. *National Affairs*. https://www.nationalaffairs.com/publications/detail/the-missing-half-of-school-reform

Hess, R. (2020, April 17). AP testing continues amid coronavirus crisis. *Rick Hess Straight Up*. https://blogs.edweek.org/edweek/rick_hess_straight_up/2020/04/ap_testing_continues_amid_coronavirus_crisis.html

Hill, H. C., & Loeb, S. (2020, April 7). Parents as emergency teachers? The research offers cautions and opportunities for schools. *Education Week*. https://www.edweek.org/ew/articles/2020/04/07/parents-as-emergency-teachers-the-research-offers.html

Hinton, E. K. (2016). *From the war on poverty to the war on crime: The making of mass incarceration in America*. Cambridge, MA: Harvard University Press.

Honig, M. I., & Hatch, T. C. (2004). Crafting coherence: How schools strategically manage multiple, external demands. *Educational Researcher, 33*(8), 16–30.

Horsford, S. (2011). *Learning in a burning house: Educational inequality, ideology, and (dis)integration*. New York, NY: Teachers College Press.

Hoxby, C. M., & Avery, C. (2012). *The missing "one-offs": The hidden supply of high-achieving, low income students*. NBER Working Papers 18586. National Bureau of Economic Research.

Human Rights Watch. (2018, November 12). *"Shall I feed my daughter, or educate her?" Barriers to girls' education in Pakistan*. New York, NY: Author. https://www.hrw.org/report/2018/11/12/shall-i-feed-my-daughter-or-educate-her/barriers-girls-education-pakistan

Ignatius, D. (2020, July 8). Congress's bipartisan national-service bill would be a powerful tonic for what's ailing America. *The Washington Post*. https://www.washingtonpost.com/opinions/2020/07/08/congresss-bipartisan-national-service-bill-would-be-powerful-tonic-whats-ailing-america

IkamvaYouth. (2019). *Alumni Survey 2019 Report*. Cape Town, South Africa: Author. http://ikamvayouth.org/wp-content/uploads/2020/06/2019-IkamvaYouth-Alumni-Survey-Report.pdf

Innove. (n.d.). Educational Counselling in Rajaleidja Centres. https://www.innove.ee/en/rajaleidja-network

Isenberg, E., Max, J., Gleason, P., Potamites, L., Santillano, R., & Hock, H. (2013, November). *Access to effective teaching for disadvantaged students* (NCEE 2014-4001). Washington, DC: National Center for Education Evaluation and Regional Assistance, Institute of Education Sciences, U.S. Department of Education.

Ixora Studios. (2017). wRite Formula (33) [Mobile application software]. https://play.google.com/store/apps/details?id=com.ixorastudios.writeformula&hl=en

Jacob, B. A., & Lovett, K. (2017, July 27). Chronic absenteeism: An old problem in search of new answers. *Evidence Speaks, Brookings*. https://www

.brookings.edu/research/chronic-absenteeism-an-old-problem-in-search-of-new-answers/#footnote-3

Kearns, D. T., & Anderson, J. L. (1996). Sharing the vision: Creating New American Schools. In S. Stringfield, S. Ross, & L. Smith (Eds.), *Bold plans for school restructuring: The New American Schools designs* (pp. 9–23). Mahwah, NJ: Lawrence Erlbaum Associates.

Kelleher, M. (2014). *New York City's Children First: Lessons in school reform.* Washington, DC: Center for American Progress.

Kendi, I. X. (2017). *Stamped from the beginning: The definitive history of racist ideas in America.* New York, NY: Bold Type Books.

Khazei, A., & Bridgeland, J. (2020, May 1). Just like the Great Depression, we need 500,000 service year jobs now. *The Boston Globe.* https://www.bostonglobe.com/2020/04/30/opinion/just-like-great-depression-we-need-500000-service-year-jobs-now

Klette, K. (2002). Reform policy and teacher professionalism in four Nordic countries. *Journal of Educational Change, 3*(3–4), 265–282.

Kneebone, E., & Holmes, N. (2016, August 31). *U.S. concentrated poverty in the wake of the Great Recession.* Washington, DC: Brookings. https://www.brookings.edu/research/u-s-concentrated-poverty-in-the-wake-of-the-great-recession

Koretz, D. (2003). Using multiple measures to address perverse incentives and score inflation. *Educational Measurement: Issues and Practice, 22*(2), 18–26.

Koretz, D. (2017). *The testing charade: Pretending to make schools better.* Chicago, IL: University of Chicago Press.

Krogstad, J. M. (2016, July 28). *5 facts about Latinos and education.* Pew Research Center. https://www.pewresearch.org/fact-tank/2016/07/28/5-facts-about-latinos-and-education

Ladd, H. F. (2017). No Child Left Behind: A deeply flawed federal policy. *Journal of Policy Analysis and Management, 36*(2), 461–469.

Ladson-Billings, G. (2006). From the achievement gap to the education debt: Understanding achievement in U.S. schools. *Educational Researcher, 35*(7), 3–12.

Lagorio-Chafkin, C. (2013, October 2). *Clay Christensen: The wrong kind of innovation.* https://www.inc.com/christine-lagorio/clayton-christensen-capitalist-dilemma.html

Laurens, D. (2020, April 7). 12 million kids lack internet access. Now is the time for the government to step in and close the digital divide. *The 74.* https://www.the74million.org/article/laurens-12-million-kids-lack-internet-access-now-is-the-time-for-the-government-to-step-in-and-close-the-digital-divide

Leadbeater, C. (2014, February 9). Innovation in education: Lessons from pioneers around the world. *Learning From the Extremes.* https://charlesleadbeater.net/2014/02/innovation-in-education-lessons-from-pioneers-around-the-world

Lee, N. T. (2020, March 17). What the coronavirus reveals about the digital divide between schools and communities. *Techtank, Brookings.* https://www.brookings.edu/blog/techtank/2020/03/17/what-the-coronavirus-reveals-about-the-digital-divide-between-schools-and-communities

Lee, S. K., Goh, C. B., & Fredriksen, B. (2008). *Toward a better future: Education and training for economic development in Singapore since 1965.* Washington, DC: The World Bank.

Legatum Institute. (2019). *The Legatum Prosperity Index™ 2019.* https://www.prosperity.com/rankings

Levitt, B., & March, J. G. (1988). Organizational learning. *Annual Review of Sociology, 14*(1), 319–338.

Lewis, K. (2019). *Making the connection: Transportation and youth disconnection.* New York, NY: Measure of America, Social Science Research Council. https://ssrc-static.s3.amazonaws.com/moa/Making%20the%20Connection.pdf

Maciag, M. (2018, February). The widening cost-of-living gap. *Governing.* https://www.governing.com/topics/urban/gov-cost-of-living-regions.html

Manduca, R. (2018, August 23). How rising U.S. income inequality exacerbates racial economic disparities. *Washington Center for Equitable Growth.* https://equitablegrowth.org/how-rising-u-s-income-inequality-exacerbates-racial-economic-disparities

March, J. G. (1991). How decisions happen in organizations. *Human–Computer Interaction, 6*(2), 95–117.

Mark, G. (2019, November 14). Singapore parents' guide to understanding (and maximising) their child's Edusave and PSEA. *DollarsAndSense.* https://dollarsandsense.sg/singapore-parents-guide-to-understanding-and-maximising-their-childs-edusave-and-psea

Matharu, H. (2015, October 22). The European capital that wants to ban homework. *Independent.* https://

www.independent.co.uk/news/world/europe/
homework-could-be-abolished-for-schoolchildren-
in-norways-capital-a6704176.html

McCann, E. (2016, November 3). Abt Associates Evaluation of Citizen Schools ELT Model. *Citizen Schools.* https://www.citizenschools.org/news/abt-evaluation

McShane, M. (2018, October 31). When did you learn your first lesson about the Bush-Obama reform era? *Rick Hess Straight Up.* http://blogs.edweek .org/edweek/rick_hess_straight_up/2018/10/when_did_you_learn_your_first_lesson_about_the_bush-obama_reform_era.html

Mediratta, K., Shah, S., & McAlister, S. (2009). *Community organizing for stronger schools: Strategies and successes.* Cambridge, MA: Harvard Education Press.

Mehta, J., & Fine, S. (2019). *In search of deeper learning: The quest to remake the American high school.* Cambridge, MA: Harvard University Press.

Metz, M. H. (1989). Real school: A universal drama amid disparate experience. *Politics of Education Association Yearbook, 75*–91.

Ministry of Education Singapore. (2018a). Co-curricular activities. https://www.moe.gov.sg/education/programmes/co-curricular-activities

Ministry of Education Singapore. (2018b). A holistic education for secondary school students—LEAPS 2.0. https://www.moe.gov.sg/docs/default-source/document/education/programmes/co-curricular-activities/leaps-2.pdf

Ministry of Education Singapore. (2020). Edusave Account: Overview. https://beta.moe.gov.sg/fees-assistance-awards-scholarships/edusave-contributions/overview

Modan, N. (2020, March 27). Wi-fi and hotspots "still won't work" for rural districts lacking connectivity. *Education Dive.* https://www.educationdive .com/news/wi-fi-and-hotspots-still-wont-work-for-rural-districts-lacking-connectiv/574826

National Academies of Sciences, Engineering, and Medicine. (2019). *Monitoring educational equity.* Washington, DC: The National Academies Press. https://doi.org/10.17226/25389

National Assessment of Educational Progress. (2015). NAEP—2015 student questionnaires results. https://www.nationsreportcard.gov/sq_students_views_2015

National Center for Education Statistics (NCES). (2018, April 10). *2017 NAEP mathematics report card.* https://www.nationsreportcard.gov/reading_math_2017_highlights

National Center for Education Statistics (NCES). (2019, February). *Status and trends in the education of racial and ethnic groups: Indicator 6: Elementary and secondary enrollment.* Washington, DC: Institute of Education Sciences, U.S. Department of Education. https://nces.ed.gov/programs/raceindicators/indicator_rbb.asp

National Center for Education Statistics (NCES). (2020, April). *Preschool and kindergarten enrollment.* Washington, DC: Institute of Education Sciences, U.S. Department of Education. https://nces.ed.gov/programs/coe/indicator_cfa.asp

National Commission on Excellence in Education. (1983). *A nation at risk: The imperative for educational reform.* Washington, DC: Author.

National Commission on Social, Emotional, and Academic Development. (2018). *Building Partnerships in Support of Where, When, & How Learning Happens.* Washington, DC: Aspen Institute. https://www.aspeninstitute.org/publications/building-partnerships-in-support-of-where-when-how-learning-happens

National Science Foundation. (2014). *About the LIFE center.* Learning in Informal and Formal Environments. http://life-slc.org/about/about.html

Nation's Report Card. (2017). *NAEP reading: National achievement-level results.* https://www.nationsreportcard.gov/reading_2017/nation/achievement/?grade=8

Nation's Report Card. (2019). *Massachusetts.* https://www.nationsreportcard.gov/profiles/stateprofile/overview/MA

Naviwala, N. (2017, October 18). What's really keeping Pakistan's children out of school? *The New York Times.* https://www.nytimes.com/2017/10/18/opinion/pakistan-education-schools.html

Neuman, S. B., & Knapczyk, J. J. (2020). Reaching families where they are: Examining an innovative book distribution program. *Urban Education, 55*(4), 542–569.

Neuman, S. B., & Moland, N. (2016). Book deserts: The consequences of income segregation on children's access to print. *Urban Education, 54*(1), 1–22.

Ng, P. T. (2017). *Learning from Singapore: The power of paradoxes.* Abingdon-on-Thames, UK: Routledge.

Ng, P. T., & Chan, D. (2008). A comparative study of Singapore's school excellence model with Hong Kong's school-based management. *International Journal of Educational Management, 22*(6), 488–505. https://doi.org/10.1108/09513540810895426

Ng, P. T., & Tan, C. (2010). The Singapore global schoolhouse. *International Journal of Educational Management. 24*(3), 178–188. http://dx.doi.org/10.1108/09513541011031556

Nickow, A., Oreopoulos, P., & Quan, V. (2020). *The impressive effects of tutoring on pre-K-12 learning: A systematic review and meta-analysis of the experimental evidence.* NBER Working Papers 27476. National Bureau of Economic Research.

Norman, D. (2013). *The design of everyday things* (Rev. and expanded ed.). New York, NY: BasicBooks.

Norwegian Directorate for Education and Training. (2007, January). *Improving school leadership: Country background report for Norway.* Paris, France: OECD. https://www.oecd.org/education/school/38529305.pdf

Norwegian Ministry of Education and Research. (2001). *The development of education 1991 to 2000: National report from Norway.* Oslo, Norway: Norwegian Ministry of Education and Research. http://www.regjeringen.no/en/dep/kd/Documents/Reports-and-actionplans/Reports/2001/The-Development-of-Education-1991-to-200/1.html?id=277458

Norwegian Ministry of Education and Research. (2016). *Teacher Education 2025 National Strategy for Quality and Cooperation in Teacher Education.* https://www.regjeringen.no/contentassets/d0c1da83bce94e2da21d5f631bbae817/kd_teacher-education-2025_uu.pdf

Nusche, D., Earl, L., Maxwell, W., & Shewbridge, C. (2011). *OECD reviews of evaluation and assessment in education: Norway.* Paris, France: OECD.

Oakes, J., Lipton, M., Anderson, L., & Stillman, J. (2018). *Teaching to change the world* (5th ed.). New York, NY: Routledge.

OECD. (2011). *Strong performers and successful reformers in education: Lessons from PISA for the United States.* Paris, France: Author.

OECD. (2013). *Strong performers and successful reformers in education: Lessons from PISA 2012 for the United States.* Paris, France: Author.

OECD. (2017). *Country Note: Singapore.* Paris, France: Author. https://www.oecd.org/pisa/PISA-2015-Collaborative-Problem-Solving-Singapore.pdf

OECD. (2019). *Education at a glance 2019: Finland.* Paris, France: Author. https://www.oecd.org/education/education-at-aglance/EAG2019_CN_FIN.pdf

OECD. (2020). *Finland: Student performance (PISA 2018).* Paris, France: Author. https://gpseducation.oecd.org/CountryProfile?primaryCountry=FIN&treshold=10&topic=PI

Office of the Under Secretary. (2002). *No Child Left Behind: A desktop reference.* Washington, DC: U.S. Department of Education. https://www2.ed.gov/admins/lead/account/nclbreference/reference.pdf

Orfield, G., Ee, J., & Coughlan, R. (2017). New Jersey's segregated schools trends and paths forward. UCLA Civil Rights Project/Proyecto Derechos Civiles. Los Angeles, CA: Civil Rights Project. https://www.civilrightsproject.ucla.edu/research/k-12-education/integration-and-diversity/new-jerseys-segregated-schools-trends-and-paths-forward/New-Jersey-report-final-110917.pdf

Perrin, A., & Turner, E. (2019, August 20). Smartphones help blacks, Hispanics bridge some—but not all—digital gaps with whites. *Fact Tank, Pew Research Center.* https://www.pewresearch.org/fact-tank/2019/08/20/smartphones-help-blacks-hispanics-bridge-some-but-not-all-digital-gaps-with-whites

Pew Research Center. (2015, December 17). Parenting in America. *Pew Research Center's Social & Demographic Trends Project.* https://www.pewsocialtrends.org/2015/12/17/parenting-in-america

Philanthropy News Digest. (2018, March 20). Racial gaps in upward mobility persist even among the rich. *Candid.* https://philanthropynewsdigest.org/news/racial-gaps-in-upward-mobility-persist-even-among-the-rich

Piketty, T., Saez, E., & Zucman, G. (2018). Distributional national accounts: Methods and estimates for the United States. *The Quarterly Journal of Economics, 133*(2), 553–609. https://doi.org/10.1093/qje/qjx043

Pinckney, D. (2014). *Blackballed: The Black vote and US democracy.* New York, NY: New York Review Books.

Polikoff, M. S. (2015). How well aligned are textbooks to the Common Core standards in mathematics? *American Educational Research Journal, 52*(6), 1185–1211. https://doi.org/10.3102%2F0002831215584435

Pressman, J. L., & Wildavsky, A. (1984). *Implementation: How great expectations in Washington are dashed in Oakland; or, Why it's amazing that federal* programs work at all, this being a saga of the Economic Development Administration as told by two sympathetic observers who seek to build morals on a foundation of ruined hopes (3rd ed.). Berkeley, CA: University of California Press.

Public Service Commission Singapore. (2019). *Public Service Commission (PSC)*. https://www.psc.gov.sg/home

Public Service Commission Singapore. (2020). *Public Service Commission (PSC) Scholarship (Teaching Service)*. https://www.psc.gov.sg/Scholarships/public-sector-scholarships/browse-by-scholarship/public-service-commission-psc-scholarship-teaching-service-PSC

Resnick, L., & Hall, M. (1998). Learning organizations for sustainable organizational reform. *Daedalus, 127*, 89–118.

Rincón-Gallardo, S. (2016). Large scale pedagogical transformation as widespread cultural change in Mexican public schools. *Journal of Educational Change, 17*, 411–436.

Rincón-Gallardo, S. (2019). *Liberating learning: Educational change as social movement*. New York, NY: Routledge.

Roegman, R., Allen, D., Leverett, L., Thompson, S., & Hatch, T. (2019). *Equity visits: A new approach to supporting equity-focused school and district leadership*. Thousand Oaks, CA: Corwin.

Rogers, T., & Feller, A. (2018). Reducing student absences at scale by targeting parents' misbeliefs. *Nature Human Behaviour, 2*(5), 335–342. https://doi.org/10.1038/s41562-018-0328-1

Sahlberg, P. (2011). *Finnish lessons: What can the world learn from educational change in Finland?* New York, NY: Teachers College Press.

Sampson, C., Moore, J., & Roegman, R. (2019). Reversing course: Equity-focused leadership in action. *Educational Leadership, 76*(6), 58–63.

Sander, H. (2017, May 30). Have 65% of future jobs not yet been invented? *More or Less* [Audio file]. *BBC World Service*. https://www.bbc.co.uk/programmes/p053ln9f

Schleicher, A., Oates, T., Kuustik, R., Saarinen, A., Heller Sahlgren, G., & Jerrim, J. (2019). The parable of Finland: PISA results can lead policymakers astray. *The Economist*. https://www.economist.com/international/2019/12/05/pisa-results-can-lead-policymakers-astray

Schwarz, E. (2014). *The opportunity equation: How citizen teachers are combating the achievement gap in America's schools*. Boston, MA: Beacon Press.

Semuels, A. (2016, December 27). Severe inequality is incompatible with the American dream. *The Atlantic*. https://www.theatlantic.com/business/archive/2016/12/equality-of-opportunity/510227

Senge, P. (1990). *The fifth discipline: The art and practice of the learning organization*. New York, NY: Doubleday.

Shirley, D. (1997). *Community organizing for urban school reform*. Austin, TX: University of Texas Press.

Shulman, L. (2004). *The wisdom of practice: Essays on teaching, learning, and learning to teach*. San Francisco, CA: Jossey-Bass.

Sim, C. (2014, November 7). Co-curricular activities in schools. *Singapore Infopedia*. https://eresources.nlb.gov.sg/infopedia/articles/SIP_2014-11-08_124430.html

Simpson, A. (2019). *Endline evaluation, Luminos Fund Second Chance Program, Liberia*. Boston, MA: Luminos Fund. https://luminosfund.org/wp-content/uploads/2018/11/QA_Second_Chance_Endline_Evaluation_Report_2018-19_Final.pdf

Singleton, G. E. (2014). *Courageous conversations about race: A field guide for achieving equity in schools*. Thousand Oaks, CA: Corwin.

Sizer, T. R. (1985). *Horace's compromise: The dilemma of the American high school*. Boston, MA: Houghton Mifflin.

Skedsmo, G. (2011). Formulation and realisation of evaluation policy: Inconsistencies and problematic issues. *Educational Assessment, Evaluation and Accountability, 23*(1), 5–20.

Slavin, R. E., Collins, M. E., Repka, M. X., Friedman, D. S., Mudie, L. I., Owoeye, J. O., & Madden, N. A. (2018). In plain sight: Reading outcomes of providing eyeglasses to disadvantaged children. *Journal of Education for Students Placed at Risk, 23*(3), 250–258.

Sloan Wilson, D. (2015, March 2). *The spandrels of San Marco revisited: An interview with Richard C. Lewontin*. The Evolution Institute. https://evolution-institute.org/the-spandrels-of-san-marco-revisited-an-interview-with-richard-c-lewontin

Smith, L. M. (2019, December 4). Singapore students lose PISA top spot to China—which wasn't in top 5 previously—despite far above global average scores. *Business Insider Singapore*. https://www.businessinsider.sg/singapore-students-lose-pisa-top-spot-to-china-which-wasnt-in-top-5-previously-despite-far-above-global-average-scores

Smith, N. (2018, April 3). U.S. doesn't deliver on promise of equal opportunity for all. *Bloomberg.* https://www.bloomberg.com/opinion/articles/2018-04-03/u-s-doesn-t-deliver-on-promise-of-equal-opportunity-for-all

Snyder, T. D., de Brey, C., & Dillow, S. A. (2019). *Digest of education statistics 2017, NCES 2018-070.* Washington, DC: National Center for Education Statistics, Institute of Education Sciences, U.S. Department of Education.

Sparks, S. D. (2010, October 1). Spurred by statistics, districts combat absenteeism. *Education Week.* https://www.edweek.org/ew/articles/2010/10/01/06absenteeism_ep.h30.html

Sparks, S. D., & Harwin, A. (2018, May 29). A third of students need eye exams, study finds. *Education Week.* https://www.edweek.org/ew/articles/2018/05/30/a-third-of-students-need-eye-exams.html

Spaull, N. (2017, January 27). Matric really does start in grade one. *Mail and Guardian.* https://mg.co.za/article/2017-01-27-00-matric-really-does-start-in-grade-one

Success for All Foundation. (2015). *Success for all.* Baltimore, MD: Author. https://www.successforall.org/wp-content/uploads/2016/03/410474000_FullDescrip_TxtCvr.pdf

Sweeten-Lopez, O. (2017). *Dell Scholars Program: Supporting students through college completion.* Austin, TX: Michael and Susan Dell Foundation. http://15ecnn2oq2dlb80aj55ssr2x-wpengine.netdna-ssl.com/wp-content/uploads/2018/03/Dell-Scholars-Program-eBook.pdf

Taylor, K. (2019). *Race for profit: How banks and the real estate industry undermined black homeownership.* Chapel Hill, NC: University of North Carolina Press.

Teng, A., & Davie, S. (2020, March 27). One day of home-based study a week from April 1. *The Straits Times.* https://www.straitstimes.com/singapore/one-day-of-home-based-study-a-week-from-april-1

Tolo, A., Lillejord, S., Flórez Petour, M. T., & Hopfenbeck, T. N. (2020). Intelligent accountability in schools: A study of how school leaders work with the implementation of assessment for learning. *Journal of Educational Change, 21,* 59–82.

Tucker, M. S. (Ed.). (2011). *Surpassing Shanghai: An agenda for American education built on the world's leading systems.* Cambridge, MA: Harvard Education Press.

Tyack, D. B., & Cuban, L. (1995). *Tinkering toward utopia: A century of public school reform.* Cambridge, MA: Harvard University Press.

UNESCO. (2015). *Education for All 2000–2015: Achievements and challenges.* Paris, France: Author.

UN Economic and Social Council. (2020, April 28). *Progress towards the sustainable development goals report of the Secretary-General.* E/2020/57-E-E/2020/57. https://undocs.org/en/E/2020/57

UN General Assembly. (2015, October 21). *Transforming our world: The 2030 Agenda for Sustainable Development.* A/RES/70/1. https://www.refworld.org/docid/57b6e3e44.html

UNICEF. (2019, October). *Literacy among youth is rising, but young women lag behind.* https://data.unicef.org/topic/education/literacy

U.S. Department of Education. (2009). *Race to the Top program, executive summary.* Washington, DC: Author. https://www2.ed.gov/programs/racetothetop/executive-summary.pdf

U.S. Department of Education. (2018). *Academic performance and outcomes for English learners: Performance on national assessments and on-time graduation rates.* https://www2.ed.gov/datastory/el-outcomes/index.html

U.S. Department of Education. (2019). Chronic absenteeism in the nation's schools: A hidden educational crisis. https://www2.ed.gov/datastory/chronicabsenteeism.html#:~:text=Chronic%20absenteeism%20is%20widespread%E2%80%94about,100%20million%20school%20days%20lost

Usher, A. (2011, December). *AYP Results for 2010–11.* Washington, DC: Center on Education Policy. https://doi.org/10.1787/9789264311671-en

Wall, P. (2015, November 11). How New York City is using Google Drive to revamp its struggling schools. *Chalkbeat.* https://chalkbeat.org/posts/ny/2015/11/11/how-the-city-is-using-google-drive-to-revamp-its-struggling-schools

Walsh, K., & Snyder, E. (2004). *Searching the attic: How states are responding to the nation's goal of placing a highly qualified teacher in every classroom*. Washington, DC: National Council on Teacher Quality.

Walsh, R., & Ross, E. (2019). *State of the states: Teacher and principal evaluation policy*. Washington, DC: National Council on Teacher Quality. https://www.nctq.org/publications/State-of-the-States-2019:-Teacher-and-Principal-Evaluation-Policy

Warren, M. R., Mapp, K. L., & The Community Organizing and School Reform Project. (2011). *A match on dry grass: Community organizing as a catalyst for school reform*. New York, NY: Oxford University Press.

Weisberg, D., Sexton, S., Mulhern, J., & Keeling, D. (2009). *The widget effect: Our national failure to acknowledge and act on differences in teacher effectiveness*. Washington, DC: The New Teacher Project.

Whitmire, R. (2019). *The B.A. breakthrough: How ending diploma disparities can change the face of America*. New York, NY: the74 media.

Will, M. (2019, October 8). Most states have walked back tough teacher-evaluation policies, report finds. *Teaching Now*. http://blogs.edweek.org/teachers/teaching_now/2019/10/most_states_have_walked_back_tough_teacher_evaluation_policies_report.html

Wilson, J. Q. (1978). *Varieties of police behavior: The management of law and order in eight communities*.

With a new preface by the author. Cambridge, MA: Harvard University Press.

Winthrop, R. (with Barton, A., & McGivney, E.). (2018). *Leapfrogging inequality: Remaking education to help young people thrive*. Washington, DC: Brookings Institution Press.

Wong, A. (2016, May 23). What are Massachusetts public schools doing right? *The Atlantic*. https://www.theatlantic.com/education/archive/2016/05/what-are-massachusetts-public-schools-doing-right/483935

World Bank. (2018). *World development report 2018: Learning to realize education's promise*. Washington, DC: Author.

Yang, C. (2016a, April 9). OBS camp for all Sec 3 students from 2020. *Straits Times*. http://www.straitstimes.com/singapore/obs-camp-for-all-sec-3-students-from-2020

Yang, C. (2016b, October 2). Tuition race hots up as big players up their game. *Straits Times*. https://www.straitstimes.com/singapore/education/tuition-race-hots-up-as-big-players-up-their-game

Yellen, J. L. (2014, October 17). *Perspectives on inequality and opportunity from the Survey of Consumer Finances*. https://www.federalreserve.gov/newsevents/speech/yellen20141017a.htm

Index

Education leaders, 11, 58
  improvement efforts, 49
  See also Leadership
Education workforce, 79
  power of, 171
Educators, 11
  beliefs, 47
  community-organizing efforts, 64
  effective/ineffective, 60
  expanding power of, 78–80
  grammar of schooling and, 39
  improvements in educational system, 21
EduLab (Singapore), 76–77
Edusave account, 139–140
Edwards School, 117
"Egg-crate" school, 37, 41, 177
EL Education, 5, 104
Emergent bilinguals, 19, 46, 50
English language arts (ELA), 19, 135
English language learners, 19
Enrollment rates, 15, 166
Equitable educational opportunities, 11
  advanced courses and, 27–28
  barriers, 24–25, 67
  defined, 23–24
  distribution of teachers, 26–27
  economic inequality and, 25–26
  inequality of, 25–30
  separate and unequal, 25–26
  vicious cycle, 25–26
Estonia, 86, 172
Evaluation reforms, teacher, 58–59
Every Student Succeeds Act of 2015 (ESSA), 20
Experiential learning, 53, 139
Expertise, learning infrastructure, 108
Extended learning time model, 118
Extra-curricular activities.
      See Co-curricular activities

FabLabs, 101, 108–109
Feedback, teachers', 59–60
Fergus, E., 68
Fine, S., 173
Finland
  capacity-building, 125–133
  curriculum-renewal process, 136–137
  educational system, 1, 2, 11, 12, 178–181
  expertise and materials investment, 126–128
  large-scale improvements, 20–21
  Mehackit program, 109–110
  National Board of Education, 128
  PISA scores, 180
  "phenomenon-based" learning, 109, 137
  race and equity, 9
  relationships and social networks, 130–133

Finnish National Agency for Education, 137
Fisher, J. F., 168
Follow-up mechanisms, Norwegian, 149, 150
"For today/tomorrow" educational system, 34–35
Foundational skills, 34
  high-leverage problems and, 65–67
  improvements in, 67–68
The Fourth Way (Hargreaves and Shirley), xxviii
Freehold Regional High School District, 72
Freehold Regional Opportunity Index, 72, 84
Funders, 49, 126
Future planning and education, 34
"Future school," 5

Game app, 77
Gardner, H., 62, 75
Gibson, J. J., 92
Goals
  educational system and, 34
  benchmarks and, 176
  in Finland and Singapore, 127, 129,
      140, 143
Gogwana, M., 82–83
Goldberg, R., 68–71
Goodman, N., 75
Gooden, M., xxvi
Gould, S. J., 114, 115
Grammar of schooling, 37–38
  ATLAS Communities Project, 43–45
  beyond school approaches, 172–173
  Brooklyn International
      High School, 99–100
  innovation, 54
  kindergartens, 43
  "niche" reforms, 52–54
"Ground-level" innovations, 77
Guastaferro, L., 79

Heritage Awareness Index, 141
Higher-education institutions, 50
Higher-level courses, 72
High-leverage leadership, 183–184
High-leverage problems, 61
  access to books, 164–166
  access to college, 166
  reading issues, 164
  chronic absenteeism, 73, 164–165
  community organizing principles, 62–64
  in different contexts, 164–167
  and foundational skills, 65–67
  identifying, 64
  New Jersey Network of Superintendents
      (NJNS), 68–72
  "quick wins," 62, 65, 72
  reading issues, 164

A SAGE Publishing Company

Helping educators make the greatest impact

CORWIN HAS ONE MISSION: to enhance education through intentional professional learning.

We build long-term relationships with our authors, educators, clients, and associations who partner with us to develop and continuously improve the best evidence-based practices that establish and support lifelong learning.